THE PSYCHOTIC ANIMAL

A Psychiatrist's Study of Human Delusion

Psychiatry Series

Retreat from Sanity: The Structure of Emerging Psychosis
M.B. Bowers, Jr., M.D.

Strategic Intervention in Schizophrenia: Current Developments in Treatment
R. Cancro, M.D. et al

The Behavioral Treatment of Psychotic Illness: Advances in Theory and Technique
W. DiScipio, Ph.D.

Overload: The New Human Condition
L. Bellak, M.D.

Psychiatry in Broad Perspective
R.R. Grinker, Sr., M.D.

The Person in Distress: On the Biosocial Dynamics of Adaptation
N. Hansell, M.D.

International Directory of Psychiatrists and Mental Hospitals
E.N. Rogan, Ph.D.

Long-Term Treatments of Psychotic States
C. Chiland, M.D.

The Psychotic Animal: A Psychiatrist's Study of Human Delusion
W.J. Garre, M.D.

THE PSYCHOTIC ANIMAL

A Psychiatrist's Study of Human Delusion

By

WALTER J. GARRE, M.D.

Human Sciences Press
A division of Behavioral Publications
72 Fifth Avenue
New York, New York 10011

Library of Congress Catalog Number 75–17112

ISBN: 0–87705–269–7

Printed in the United States of America
6789 987654321
Library of Congress Cataloging in Publication Data

Garre, Walter J.
The Psychotic Animal: A Psychiatrist's Study of Human Delusion.

CONTENTS

ACKNOWLEDGEMENTS

The author wishes to gratefully acknowledge the cooperation of the following authors and publishers in granting permission to reprint portions of their works:

AMERICAN PSYCHIATRIC ASSOCIATION. *Diagnostic and Statistical Manual—Mental Disorders.* Special printing November, 1965, page 24.

MACMILLAN PUBLISHING CO., INC. *The Golden Bough,* by Sir James G. Frazer

PRENTICE-HALL, INC. *Psychic Discoveries Behind the Iron Curtain,* by Ostrander and Schroeder

TIME, INCORPORATED. *The Epic of Man*

WILLIAMS AND WILKINS COMPANY. *Comprehensive Textbook of Psychiatry,* edited by Alfred M. Freedman, M.D., and Harold L. Kaplan, M.D., Chapter 13, written by Louis Linn, M.D.

I wish to express my deep appreciation to Lisa Davidson who gave me great emotional stability over many years; to Wendy O'Donnell who did an excellent job of editing my manuscript; and to Lorraine Pantalena who did an outstanding job of typing and retyping my manuscript, even when it was barely readable. I wish also to thank Mr. Philip Mankoff, psychologist, for his permission to use his test results in Chapter 7.

Finally, I wish to state that this book was especially written to show my children what their father really amounted to.

Walter J. Garre, M.D.

DEDICATION
(very much with tongue in cheek)

To all the vicissitudes of my life which I had to overcome in order to avoid becoming another casualty on the battlefield of life; my early inferiority feelings; the political upheavels in my native Austria in 1938 which forced me to continue and finish my medical education in a new country under sometimes very, very difficult conditions; to my ex-wife who left me after two wonderful children were born and therefore forced me to mobilize every possible emotional resource within myself so that I would not fail . . .

Don't misunderstand—there are some facts for which I cannot even facetiously be grateful.

Foreword

I do not think that I will say many things which have not been said before, but I will come to conclusions, which may sometimes be startling in their bluntness, and, as I like to believe, objectivity. How I achieved this objectivity will be difficult to convey to any reader—I will give a short account of my life in a postscript which may, partially at least, explain the conclusions which life itself forced upon me so that I would not succumb to the emotional stress to which I became subject. In order not to perish, I had to develop emotional resources within myself to such degree that life itself became not only bearable but ultimately worthwhile. When such pressure is exerted in a human being, and at the same time is matched by an absolute determination not to give in and to die rather than to fail, then all human emotional resources are mobilized and insights become overt or clear. The average person who is not exposed to such experiences never has the necessity or the circumstances in which to develop these resources.

I will summarize the thesis of my exposition and elaborate on it as I go along. Let it be said to start that I do not write this book in an attempt to gain either economic advancement or glory for myself. Economically, I have done quite well in my profession as a psychiatrist, and I long ago learned the limitations of applause and glory—applause is so easily given by people who do not fully understand what is being presented to them that their applause cannot be satisfactory. People who thoroughly understand all that one presents are not so forthcoming, particularly if new and controversial subjects are discussed.

Finally, it is to be pointed out here that because the ideas expressed in this book stem from my very strong personal conviction, I was particularly concerned that every nuance of my meaning be preserved intact. Thus it was my decision to forego virtually *all* editorial service and counsel typically rendered by the publisher.

—Walter J. Garre, M.D.

INTRODUCTORY

SYNOPSIS:

This book is as fundamental and epochal as the *Origin of the Species* was a century ago. It points out that as Man evolved from the animal kingdom and gained dominion over the other animals by gradually developing tools and weapons, a sense of grandeur must have pervaded him.

This new-found feeling of grandeur and power was, however, incompatible with his own helplessness against the overwhelming forces of nature—floods, droughts, earthquakes, lightening, fire, etc. To preserve this newly developed feeling of grandeur and vanity, he tried—in his own mind at least—to influence these forces over which in reality he had no control. He imbued these forces of nature with human features and tried to influence them to his will through sacrifices and rituals. (Magical attempts are basically delusional and not realistic and serve only to maintain the basic human vanity.) Out of this magical thinking, religious beliefs gradually evolved—first encompassing many gods; later less; and ultimately one. The principle remains, however, the same. It is delusional; it is not realistic; it is the socially accepted form of insanity.

No human being can be totally free from the basic human vanity, and, therefore, every human being in one way or the other shares, to a certain degree at least, a modicum of irrationality. The acceptance of one's own irrationality is the highest degree of emotional adjustment and normalcy. Once this point is clearly recognized, our attitude to ourselves and to our fellow human beings changes drastically.

In the chapter on Basic Anxiety, it is pointed out that no infant, even under optimum conditions, is accepted as a total blessing by his parents, and specifically, the mother. To the degree that he was unwanted, he will on a subconscious level sense this resentment as a threat to his very existence and, depending on how this threat was perceived, some form of reactivity will result.

A total concept of the four aspects which man shares with the animal kingdom are elaborated upon in the chapter on the Holistic Approach to the Human Personality; namely:

a) physical health or sickness;
b) socio-mental health or sickness;
c) self-sustaining economy in maturity; and
d) reproductivity.

It is pointed out that man has a fifth specific aspect—"self-awareness"—which has to derive its strength from one or a combination of the above-mentioned four other aspects which thusly have invariably to be depleted, to a certain degree at least.

In the chapter on Psychophysiological Reactions, the emotional component to diseases is considered —diseases which heretofore were primarily viewed as being basically organic. Most interesting and challenging examples are discussed and exciting new vistas opened. It is clearly pointed out and elaborated upon that each individual is nothing but the result of his heredity (whatever heredity stands for) and his environment—factors for which he is not responsible.

The Illusion of Freedom of Will—so cherished by man—is another form of his unrealistic vanity.

There are in total 24 applied chapters which elaborate on the basic thesis, some of which are arresting and most startling. A postscript is provided to give some hint as to the circumstances which combined to ultimately bring forth the insights contained in this book. . .

WJG.

GENERAL THESIS

The thesis which I offer is this: Man, in the course of his evolution from the animal kingdom in a Darwinian sense, reached a point whereby his tool-making ability provided a considerable mastery over other animals and certain forces of Nature. Indeed, human beings have been called tool-making animals. As this tool-making ability reached a stage where mastery over predatory animals could be accomplished, a certain vanity might well have overcome our very early ancestors. When, after perhaps not only thousands but hundreds of thousands of years, a cause-and-effect connection was noted between dislodging rocks and their effect upon persecuting predators, or when, at first by accident and gradually over thousands of years, deliberate effort was made to break off boughs of trees which could be used to slay a threatening predator, the very earliest weapons were created. With the use of these weapons, which were, of course, gradually improved—stone axes and missiles of more refined shape and form—a certain feeling of power must have been felt by these very early ancestors. Since I am not an anthropologist, it would be difficult for me to point out at what period in the anthropological development this emotional feeling of powerful sensation may have gradually begun to enter and to what degree it had to develop for the first step to be clearly felt—whether it was 500,000 years or one million years ago or perhaps only during the Neanderthal period—would be only an educated guess. I will leave it to the professionally trained anthropologist to pinpoint more precisely the period of time over which such a development is likely to have taken place. Suffice it to say that this can only be assumed—no proof can be given and this has to be kept in mind. It is a theory, just as relativity was a theory which subsequently proved its value functionally. If this theory is correct, let us assume also that this feeling of grandeur was greatly jeopardized by the helplessness which these early ancestors felt in the face of the overpowering forces of Nature which burst upon them every so often—earthquakes, floods, storms, winds of tremendous proportions, fires caused by lightening, drought—all these were forces of Nature over which Man obviously had no control. It is my supposition and assumption that the feelings of power, grandeur, and vanity gained from mastery over other animals by weapons, however primitive, and the feeling of helplessness against the overpowering forces of Nature, were incompatible. Man had to seek in some form reconciliation of this new-won vanity—so pleasant to his own feelings—with the reality of forces over which he had no control. I have elaborated on this point in some detail in my earlier book *Basic Anxiety,* which was published by the Philosophical Library of New York in 1962.

We come now to the point where magic begins by projecting humanizing features onto all these forces of Nature. As these forces were visualized as possessing humanized features, beatification or spirit projection developed. Man in his own fantasies had a mechanism to preserve his own feeling of grandeur—in other words, his vanity. He might give thanks for favorable events such as rainfall, sunshine, or the new warmth of the sun after the winter solstice. He might bring prayers and sacrificial gifts to unfavorable forces which he had humanized and called first spirits and later gods, and try to reconcile them by his devotion in bringing gifts and performing ritual actions which were thought to be pleasing to these forces. Here I certainly will refer the reader above all to *The Golden Bough,* the well-known work by James Frazier. Now it cannot be denied, and this is part of my thesis, that any attempt to try to influence forces over which in reality Mankind has no influence—whether by prayer, by magic, or by sacrifices or deeds—in reality did not change the course of natural events. But in his mind Man made the assumption that these rituals, sacrifices, prayers, etc., would influence these forces or might influence them if he adopted the proper attitude—that is, if he said, on bended knee, "It is your will, but please listen to me—maybe you will pay some attention to my request." So, in a form, this is a most unrealistic attempt as it is unrealistic when we wish somebody well and feel that our wish will bring about good fortune or, conversely, that our curse will be harmful to another person. When we clearly realize that these attempts to control the forces of Nature, which are beyond our control, are not realistic, we do not have to shrink from or shy away from calling it unrealistic or psychotic and, therefore, insane.

Since every human being shares the fate of Mankind, which means having vanity in his own personality and to the degree that this vanity has to be reconciled with the forces of Nature in one form or another, we can postulate that every human being, to a certain degree at least, is unrealistic and, therefore, insane. To accept this insanity as the norm of Mankind is in all likelihood the highest possible degree of objectivity and self-acceptance. As long as we define the word "normal" as an absence of abnormality, we are likely to miss the boat completely. It is actually acceptance of the fact that insanity, to a certain degree at least, is part and parcel of Mankind which will ultimately convey the feeling of peace of mind. I will draw, therefore, the conclusion that any form of magical thinking, and subsequently what we call religion, is an unrealistic attempt to influence forces over which in reality Mankind has no influence and, therefore, is insane and psychotic. I wish to state that it basically makes no difference whatsoever whether a man has 10,000 gods, fifty gods on Olympus, or ultimately one god—the principle remains the same—it is a socially acceptable form of insanity, and the more emotionally disturbed a human being is, for reasons which I will point out in a later part of this book, the more he is likely to take refuge in this socially acceptable form of insanity which today we call religion and which is perhaps shared by practically all human beings, at least in the hour of their need when they wish to hold on to something and perhaps only utter to themselves, "Please, Father, help me." On the other hand, some people are so insecure that they embrace this soothing concept so totally that their lives are completely dedicated to religion. We, of course, know very well that religion in virtually any form is exclusive of any other similar adjustment, inasmuch as each feels it has the only right answer—the truth—and, therefore, this is incompatible with the equally strong conviction of another person or another group of people. Sooner or later, therefore, clashes will take place—clashes which have caused bloodshed all through history. It is people who are basically psychotic who rigidly hold to their own adjustment—they cannot jeopardize their own adjustment because they would thereby see themselves as deeply disturbed. This is not their own fault, as I will point out later, but, nevertheless, since those who are deeply disturbed are not equipped to see themselves in an objective light, they become exclusive, clashes have to take place, and the bloody consequences are so well known to all of us.

At no time should these thoughts be interpreted as basically anti-religious or as a crusade against religion. This is not at all the deeper purpose of this book. The purpose of this book is to have the maximum amount of objectivity about Mankind and its emotional adjustment, and to see that by the very fact that we are human beings split off from the animal kingdom (with the subsequent vanity which resulted from our gradual mastery over other animals and by our desire to rule and influence forces of Nature over which in reality we have no influence), we have to be unrealistic and, therefore, psychotic. For a long period of time religion in any form, including magical thinking, has given the illusion of mental balance and has been an outlet for the emotionally disturbed, enabling them to appear balanced, although their attitude showed its basically disastrous maladjustment, if not on the individuals themselves, certainly on subsequent generations.

The time has come where perhaps a short pause should be made to distinguish between fault and cause as they are usually understood in human thinking. Let us, for instance, make the supposition that a mother dies in childbirth. Obviously, the newborn infant can in no way be at fault for the death of the mother; nevertheless, nobody can question that his birth caused the death of the mother. In this sense perhaps, the feeling of guilt for causing some ill effect and any subsequent blame become unrealistic, particularly if we see that human beings are, in a way, just as programmed into their behavior pattern as computers are in their functioning. Indeed, I would compare human beings to computers with the additional property of vanity. I mean to say that human beings certainly are not responsible for whatever heredity they received. Whatever heredity may stand for, we certainly are not responsible for it. Later we will delineate what the influence of heredity is, whether heredity has any influence at all on the personality pattern and the emotional adjustment of the individual, or whether heredity is confined solely to the physical and organic basis of a living being. If we are not responsible for our heredity, which certainly we are not, the next question is, what are the other influencing factors which determine the development of a human being? The factors are, of course, what we call environment; in the same way as the environment of a plant seed determines its growth and appearance, environment determines the growth of an animal or a human being.

Let me introduce here a very simple mental supposition which certainly will hardly need to be repeated experimentally because it is convincing. If we take seeds from the same plant and put some of those seeds in excellent soil and take the best possible care of them, if we give them the proper light conditions and sunshine, and if we supply them with all the other necessities such as water, minerals, etc., we can ultimately expect prize blooms. If some of those conditions are only somewhat altered to a less favorable degree, the results of the bloom will perhaps still be satisfactory but certainly not as extraordinarily beautiful as under perfect conditions. If conditions become worse—particularly in the most vulnerable early stages of the plant—serious stunting and damage will take place. Ultimately, if a forbidding environment is found by these seeds, then we see no development. We see, in other words, in this simple example that in a plant the hereditary endowment obviously will determine what type of plant we deal with, but the quality of the plant will be determined completely by the conditions of the environment. It is very true that in certain plants—let us think of some fruit trees—excellent fruit may be obtained when excellent care and environment is given to this tree; however, here and there some stunted fruit will be found on some branches. This is most likely due to mutations, which are apparently unavoidable in the interplay of the forces of genetics, but this will be the rare exception.

When we postulate that each newborn child will be raised by parents who are the products of their own childhoods, we see that the degree of emotional endowment carries over from one generation to the next. Generation follows generation and each parent does the best he knows how, inadequate as it may be. Therefore, to blame parents for the faults or deficiencies of their children is uncalled for and unrealistic. We should bear in mind that, even though they did the best they could, they were still inadequate, and, therefore, they caused the disturbance without actually being guilty. This is a very important point when we deal with adolescent and child psychiatry. As long as we blame parents for the inadequate development and disturbance of their children, it is small wonder that they become defensive and react negatively to any such suggestion because in reality they cannot be blamed. They only convey to the new generation the emotional strength which they in turn received from their parents and their environment when they were young themselves.

It remains to be seen to what degree the mother seems to be the overwhelming influencing force (because, after all, the infant deals for the early part of his life entirely with the mother, and the mother, according to biology, has the breasts containing milk and milk is food and food is life and little does the infant know that in order for the mother to have milk she has to eat and the father has to go out and provide the food). It may take a long time to see the importance of the father as not only the economic but also the emotional support of the mother. To the degree that he is available for this emotional support he is equally important in development of the child; however, it is not quite evident to the infant who could be raised, somehow at least, if the father were absent and the money were provided for the mother to sustain herself and her offspring. The emotional deficit, of course, would sooner or later make itself felt.

Perhaps I should revert here to my earlier concept of human vanity. We see we are not responsible for our heredity, and we certainly are not responsible for the environment into which we are born. These, to my understanding, are the only two factors which determine our development. Any assumption that these factors in one way or another will not ultimately and realistically determine our programming is fallacious; however, it is very difficult to convey these thoughts clearly because they clash head on with the deep-seated feeling of human vanity which tells us we are the masters of our own souls, the captains of our own ships, and that by volition and determination we can ultimately determine the pattern which we wish to take. We know, for instance, that criminology is based on the fact that we hold an individual responsible for his action and act upon him, therefore, with punishment, incarceration, or disapproval—whatever seems called for. We are, however, not realistic enough to see that the individual, due to the pattern which was programmed into him, could not have acted differently. It is, however, very important that the reader not misunderstand me at this point and feel that the conclusion to be drawn is that, since nobody is really responsible for what he does, society has no right to take any steps to curtail anybody who functions in any anti-social or asocial form. This is not at all what I wish to say—the highest law of Nature in the animal kingdom, or in general, as far as I can see, is not the preservation of the individual but the preservation of the species. The species has a right—and one can substitute the word "society" for "species," if one prefers—to restrain anti-social or harmful individuals or at least to make them innocuous and render them harmless until they can conform to the requirements of society. It would, however, be more honest and realistic if society clearly stated that the offender, whatever his offense may be, is in the truest sense not really guilty or at fault for his personality pattern; however, it is deplorable that his formation and programming took such shape that it is disastrous and harmful to society and that society, or the herd, cannot tolerate such action and behavior because this would permit its own destruction. This, in a way, could be seen as another form of the law of the survival of the fittest, or rather the natural selection of the fittest for survival. The same misfortune which befalls the seed on rocky ground which prevents germination befalls human beings who come from poor emotional backgrounds. If anything can free them it is the insight that their progress in life, whatever it may be, only conforms to the law of Nature.

Perhaps this insight is the one specific human factor that may free us ultimately from the forces of Nature as they are biologically programmed into us. With the realization that we are responsible neither for our environment nor for our heredity, the concept of pride in our accomplishments and, on the other hand, guilt for our faults falls away. In other words, we are neither responsible for our desirable features nor responsible for what society or the herd may call the undesirable features. Guilt and pride, therefore, are equally unrealistic. Several thoughts, of course, come immediately to mind; for instance, that in some families there are many children and some seem to do very well in every respect of human evaluation while there may be one or more that do not seem to function at all well. This thought deserves further investigation—how is it that such diversified results can come from what is apparently the same background? In addition, it is obvious that extraordinary and useful human beings sometimes come from apparently deplorable backgrounds. Other additional concepts will have to be introduced to appreciate this situation fully; I shall discuss the holistic approach to human beings in a later chapter.

I feel that one cannot do justice to a total human personality unless one considers various aspects of the human condition: (1) physical health or sickness; (2) socio-mental health or sickness; (3) economic independence and self-sustaining activity in the mature individual which, of course, includes homemaking by the mother who raises the children; and (4) reproduction. Nowhere in the animal kingdom (except for domesticated animals) is sexual abstinence or celibacy practiced. The preservation of the species is the highest law of biology and nature. There are only few exceptions under extraordinary conditions. Therefore, when we see human beings who seem to function exceedingly well as far as society goes, but, who for some reason, either willfully or unknowingly, abstain from reproduction, we have to consider this a very high price paid for their otherwise social acceptability. From a higher viewpoint they are deficient. They do not fulfill the laws of biology and nature; however, human adjustment has been so broadminded that, unless a human being is completely intolerable to society, we close our eyes, we let him have his own shortcomings, and we do not judge his mental adjustment as deficient. They are functioning on a lower level of the optimum of biological requirements. But these deficient adjustments take place and one has to be broadminded in order not to draw the limits too narrowly because, in fact, all human beings are disturbed, some less, some more, depending on their adjustment—as long as it is not harmful to the herd in general, we will let them pass and find them acceptable.

The animal kingdom, and certainly the higher mammals, also experience these four elements of individual behavior. The specific human feature is what we call self-awareness. Self-awareness derives from the feeling of vanity and this is the feeling which a human being has in distinction to animals. For some reason this feeling of self-awareness has to derive its strength from one basic aspect of biology or another, and, therefore, causes some curtailment on either the physical health level or the socio-mental health level or in the ability to become economically independent or to reproduce. This I have called the holistic approach, and it is inconceivable that any human being could be completely adequate in all these four aspects of life in addition to possessing full self-awareness. This would be a condition which would be ideal but only an approximation can be achieved at best. We can measure the quality of the human being and his degree of adequacy by how close he comes to this ideal, perfect concept of adequacy in all these five aspects. It should be kept in mind that this perfection can never be realized. A yardstick, however, is given as to what degree we deviate; in other words, if one of, or any combination of, these five requirements is deficient, we can measure the degree to which it is lacking or in which combination it is lacking.

It is easy to see that, for instance, a person in whose pattern some physical health is forfeited might have great emotional strength gained from the depletion of his energy supply for his physical health. At the same time, we can visualize physically healthy individuals who seem to be quite reproductive and perhaps economically independent who are, however, socially unacceptable, or, on the other hand, human beings who are socially acceptable and even physically healthy, but who have to forfeit reproductive urges in order to have feelings of self-awareness.

I do feel that some additional discussion of the concept of freedom of will is called for, because this is one of the most cherished human beliefs and vanities, and readers who have come a long way in understanding what has been said so far may stumble over the concept that in a way they only act according to the programming which their environment placed on their hereditary faculties in their developing years. Of course, it is well understood that the parental, particularly (directly at least) the motherly impression, is all-powerful in the very early stages of life. I will elaborate on this concept later. At this point, I wish above all to discuss the concept of freedom of will, so dear to and cherished by mankind.

Heredity and environment are beyond our influence. I cannot conceive of any other factor which might program us, but still we believe that sometimes we, by dint of will and determination, can say, "All right, I will change my attitude and change previous habits and thought processes." It takes a considerable amount of objectivity to realize that even the determination to say to oneself, "I will now adopt a changed attitude," is in itself only the result of a predisposition to make such a decision—in other words, the decision itself is only the result of the forces which programmed us. I realize that a personality pattern might meet with circumstances and attitudes incompatible with life, health, and existence. Unless this individual is forbiddingly rigid, which may lead to his destruction, some readjustment will take place. But this readjustment will necessitate stress on another aspect of the personality according to the holistic approach described above.

Perhaps, a comparison can clarify this point. If we release a rock of very irregular shape from the summit of a mountain with a very irregular mountainside, we certainly can say that the forces of gravity will pull this rock downwards. It will, according to the laws of gravity, fall with increasing speed towards the valley where it finally comes to rest. But even the best mathematician or engineer will not be able to predict exactly every bounce of this rock because the influencing factors are so complicated that at the best we can only guess what bounces the rock might take. If we consider, in addition, not only the irregular shape of the rock itself but the mountainside and the surface of all the rocks on which the falling rock bounces and rebounces, and if we also consider the temperature which has some influence and certainly the barometric pressure and wind conditions, and (if we want to be exceedingly subtle) the lesser density of air resistance on the higher levels of the mountainside, we will see that the eventual resting place of that rock in the valley will be only approximately predictable. Now, if we consider the development of a human being, at least as complicated and influenced by as many variable factors as the mountainside and the irregular formation of a rock, then we have to realize that even the best of our predictions of reaction will not be accurate. Only in more simplistic circumstances when a personality pattern is pretty well known and the influencing factors are quite outstanding, can we have a reasonable prediction about the reactivity of a person under certain conditions. This is very difficult to prove; on the other hand, many examples will seem to justify this theoretical statement, which to me is not theory but a factual situation. Now, if we dispose once and for all of the concept of freedom of will, and see ourselves only as reacting to the various situations which we meet in life (depending, of course, on the programming and pattern formation which is generally called personality), and if we at the same time keep in mind that each bounce which the rock takes somewhat changes its shape, so each event in itself which we experience leaves its impression on us. We will then see to what degree our reaction to a given situation is, if not predictable, at least determined. If we, therefore, can dispose of the concept of freedom of will, we have to rethink many of our ideas concerning human behavior and human attitudes as drastically as astrophysicists have to rethink the entire concept of cosmic events with the recent discovery of black holes in the universe and the continuous creation of positrons and electrons out of the vacuum.

Many of our cherished beliefs and thoughts will deserve rethinking and objective evaluation. With disposal of the concept of freedom of will, the concept of good and bad fall by the wayside, and we can only speak in the context of useful and not useful—useful to us, useful to others or to society, and useful ultimately to the preservation of the species.

From this viewpoint we see that good and bad and moral and immoral issues are to the highest degree predetermined.

In this book, I wish above all to lay down the basic theoretical principles of thinking and will leave it to later writers to investigate in detail the degree to which the various concepts of thinking have to be changed. We do not think in terms of guilt and proud accomplishment, but rather in terms of useful and not useful, and useful above all to the preservation of the species. Ultimately, the question narrows itself down to the question by Hamlet: "To be or not to be?" Do we believe in life as known to us or do we not believe in life as known to us? No compensatory mechanism which promises us a life hereafter will repay anybody for deficits and hardships which he endures in this world. We can easily, right here, see the unreality and, therefore, the insanity of taking promises for rewards or threats for punishments after our earthly life has come to its conclusion. These are all unrealistic and, therefore, insane concepts which are meant to compensate mankind for the unbearable hardships and difficulties of our earthly existence. Psychiatry at its best ultimately aims at facing up to the reality and facts of life as they are, but only the strongest of us will be even approximately strong enough to face up to the reality as it is and adjustments at times must be made for unbearable situations.

I will, for instance, give an example which I had in my practice recently—a young boy who was greatly disturbed came under my care. I tried to be of as much support to him as possible. His mother related that the man whom the boy considered to be his father was not his father. In reality, he was the son of his own grandfather; in other words, the father of his mother had intercourse with his daughter and the boy was born as a result of this incestuous relationship. I felt that this young man could not realistically face up to the reality of his own origin and felt that he most likely would either commit suicide, or perhaps murder his mother or grandfather-father if he learned the reality of the situation.

Therefore, we have to see that, if a disturbance is beyond toleration, a psychotic adjustment is actually Nature's way of preserving the disturbed one and making it possible for him to exist. Psychosis is, in other words, the adjustment to an intolerable situation, exactly as if physical pain becomes unbearable and shock, fainting, and cardiac arrest take place. In an emotionally unbearable situation a psychosis will occur since human vanity apparently does not permit us to see ourselves as completely powerless in the play of forces of nature. Since this concept, which is unbearable to our sense of self-vanity, which I equate to unrealistic thinking, is, therefore, unavoidable in human affairs, the question is only to what degree this insanity or deviation from a realistic, objective evaluation of the reality and facts exists. Just as the theory of relativity deals with assumptive experiments, which in reality cannot be carried through because the conditions cannot be duplicated which the assumption requires but which are so convincing that such supposition certainly seems justified, I wish here to give an assumptive experiment which would be highly convincing even to skeptical observers if it could be carried through.

If we could take a complete follow-up motion picture, including sound, of every second, minute, hour, day, week, month, and year from the moment of birth of a child—every word, every action, every touch recorded clearly through the formative years —and subsequently played in proper sequence and not speeded up and not slowed down and not even abstracted but in complete sequence—if this could be projected, then we could clearly see and the individual could clearly see what the influencing factors which went into his own pattern formation or personality were. If we deal with a child who is three years old, we see an already formed human being very clearly and, if we are astute observers, we are in a position to make certain predictions about his future development or mentality and attitude toward life. Nevertheless, we know that it is impossible to remember anything which takes place in the first few years of life because myelinization of the neurons of the brain is incomplete until somewhere between the 18th and the 36th month. Therefore, we can never have a clear memory of the factors which went into our own pattern formation and can never be totally objective about ourselves. We can only, from little features of events which took place later, try to form, like an antique mosaic, a picture which has to be filled in by our imagination. If we remember in later years, for instance, that our mother never seemed to have time for us, or that whatever she did for us she did with a certain amount of impatience, we are certainly permitted to draw certain conclusions from these facts. In a way, what we know about ourselves can be compared to an iceberg where one-tenth of the mass of the iceberg sticks out above the water and this is what we know, feel, and think about ourselves, but nine-tenths is submerged, and we have no knowledge whatsoever about the basic pattern of our personality which prompts our subsequent reaction to events and occurrences to which we are exposed. This sum total of all the events and exposures which took place throughout our lifetime—events of which we are not conscious or which in later times we have forgotten—has still left its imprint on our own pattern formation. We call this imprint the subconscious. The events may not be totally forgotten, and at times break through in dreams or flashbacks. If we are able to disabuse ourselves of the fond vanity that we are the masters of our own personality development which, of course, gives a sense of grandeur, but at the same time accounts for our guilt feelings (for example, a belief that we could have done differently or that we deserve every bit of adulation because we have done rather well); if we can disabuse ourselves of this knowledge and fondness for our own selves, this self-idolatry, this self-love, and rather see ourselves as imprintable and impressionable recipients upon which every experience and certainly the early formative experiences of infancy leave indelible marks, then we can only say that we have a more or less fortunate background. Many very practical conclusions can be drawn from this. This assumption, which appears theoretical, nevertheless, goes to the heart of our relationship with other human beings on personal and societal levels and even between tribes and nations.

We will arrive at much more objective perspectives. We will not deal with persons as worthless and despicable, but rather as persons whom we cannot permit to have destructive influences upon us for the sake of our own self-preservation; not, however, because they are inherently bad, but because they were unfortunate enough to have imprints which formed unacceptable attitudes. Once people feel that we do not reject them for their character, but rather because we cannot put up with their attitudes and that we are understanding of the circumstances which formed them, their own reaction to us may be completely changed and perhaps a more peaceful co-existence between human beings will be possible. I will go into more detail on many of these points in a later part of this book.

At this time, I wish to come to grips with a rather paradoxical phenomenon which characterizes human personality formation and existence. The specific difference between the animal kingdom (by which I mean the higher mammals, closest to human development) and human beings themselves is what can be called human self-awareness—the feeling of "I am somebody." It has to be made very clear that, first of all, in human affairs, the degree of emotional self-acceptance of the infant and later of the child and adult originates directly from the mother and indirectly from the father. Inasmuch as the husband gives emotional support, approval, and acceptance to his wife and to the degree the joy of having a child (a joy that is never unmixed, pure, and perfect—a fact which I will discuss in subsequent chapters) is felt by the mother, the infant reacts with pleasure and gradually forms a feeling of being accepted and being enjoyed. Very gradually, the child develops a feeling of "I am accepted; I give joy to my mother; I give joy to my parents. I am somebody." In other words, we only incorporate within ourselves, or a mechanism takes place which incorporates into us, a feeling of "I am somebody" to the degree that we are accepted. We see again we are only reacting to the situation we find when we are fortunate enough, to put it bluntly, to be accepted by our mother. It is, therefore, not really our own accomplishment but our very existence which leads to our self-acceptance. So, the very human factor of feeling "I am somebody," this self-awareness which we rate so highly as the highest accomplishment which humanity and the individual is able to experience, is nothing but a reaction to the environment which we originally found. Therefore, the paradox should be noted and kept in mind.

That this attitude, which we form toward ourselves, is the key to our subsequent adjustment to life and the events which we will meet on our course of life will become quite obvious. This is our pattern formation by which we will experience subsequent events, but the point has to be kept clearly in mind that our own reaction to ourselves is ultimately not a result of our own accomplishments, of our own doing, but only of the reception which we fortunately or less fortunately received when we were born.

When we, therefore, tell children, "Be somebody; be proud of yourselves; feel that you are worthwhile," this is preaching as one might to a plant: "Well, I do not quite feel that your leaves are adequate—just be better, have better leaves, have better blooms, shine more and be more productive." In reality, the plant did the best or reacted the best way the circumstances permitted it to react, as any other substance in Nature, but it is nothing but a reaction due to the determining factors. In human affairs, therefore, I feel it is much more justified to speak only of reaction formation when we speak of personality. At no time should one indulge in preaching and exhortation as to how people ought to be if they were not given the ingredients which permitted adequate development. Now, of course, it should not be forgotten that deficits can be switched around, and I will elaborate on this more when I come back to the holistic approach in human affairs.

I can deplete my physical health in order to be entirely socio-mentally acceptable. I can deplete my reproductive strivings in order to be socio-mentally acceptable or I might be very reproductive but at the same time become an economic burden to others, to the society, or the herd. I would like to make a comparison, which seems rather simple, but, perhaps will illustrate the point. If we, for instance, have a plastic tarp on the floor in a room and there is an air bubble in one place and we would like to get rid of the air bubble in this place, we press on it; however, the air bubble will not disappear if the edges are well fastened down but will appear in a different place. In turn, when we push down on the air bubble in the new place, it will show up again in yet another place. We displace, in other words, our shortcomings from one manifestation into another —from a physical level, perhaps, into a socio-mental one—from a socio-mental one perhaps into a reproductive one, or an economic one, or any combination of shortcomings. No human pattern will change unless the necessity for change presents itself. If we form a pattern that permits us to exist very well, if our shortcomings manifest themselves in asocial or anti-social behavior—let us say, in shoplifting—we will persist in this behavior whether we are proud of it or not, as long as we don't run into serious difficulties. Once we run into serious difficulties, it is like water meeting a stone wall. It has to get around. We have, therefore, to take another pattern; we have to abstain from shoplifting in order to avoid the consequences. Then, unless we receive adequate psychiatric treatment for support or gain psychological insight so that we understand our own pattern formation which got us into this predicament, some other manifestations may take place. In other words, a disturbed social behavior, unacceptable to society, if it runs into trouble may suddenly convert itself to serious physical ailments or outright psychotic manifestations or to a dependency attitude which necessitates that society step in and in some form or another take over the support of the individual. Strictly speaking, patients who have to spend part of their lives in state institutions are really the result of reaction formation. They are not equipped to have a constructive, self-supporting attitude in competitive life and have to be supported in an institution by the work of others. Being supported, they are able to function on a very reduced level, but, nevertheless, are able to exist.

I wish now to come back to the concept of basic anxiety. I feel that the degree of acceptance and joy which a child receives from the moment of birth will determine the emotional security and absence of stress within the child. Such a totally ideal state can never be reached in human affairs because, as pointed out previously, the parents themselves were received by human beings with their shortcomings, and even at the best conveyed only what they received but could not convey more than their own emotional endowment permitted them to. To the degree the joy is absent or the child is actually experienced as an imposition, a burden, and an interference, the child must feel, not on a conscious level perhaps, that his presence is not welcomed. To that degree, a completely subconscious biological feeling of insecurity develops on the level of the autonomic nervous system. This can go from the slightest degree to the most disastrous degree if an infant is surrounded and received by a mother who could just as well drown the child and do away with him and who certainly shows her impatience in every gesture, word, intonation, and action. In such a case, the child must feel that his very existence is threatened.

I postulate also that within human affairs, total acceptance is unthinkable and a certain degree at least of fear, unacceptance of the child, and a sense of the burdensomeness of the infant is unavoidable. To the degree that the mother feels the child is an imposition, the child, on the biological level of the autonomic nervous system, must feel his life is threatened. This actual fear for his existence, which the child must have in a certain, not clearly circumscribed but, nevertheless, reactive way is sensed and reacted to by the child, I call "basic anxiety." I feel this basic anxiety obviously goes hand in hand with the degree to which the mother feels the child an imposition, or, in other words, to which the child is unwanted.

This basic anxiety takes three different forms, depending on the attitude of the mother: (1) If the child intuitively senses that the mother wants to destroy it, his life instinct would react to an outright threat and destructive impulse in the only way, according to established thinking, an animal can react —by either fight or flight. A stimulation of the sympathetic part of the autonomic nervous system takes place and I postulate, therefore, that this overstimulation of the sympathetic nervous system predisposes the infant to disturbances which are influenced and caused primarily by the sympathetic nervous system. Here I would think of high blood pressure and all other diseases where an over-excitation of the sympathetic nervous system is present.

(2) If, on the other hand, the threat is experienced by the infant as a fear that the mother might abandon him, which ultimately would cause the death of the infant, then the reaction would be felt as death by starvation. Ultimately, in order to avoid starvation, any form of nourishment might be called on, even to the point of self-digestion. This self-digestion of the stomach is, partially at least, present in peptic ulcer formation and, therefore, we can say in similar cases of abandonment we might have an over-stimulation of the parasympathetic part of the autonomic nervous system as in peptic ulcer formation, colitis, and all those conditions which are characterized by vagototony in distinction to sympathotony in the earlier described fight-or-flight reaction.

(3) I postulate as a third possibility that a child may feel that his life is in danger indirectly through the mother; namely, that the mother would not defend him adequately against external dangers. We cannot imagine a cub feeling that its mother would not take every possible step to the point of risking or even sacrificing her own life in defense of it. In certain species, this will also hold true for the male; particularly when it comes to the defense of the territory in which the female raises her cubs. If an infant senses that he will not be adequately protected against external dangers, we can postulate that he may exaggerate his own reactivity to external dangers: he may become hypersensitized to his environment and perhaps allergic reactions and over-sensitive reactions to noxious and unpleasant stimuli or experiences may subsequently take place. Perhaps in the mental field a certain paranoid adjustment might be the analogy to such allergic reactivity, although other factors also enter, as will be pointed out.

I postulate that our entire concept of personality development and personality evaluation deserves a complete rethinking similar to the rethinking needed to change from the Ptolemeic concept that the earth was the center of the universe to the Copernican insight that it was not the sun which orbited around the Earth, but vice versa. Today, of course, we know in the sense of relativity both rotate and orbit about each other. In the same way as we have to re-evaluate in order to understand that substance is nothing but, in the strictest form, a manifestation of electronic charges, which at first is difficult to perceive, we must also come to grips with and rethink our entire traditional concept of the creation of the universe. The general human attitude is that everything must have a beginning and must have an end, or at least must have a beginning. This is a human postulation from our own limited human viewpoint. I certainly can conceive of, in a static universe, which the astronomers consider a possibility, that there are changes on a universal cosmic plane going on continuously, but, in itself, the universe has no beginning and no end. There are other theories about the existence and creation of the universe, and while I certainly do not feel entitled to speak here as an expert, a certain degree of acquaintance with the basic facts of modern science permits us to come up with a realistic, although limited, evaluation. At no time should it be interpreted that we are able to come up with the final answer, nor do I imply that we ever will be able to come up with a final answer. This is definitely beyond human experience, but at least we should have some knowledge of how far scientific thinking is permitted to draw definite knowledgeable conclusions.

We speak of a pulsating universe and the cosmologists say this theory implies that after a period of many billions of years of universal expansion, a contraction will take place to an unbelievable degree of density, perhaps even to almost non-existence with a gravity of incredible, indescribable intensity, and then another period of billions of years of expansion will follow. If such a theory is factual, by the very nature of contraction to non-existence, every trace of previous existence would be annihilated and, therefore, no trace could ever be found of a previously existing universal expansion period, which was followed by a complete contraction into a nucleus. Then there is a theory, held by some astro-cosmologists, that the universe created itself in an explosive fashion billions of years ago. The question then, of course, could be asked, how such an event took place? Well, we have to acquaint ourselves with the various theories of physics that waves can neutralize each other.

Apparently, if the theories of the black holes in the universe have justification, substance might fall into them, forming situations which transcend our hitherto-held concepts. The interested reader can consult the adequate literature on these theories in astro-physics and cosmology. My only implication is that our concept has to be very broadminded to have any form of orientation and that no shortcut is permissible. This is the background against which we live: a small planet rotating with eight other planets around a mediocre star which we call the Sun and which to us seems enormous, which in one flash of a flare discharges energies beyond human comprehension. There are billions of stars in our galaxy with an unknown number of planets circling them. The closest star is four light years away from us. There are billions of other galaxies and other manifestations of the universe of which we have only limited concepts, such as the quasars and pulsars. This is the limited extent to which the universe is perceived by us and we cannot answer yet what lies beyond our best perceptive instruments. The relationship of one form of energy to another must always follow certain patterns, and these patterns we can call the laws of nature and out of these laws of nature, more elaborate manifestations will result.

It is well accepted in scientific thinking that, when it comes to living substance, the laws of adaptability and survival of the fittest will take place. We have a closed system and have some understanding of the development of what we rightly consider a highly integrated and basically well-balanced pattern. These laws of interactions of energies and forces will at all times prevail and as much as Man tries to understand and to transform and use the energies according to his own desires, ultimately, he himself is subject to these forces. If nothing else, the aging of protein ultimately limits our lives. In a small way, we have seen in recent days that the industrial process is highly limited in its development by the requirements of ecology, of air and water supply, and the natural resources which, to a high degree, limit further industrial development. New sources of energy supply will have to be found and these sources, on the other hand, as they are used have to remain compatible with life and existence on this planet. Otherwise, by necessity, a self-destructive process will take place which can easily lead to Nature catching up with the endeavor of Man; that is, putting him in his place and limiting his existence on this

Earth, destroying him as so many other species have faded away when the living conditions went beyond the individual species' adaptability.

We speak of conquering the planets at this period of time, and, in a way, this is not beyond the human grasp. Just as a new world was found when Columbus set sail for what ultimately turned out to be a new continent, the same unheard-of possibilities might open up if other planets become reachable and usable, but, ultimately, we are still limited at the most to the planets in our own solar system, far-reaching as this might be. It is still unknown which planets are at all adaptable to human existence, if any. However, when we realize that the very next star to the Earth is four light years away, and if we realize what the implications of this statement are, and if we know the laws of relativity—that no substance can exist as we approximate the speed of light—then we realize that dreams of ever reaching the stars by human beings are just what they are—dreams that have no possibility of materialization. This is the overall setting and in this setting man has to make a livable adjustment so that he finds his own days justified and enjoyable and has as little conflict as possible in order not to waste energies unnecessarily and by depletion show stress symptoms which we call sickness or emotional bankruptcy.

Ultimately, all our substance by the end of the life cycle falls back into the chemical structure of the Earth. This is, of course, a truism and from this viewpoint we can speak of reincarnation, but it should be clear that this is justified only on a chemical energy level and no other thought beyond that is realistic.

I wish here to come to grips with the concept of God—of a personalized God—or at least of some force which takes a direct interest in human beings and in all kinds of events on this Earth. There is no question that as little and as insignificant this planet and each individual is, nevertheless, just as any grain of sand is part and parcel of the seashore, so every human being is part and parcel of what we consider the energy interplay of the universe and, therefore, subject to the same fate as the universe at large and of this planet in this solar system in particular. Now, if we consider the interrelationship of energies in one form or another, following certain adaptations to each other, we can call this interaction of energies the laws of Nature. Now, obviously then, these laws of Nature, this interaction of energies, will take place from the smallest form to the most extended form—the level of the universe. It seems, then, that any concept of a planned and goal-directed preconceived concept about the functioning of these energies is unrealistic. It is only an interaction of energies which leads to the resultant manifestations on a cosmic level and a solar system level, on a planetary level, and what we consider life itself in human existence on this Earth.

The best mathematician could not predict every bounce of the rock released on the summit of a mountain. The best physicist cannot predict exactly the ongoing interplay of energies and their manifestations. Now, to go a step further—we assume such a personalized God concept takes a personal interest in us. We even assume that this personal interest supersedes our own primitive desire to manipulate the forces of Nature, and becomes a source of personal love toward us. We are, therefore, substituting in a most unrealistic and imaginary—that is, psychotic or insane—way for the lack of acceptance which we experienced during our own infancy and childhood.

I wish now to point out that human vanity, which actually is nothing but self-love, can take many other forms besides a feeling of control of the natural forces by religious and ritual means. Science, in itself, can become a religion if underlying the scientific thinking is the conviction that nothing is impossible to the human mind, with more and more research and deeper and deeper penetration into the secrets of the universe. Science is a method of increasing understanding, but that is all. There is no doubt that the greatest force of Mankind is the continuous search for better understanding of natural energy relationships and prevailing forces; nevertheless, the assumption that the ultimate answer will ever be forthcoming and be obtainable and within the reach of Mankind seems an utter fallacy and the epitome of human self-love, which is vanity. If we visualize that as we have penetrated in our understanding from molecules to atoms and from atoms to electronic charges, wider and wider—or should I rather say narrower and narrower—concepts and unanswered questions present themselves. I am not a physicist able to discuss these points in a scientific way and must suggest that the reader consult studies in this area. At the same time, if we assume there is a static universe without end, this, in itself, would preclude an ability to perceive limits in the face of infinity—just as in a universe which started with what is called the big bang, it would not be possible for us to perceive clearly what caused the big bang or what preceded the big bang and why such an occurrence took place. The same would hold true for the pulsating universe which has been postulated. Recently, I have heard theories expounded that positrons and electrons are continuously formed from nothing out of the vacuum and, vice versa, that forces of energy can disappear without trace in what are called the black holes of the universe with infinite gravitational pull.

To come up with a statement: "Well, God made it all and since we cannot know His will, we should rather be quiet and not make any further statements" seems only to appease our anxiety and feeling of insecurity at the price of insanity—insanity because we substitute a delusion for the reality. It seems much more justified and realistic to me to go to any end as far as science can lead us; we must remember, however, that as we go on and the more deeply we penetrate into understanding, the more vistas will open up. A final answer will never be obtained, but, nevertheless, the endeavor of mankind to research and gain deeper understanding is the positive part—as Goethe in his *Faust* so clearly pointed out: "Striving forward is the positive part of human endeavor."

To the degree that we were not accepted by our mothers in infancy and indeed did not receive the feeling of being a person because we were enjoyed and, therefore, felt that we had personal value, this feeling was unbearable to us.

I now go beyond the concept of basic anxiety, which I previously outlined as nothing but that we felt threatened and an anxiety arose in us that was unbearable. Here I go to the absence of the feeling that we are somebody, which is an indispensable necessity for the human personality. To the extent that we did not receive this feeling of, "I am somebody," by acceptance first by our mother and subsequently by other people, depending on our first imprint in infancy, to this degree we have to obtain this feeling of personality in many other ways. Constructive accomplishments which are acceptable to other people and the public at large—in other words, recognition by other people becomes then the substitute for our own lack of self-acceptance. Here we have the long list of attempts to get public acclaim and recognition for our economic endeavors, scientific endeavors, artistic endeavors, altruistic attitudes, etc. There is no limit. If we have, at the same time, an anti-social component of considerable dimension, then the recognition will be sought from people who have similar attitudes and then groups might be formed, whence we want recognition in our anti-social or asocial behavior. We will at times use force to impose our will on others to their complete destruction or only to take advantage of them and feel that we have, therefore, gained superiority and mastership and personality values. We can see how difficult it would be to change such a pattern once it has formed and convert it satisfactorily to a more acceptable form of pattern because, strictly speaking, we would have to give such a person all the acceptance which he was deprived of in his infancy. This would mean the feeling that, like the adequate mother would if need be, as in the animal kingdom, risk her life in the defense of the cub, we would have to secure within him the feeling that we would not abandon him under any conditions and indeed would be willing to die for him, if need be. Obviously, this is an impossible assumption. We know that so many times adopted children are not quite able to identify with their adoptive parents because they feel they actually would not go to that length in defense of them. In addition, we see that even children with their own parents will not have this unquestioned feeling. Since the feeling of "I am somebody" depends, therefore, on such strong dedication from the mother, it is very difficult to visualize that we might be so important to the other person that they would go to such lengths for us. In addition, it is not satisfactory just to know that somebody would die for us because they might ultimately do it for their own glorification, for their own self-respect, and not necessarily out of love for us and dedication to us as a person. We have to differentiate strongly between emotional dedication and intellectual dedication. Many persons for self-indulgence and self-glorification will go to any length, even that of self-sacrifice, for other people in order to feel their own sense of personality value and glory, but it is not the emotional attachment which motivates them, and so even the highest sacrifices do not contribute to the emotional enrichment of the recipient; indeed, the recipient may only feel that he is the object upon which the do-gooder, so to speak, focuses his own activity in order to be able to indulge in his own self-glorification. We have to differentiate between actions undertaken out of emotional need and for intellectual rationalization, reasonings, or self-glorification.

Another concept has to be disposed of and this is the concept of immortality. In Nature, we see that in the animal kingdom, above all, the highest law is the preservation of the species. It is not at all necessarily the preservation of the individual, but rather the preservation of the species which matters; indeed, let it be mentioned at this moment that the individual many times will be called on to sacrifice himself in order to serve the preservation of the species. It is considered quite natural that the parental generation, and certainly the female, will risk its own life, not unnecessarily, of course, but if necessity should arise in the defense of the cubs. Naturalists tell us that many times cows and calves, in moments of attack by predators, will be taken inside of a circle, while the bulls form a protective ring around them and risk their lives in defense of the cows and calves, which, after all, represent the next generation. This law of preservation of the species is certainly incorporated in the old law of the sea. When a ship sinks, the traditional cry goes up, "Women and children first!" and a dim view is taken of a male who tries to save himself before the women and children are rescued. Divorce laws also favor the mother, which is compatible with the first thought upon survival of the species.

Now, it is obviously understood that, from an objective, long-range viewpoint, our solar system and, therefore, our planet Earth, has a limited existence. We speak of ten billion years or perhaps ultimately double that lifetime of our solar system, but this, for practical purposes, is considered theoretical because human beings do not think in those long terms normally. Nevertheless, these are newer concepts which science has opened up.

The concepts of early mankind did not permit an individual to disappear for all time to come. We can, therefore, surmise that the natural instinct of preservation of the species has turned, influenced by the basic human vanity, to the desire for immortality. The immortality was fantasized to take place in some form of afterlife and mythology and early religion certainly tell us of the various concepts which the tribes and religious groups conceived. Best known to our Western world is the concept of the ancient Greeks, where the souls of the deceased go to Hades and are the shadows, which in some form or other, still form an afterlife. The Teutonic form of mythology sees the survival of the heroes in Valhalla where they mingle with the gods. Studies on the development of myth and religion give all the necessary information to elaborate on this point. The burning or burial of the deceased was an integral part of many religions in order to permit "the soul of the deceased to find his peaceful resting place." Pyramids and mighty buildings of antiquity are witness to the beliefs that an afterlife was an accepted concept. It was unthinkable for human beings and certainly for primitive human beings that they should completely disappear from this earth without any trace. Vanity had to create one form or another in which a persistent human existence could, in imagination at least, be preserved.

The inborn biological instinct of procreation and preservation of the species had, to a high degree, the emotional connotation of living on in one's children and the desire to have specifically male heirs, which was and is so prevalent all over the world in different cultures, reflects the particular male vanity to live on in their male offspring.

Religion has, to a high degree, been identified as the guiding lines for human behavior in the human interchange and relationships among themselves, other tribes, and the world at large. Indeed, it is not infrequent that human beings are found who basically do not share the concept of creation as related by religious tenets, nor believe in an afterlife, nor in god-personification in any form whatsoever; nevertheless, they feel that there is a positive part in religion inasmuch as religion seems to be the teacher of moral laws. I like to challenge even this concept very definitely because the morals depend, to a large degree, on reward and punishment, so well known to everybody that I certainly do not have to elaborate on this at this time. The assumption would be if the highest level of human development would be the realization of one's own personality value, one would, under no condition, wish to diminish this feeling of personal value and self-awareness and avoid for very direct, personal reasons any infringement of this feeling of self-respect and, therefore, the moral outline of behavior would intuitively be followed without having to depend on the primitive fear and reward mechanism.

I am fully aware that it is an idealistic assumption that human beings will reach such a state of development, and at no time do I wish to be misunderstood as an idealist without any realistic appreciation of facts. Nevertheless, the facts have to be seen as they are if we want to have any objective appreciation of human adjustments. There is no question that in all this there is a recurrent paradox. In one way, we are not responsible for our basic personality; in the other way, it is the personality which has been formed upon us which dictates to us our mode of behavior. Again, I have to emphasize that, in a broad sense, this is the law of the selection of the fittest. The question remains unanswered and is speculative as to what degree an objective appreciation of facts, which disposes of the basic human vanity as much as possible, will change also the reactivity of human beings. On this point, of course, such speculations can go on, but it should be undertaken, although they may appear only theoretical at the moment.

We have to come to grips with another concept and that is the fatalistic concept which is, perhaps, not in practice but in theory, far spread—that things take their place, events will follow, and human endeavor will not be able either to influence the events or change the course of developments. As much as, on the surface, this thought has the appearance of reality after all that has been said, nevertheless, it is a limited concept because it does not take into consideration and account for the human need for feeling active in his fate. In reality, events will take their course according to the pattern of the human beings involved; however, in our vanity again we have the feeling that our actions are greatly influenced by the decisions we make. In order to fulfill, then, the imprinted need of vanity, we will face with action the events which we meet, action and reaction, but certainly with a decision toward behavior. Complete passivity at no time does justice to the basic human needs of reacting to events. In the chase of a pursued animal—let us say, by a lion—the eventual outcome could be predicted if we would know all the factors involved—the age, speed, health of the hunted animal; the skill and development of the lion; the countryside with all potential hiding places; and a million other elements which arise. Nevertheless, the animal will, under normal conditions, do everything to avoid a disastrous end that means his own death at the fangs of the predator. The same is true of a human being who will do everything that the situation permits him to do to overcome difficulties successfully. To assume in a limited concept that the outcome is therefore predetermined and no action has to be taken is fallacious because it does not take into account the reactivity of the individual or of the herd at large. Therefore, a passive, fatalistic attitude is unrealistic. As the comparison previously taken with the rock released from the summit may apply here also, although from a higher objective viewpoint far beyond the reach of human foresight, the ultimate outcome of the boundings of a released irregular rock from the summit of a mountain may be predetermined. Nevertheless, human insight is inadequate to foretell the exact outcome and the same comparison holds for human action. We cannot speak of a fatalistic outcome without taking our own reactivity into account and this reactivity, in itself, demands active reaction, whatever seems appropriate, and not passive toleration of a given circumstance which might be equated to suicide at times. This is, of course, contradictory to the instinct of self-preservation and certainly of the preservation of the species.

The question of the desire for leadership has to be discussed now—maturity against immaturity. To the degree that we have been happily received in our infancy, we accept ourselves and follow through the biological and psychological development in self-acceptance with the desire to exist and take care of ourselves as individuals and eventually to procreate within the biological urges of Nature itself. To the degree, on the other hand, we were not adequately and happily received by our mother, an unfulfilled desire for parental security and guidance remains in us. We remain subconsciously, unknown to ourselves, followers rather than independent, mature human beings because in following we receive the emotional compensation for inadequate emotional endowment in our own childhood. Maturity, therefore, is manifested by self-preservation and self-manifestation with justification to carry over one's own image into the next generation, whereas immaturity will not feel justified in so doing because of inadequate emotional investment and will, therefore, in some form or other, deviated as it may be, interfere with self-reproductivity. Now, a long line of maladjustments so familiar to established psychiatry could be enumerated here, if my purpose were to write a textbook on psychiatry. I wish, instead to focus on the deeper concepts which may shed light on a better understanding of human instincts and behavior patterns.

Another paradox has to be considered; namely, that sometimes the very immature, wishing to influence other human beings, will seek positions of influence in religious, political, economic and other forms of human endeavor in an attempt to amass followers. In order to feel powerful and important, the immature become leaders, not so much by their own accomplishments and not that the followers do so of their own volition, but because of the high degree of solicitation of and preaching to the followers. This attempt to obtain influence is necessary to compensate the immature for their basic feeling of inadequacy, although, as previously pointed out, it is recognized they ultimately are not responsible for their pattern, but, in their vanity, they think they are.

At this point, some thoughts should be given to the inborn human need for companionship and the horror and basic unbearable feeling of lonesomeness. Basic biology requires reproduction. This is the law of Nature and the manifestation of the preservation of the species is biologically conditioned. Therefore, in the mammals—certainly in the higher mammals of which Mankind is a member—it takes a male and a female to follow this law of Nature. In itself, complete withdrawal, including withdrawal from the opposite sex, therefore counteracts the basic biological urge and law of reproductivity, as well as the herd instinct. It seems to be a well-known fact that the closer two human beings of the opposite sex are emotionally intertwined, the less they need, or even want, the companionship of other people since they are very sufficient for each other and, indeed, often seek their own company to the exclusion of others. On the other hand, if such an ideal condition does not prevail, at least not for any length of time, substitution has to be made and a certain amount of toleration of the other person's attitude is necessary if a peaceful exchange of communication and enjoyment of that person is to take place. If our thinking becomes self-serving and exclusive of other people, they will not be able to feel at ease with us—we will not attract them and they will not feel attracted by us and some lonesomeness will result which becomes practically unbearable.

Whether we then seek the company of other people in fantasy only, whether we communicate with imaginary persons (which is psychotic), or whether we lower our communications to an animal level instead of our own species, substituting animals—be it dogs, cats, other pets, or animals at large—for other human beings, this certainly is a deviation from the norm or from a mature adjustment. Since a degree of immaturity, however, is unavoidable in human affairs, as pointed out, the toleration threshhold is of a high degree. We see, however, that deviation can go so far that under some conditions animals are used as substitutes for sexual partnership. This certainly is a deviation of high degree inasmuch as it not only substitutes animals for our own species but, at the same time, does not give the animal a choice of rejection since the more powerful human being can use it at will, which in itself is characteristic of the brutishness of an individual parallel to rape where the so-called partner is used as an object by force. The human species has long been recognized as social animals, herd animals only able to survive in groups. This basic requirement necessitates the emotional dependence on human companionship also. Even if we retire to a mountaintop or retire into the desert, we carry with us the experiences of millennia.

In infancy and childhood, to the degree that our needs for emotional acceptance were not fulfilled, we had a feeling of lonesomeness and helplessness. Children at times live in an imaginary world. They invent imaginary playmates to make up in fantasy for their lack of human closeness, companionship, and playmates. In fantasy, they can answer temporarily to all their emotional needs. We see again and again, therefore, that fantasy is the imaginary substitute for deprivation of realistic needs and wish fulfillment. An individual is seriously disturbed only when fantasy goes beyond the average degree. It should be pointed out that an unrealistic belief (expecting influence and results from forces which are beyond our control) cannot only be expected in terms of organized and traditional religion but also in the belief in the power of organized and traditional science. This attitude basically postulates the invincibility and limitless power of the human mind to discover the last secrets of Nature and, therefore, truly becoming universal in the understanding of every secret of Nature, certainly implying grandeurs, psychotic thinking, and exaggeration of human comprehension. This would imply that the particle can understand the whole—the totality. It can manifest itself also in the innumerable pseudosects and fringe groups, which, in spite of bearing the connotation of being off the mainstream, always attract certain other more or less smaller groups of followers, or splinter groups, for examples, astrology, which since time immemorial attributes forces and influences from the stars and from the universe at large upon events and occurrences in human life. In all these limited splinter groups, there is a modicum of truth—it is very true, for example, that the constellation of stars in the universe, etc., had a tremendous influence on a universal basis. Certainly, the influence of the moon and the sun on life on this earth is more than obvious, but to construe that a certain constellation of planets prevailing at the time of one's birth has a significant influence on our character formation and, therefore, on our life, seems to exaggerate reality and carries a single factor to extremes to the exclusion of other more determining influences.

Then, too, there are always various pseudo-scientific, rather charletan-type groups which believe in telepathy and supernatural occurrences, basing their belief on the fact that somehow minimal energy can be conveyed over long distances, although not bothering to explain how energy transportation in the form of waves can be received over long distances by a properly attuned recipient. Here again, there is a minimum of truth; namely, that under similar or equal circumstances, various organisms will react in the same way. We can only say that similar occurrences will create similar thought patterns. Innumerable instances could be cited, but these examples would only show that the human mind will, in part, exaggerate the importance of certain happenings, and if an individual was convincing enough to acquire enough followers, a pseudo-scientific cult would again be formed, attracting the non-stabilized mind since it seems to give play to the inborn need for grandiosity and human vanity.

The issue becomes much more complicated when we deal with traditional and scientific medicine. The question cannot be overlooked as to what degree medicine itself, scientific as it may be, becomes, nevertheless, a religion—a belief of the patient in his doctor and his administrations, who, in a way, represents the source of power, influence, and capability. The person who is under stress conditions and receives reassuring words from the doctor; the patient who receives medication, which may or may not bring about a material change in the condition; nevertheless, the trust he puts into the procedure will, in a way, follow concepts of his own beliefs. The physician becomes to the patient, not only the scientific administrator of procedures that respond exactly to the cause-and-effect principle, but also the high priest of chemistry and the scalpel, which in these cases are only believed to be curative.

I wish to give a few examples: if a vague pain is experienced in the abdomen, for instance, for some time and finally a laparotomy is chosen in order to explore the abdominal cavity and all the organs are found to be sound, and if basically no far-reaching procedure is carried out, the abdominal wall is closed and healing takes place, it is quite possible the patient, being reassured that nothing was found, shows considerable amount of improvement, if he is not cured. Carrying this point further, adhesions—very mild and insignificant—are found, not by any means of such magnitude that they really cause disturbances, but of completely mild and insignificant nature. The surgeon removes them, explaining to the patient what has been done and the patient may attribute to the procedure curative and healing powers which, in reality, the procedure does not justify—especially if the surgeon believes in the procedure himself. This, of course, would clearly show to what degree we generally like to believe medical science is also a form of religion. We know that many procedures have been used in the past which today are rejected. We have no reason to question that at the time they were to a high degree effective, although they may also have been harmful. Blood-letting, poultices, and other forms of administrations are examples which come to mind as having fallen into disuse; however, they were believed by the physician, as well as the patient, to be functional. One point, therefore, that cannot be stressed enough, is that the patient has to feel that the administrator—the physician himself—believes in the procedure. Nothing is more convincing than an inspired leader who is enthusiastic in his belief or a physician who sincerely believes in the rectitude of his approach. It is apparently this need to be led, to entrust oneself to the leadership of another—a carry-over from our infancy and childhood when our own infantile dependency needs were never adequately answered—that has to be answered in various individuals to the degree that their own maturity, independence, and self-reliance were inadequately developed.

Again and again, the purpose of life itself on this earth is questioned, or, on a broader scale, the purpose of the universe. "There must be some sense to it," human beings are fond of saying. They cannot perceive that things just exist for themselves. Traditional religion answered this point in its own way by stating that the universe was created—"AD MAJOREM GLORIAM DEI" ("To the higher glory of God" and don't ask any more questions). Well, we can go a step further and say the universe and life itself exist and that is a fact. This is quite realistic and objective, to my way of thinking. At the same time, human vanity requires the need, as individuals, to have a purpose in life because our vanity will not be satisfied by just existing. We think that a life spent only on one's own pleasure and primitive enjoyment is one ill-spent, and does not give the individual the highest fulfillment which we feel is in the realization of self-respect and self-esteem in the sense of a realistic worthwhileness to the group—a contribution to society at large, in whatever form it may be. This would be the humanized form of contributing to the survival of the species.

A primitive attitude is that all events in life follow a predetermined fate; that the wills of the gods cannot be changed and events take place as they are ordained. All is written in a book of life pertaining to each human being and we follow our predestined course. Then along came the philosophers who claimed we actually are, according to their concepts, our own masters of destiny, and fate is nothing but what we make it; therefore, it is our own personality that determines the events we meet in life because our own attitude reacts to situations as they arise and, in the strictest sense, we are masters of our ships and our events. This conforms with the feeling of personality—"I am somebody; therefore, I can direct my fate."

My own concept goes a step further and that is that our own personality is predetermined by the circumstances that formed us, and it is vanity which makes us think that we are somebody with a free will so that we can shape the events of our life inasmuch as we have a free will to determine the happenings as we react to the situations that we meet. This, again, in the broadest sense, is pointing to a determinism which could lead to fatalism—whether things are predetermined only to the degree that not only the events themselves dictate the occurrences, but our own reactions to the events are reflected in the outcome. Strictly speaking, we are only predetermined through our own life experiences and, therefore, from the highest viewpoint, a determinism cannot be questioned. This determinism, however, is of such a complicated nature that at no time can we foresee the outcome in any constellation of events because it far supersedes human predictability. The definition of maturity is comparatively simple when we relate it to the animal kingdom and say that maturity exists when reproduction can take place. The same holds true for the plant kingdom. As far as human beings go, we can take the broadest view along these lines, if, we at the same time, associate reproduction to uphold the preservation of the species with an attitude of joy at having the opportunity to reproduce, and not as an imposition on our own pursuit of happiness, but rather a fulfillment. We are in a position to not only reproduce life but to secure it until such time that our infants and children grow up, become adolescents, and take their own rightful place on this earth, and to the degree that we enjoy this process of responsibility, to that degree we are certainly considered mature. Any deviation, in whatever form it may be, to the degree it is experienced as a burden and also to the degree our physical inability has been brought about by emotional constellations which then interfere with our joyful execution of this basic natural dictate, would have to be considered immaturity.

It should be pointed out that when we fall in love, we fall in love according to our own emotional needs. Courtship in the animal kingdom—certainly in higher species of the animal kingdom where a testing-out of the potential mate takes place—has the equivalent in human courtship in that we feel out our potential mate for the emotional fulfillment of our own emotional requirements. If I have to hate a woman, basically because my own attitude is one of fear derived from my experiences as a child, then I will ultimately fall in love with a person who, in close relationship, will justify this emotional attitude.

Suppose we learn that a father of a son has died comparatively young of a heart attack. On the surface, the son and the mother seem to get along very well; however, because the young boy knows his father died while married to the mother, he has to feel that perhaps repression of anger in the father caused tension, which the father had no other way to express but inwardly, ultimately suffering a heart attack, resulting in his death. Completely subconsciously, this boy must feel that association with a woman would shorten his own life and lead to his death in early years; therefore, he will be afraid to give himself into the hands of a woman, to fall in love with her, because he feels this may be an outright threat to his life. To say he will "feel" is not a correct expression. We should rather say subconsciously this attitude prevails, although on a conscious level he may adore women, he may feel his mother was wonderful, had provided for him adequately working after the death of the father, and seemed on the surface a model of motherhood. However, on a lower, more subconscious level, we can see that he may ultimately feel the mother is a destroyer and only at the price of the death of his father could she function adequately. This is a good example of how emotional attitudes are formed and, thusly, our attitude to the opposite sex takes place.

Somehow we can compare domestication of animals also to maturity and immaturity. To the degree an animal is willing to sell out, so to speak, its own independence for a certain degree of security in food reception, he accepts the fate which is then, unknown to him, bestowed by the owner or person who gets control of his existence. We can say the same applies to maturity or immaturity. To the degree we are willing to maintain or achieve independence and responsibility for our own fate and actually enjoy its responsibility and the ability to function, we are not dependent on the good will or the ill will of other people. This in itself, besides the good feeling that independence gives us, will justify the desire to be independent and mature because we at least have then the illusion that we are free in our own choosings of decisions, whereas, when we are dependent on others, we certainly lack this illusion of independence.

We all need the illusion that whatever we do serves a purpose and the idea that somebody dies and has not accomplished something, through his death at least, is unbearable to human vanity. If a child dies, we always like to construe some usefulness in this death. If nothing else can be said, we ask what can medical science learn from this death? If death seems not to have benefitted a single person in one way or another, we like to create a purpose by dedicating the body to science for additional medical research or feeling that additional lessons may have been learned which now may be useful to surviving individuals. This certainly is human vanity which cannot accept that our life does not serve a particular useful purpose.

As previously pointed out, a dualism between body and emotion, or body and mind, is certainly outdated. The human being is indivisible: body and emotions are part of the same individual, indivisible and with mutual influence upon each other. Subconsciously, we have a feeling of our potentialities, of our maturity and the joy which the functioning in a mature, independent life situation would give us. Anything which interfered with our full mature development, particularly all the factors which surrounded our own infancy and childhood, would, therefore—if we were conscious and aware of it—cause hostility and a very strong anger, that we were deprived of our full development of the best which life has to give, the feeling of our own value of self-esteem and self-respect. Therefore, we can say that there is a repressed, unconscious hostility and anger to the degree we were prevented from receiving the emotional ingredients to give us a chance to develop to this highest degree of emotional fulfillment. Most of us are not conscious of these hostilities; nevertheless, we can postulate that they would be there if we were conscious and aware of what happened to us. In psychiatric practice, we can see clearly the degree of improvement which follows to the degree this subconscious hostility is expressed. The repression of hostility is actually the retarding factor in our own emotional fulfillment. It has to be clearly understood at the same time that a free expression of our hostility against other people is inadmissible. Strictly speaking, they are not the cause of our difficulties. Our parents are the cause, but still they are not aware of it and certainly did not consciously, voluntarily retard us. It seems, therefore, a vicious circle—we cannot express the hostility outwardly if we want to be acceptable according to socially accepted lines; we can, however, express hostility against ourselves, but this, to the highest degree, is the cause of somatic disturbances. We can express it against ourselves by repressing reproductive urges—in other words, we do not create or bear children. We seek highly philosophical attitudes or attitudes of a religious nature, which are ultimately anti-reproductive, which lead to an unfertile and sterile life in the physical sense. Unproductivity is ultimately a life-denying attitude. If everybody on this earth abstained from reproductive sexual relationships, this would obviously mean the extinction of the human race within one generation. This is the case even if this attitude is hidden behind high-sounding philosophical or religious thought processes.

The rejection of life itself may be completely disguised and sometimes these people will show, on the surface at least, great sympathy for other human beings, many times saying that they love children. Of course, it is well understood that when we speak of the wish to remain childless, the wish is only the illusion of our freedom of will. In reality, we were patterned and programmed to this attitude. The basic hostility which we subconsciously feel because we were deprived of a mature, responsible, and joyful attitude toward life can either be taken out on our surroundings or on other human beings, and this, to a large degree, accounts for anti-social criminal attitudes.

If we reach an adjustment more acceptable to society but with a basic emotional deficit, this adjustment may be turned against ourselves. It may lead to somatic disease, whose form depends on some triggering mechanism, which certainly deserves further investigation. This may lead to a lack of self-acceptance, which is expressed in a psychoneurotic attitude in the form of self-disapproval, which seems subjectively justified. To the degree we lack maturity which, however, implies the vanity that we could have done better on our own, we have guilt feelings. To the degree that we feel we are worthwhile, we certainly have an attitude that our own life is justified; we are not our own enemies and we do not provoke physical or emotional difficulties for ourselves. This is—strictly speaking, of course—only a reaction to the circumstances which programmed our personality; however, in our vanity we feel subconsiously that we are worthwhile. To the degree that we feel in our vanity that we have shortcomings, we feel we should not exist; we become our own enemies and become self-destructive. Freud, of course, has correctly called this the "death wish," shared to a lesser or greater degree by every human being, with only the degree differing from one individual to another.

We can almost say that we lead our life under a post-hypnotic command. Although we were patterned according to the acceptance and circumstance which surrounded us and that pattern was incorporated into our own self, we had the feeling that it was our own free will and volition that patterned our reactions to life situations. However, we were no more free than a person in a hypnotic state, who is given some commands to follow upon awakening. He may find himself acting in a certain predetermined pattern which he may consider his own volition, not realizing that has has been given the command at an earlier, nonconscious level. When we speak of thinking, we can almost compare it to the time a computer takes to come up with an answer by reviewing all the factors which must be considered in order to arrive at a decision consistent with all the pre-programmed information. Thinking may be considered a review of all the influencing factors which determine the ultimate result of the forces which our experience has programmed into us. As we review all these forces, we come up with an answer, and this process in itself we can consider thinking.

When we speak of maturity and immaturity in the parental relationship, we can see that a mother who wants to be loved basically and above all by her children is immature and inadequate; however, to the degree she is able to give love, she is mature and adequate. To the degree we seek to be loved, we are still in an immature relationship to another person. To the degree we are able to give love and give warmth, we have maturity—the higher joy of loving instead of seeking love becomes obvious to the person who has reached that level of emotional development.

The various psychic groups, which have become so prevalent in recent days, connote only a form of human vanity, an aggrandizement, by seeking to possess more power than rational thinking, scientific research, and established facts jusify. Theoretically, we can certainly construe a relationship between any event in the entire universe and any other. Any event, as far away and as insignificant as it may be, if we split hairs thin enough, must have some effect on every other existing force in the universe, but the influence has to be of such minuscule proportion that to discern a noticeable and measurable result seems inappropriate. Strictly speaking, a human being jumping several inches off the ground is, as relativity certainly will maintain, in a mutual relationship—he pushes himself off the earth, he pushes the earth away from him. However, the degree to which he has pushed the earth away from its pre-set path is so minute that this is only a theoretical consideration. The same waves emanating from every cell in the sense of electric radiation may certainly be registered on our scalp by electroencephalography. However, the electrodes have to be placed directly on the scalp and the resulting electric currents have to be magnified tremendously to become visible. When we assume that these currents and wave radiations can be measured at some distance from the scalp, it is possible to speculate that they can be registered at any distance; however, this is again only theoretical. Therefore, to build an entire system out of the ideas that human beings can generate radiations across great distances and that the mind can bring forth definite noticeable cause-event sequences in distant objects or human beings is so far-fetched that it can only be considered as self-aggrandizement of disproportionate degree. This, therefore, falls into the category of human vanity—that is, seeing oneself out of proportion.

Since time immemorial, the words of wisdom were "Know thyself." Why is it so difficult to know ourselves? First of all, at the very best, there is no memory of the most important period in our life—the early formative years. We can only reconstruct through later events what may have preceded them. We may remember that our mother was impatient and subsequently abused us on many occasions; that our father went out drinking or beat our mother; and we can assume that our reception onto this earth was not necessarily a very welcomed one. We have to become objective about our mother. The mother, for practical purposes, is the very foundation of life for the child and if mother is life, mother cannot be wrong. If our mother thinks that we are no good, we ultimately have to incorporate this self-depreciation and, if it is unbearable to us, we have to overcome it in the most twisted forms. We either have to suffer the most devastating types of diseases or make adjustments which society will object to in order to feel that we are somebody despite the fact that we were actually rejected. We have to come to the realization that the shortcomings of our mother, which were part of her personality pattern, made her look upon us as undesirable and unwanted.

Of course, the role of the father should not be overlooked because it can be said that each child in reality is only wanted as much as the mother enjoyed not only the intercourse but her mate as well. She must want to give life to an offspring of this highly adored, desirable mate. The degree of warmth, in other words, that the mate conveyed to the wife, making her feel desirable and, therefore, somebody, conveyed itself to the offspring. The offspring, in turn, reflected this joyful acceptance in his own self-acceptance or, more precisely, in the degree of his self-acceptance. This objectivity about our parents, and particularly about our mother, is almost impossible to obtain, and only the greatest motivation will lead us to an objective appraisal that all parents do the very best they can with their own endowments. This repeats itself from generation to generation; nobody completely escapes this pattern, even though in some families, some children seem to be more fortunate and some less fortunate. This, however, is only in appearance because the weakness will break through or show itself openly in some manifestation or another later in life, or even in the next generations. We have to look at life from a very objective viewpoint. It is only to the degree that we can become objective about the forces which programmed us that we will be able to free ourselves from imprints that were put upon us.

chapter 1

REALITY AND PSYCHOSIS

This book is by no means intended to be a textbook on psychiatry. A textbook should present accepted ways of thinking and, at the best, review all reasonably well-known attitudes, divergent as they may be. Anyone who is only superficially acquainted with psychiatrists and their attitudes cannot help but be overwhelmed by the diametrically opposing viewpoints taken by them, even by prominent psychiatrists at times. Indeed, we can sympathize with the bewilderment of some patients and potential patients when they see how much psychiatrists, to whom they are about to entrust themselves, differ amongst themselves. Some psychiatrists are definitely outright organicists, feeling that mental and emotional disturbances are overwhelmingly, if not exclusively, conditioned by organicity. Their attitudes are greatly steeped in an unshakable belief in the righteousness of the tenets of accepted genetics.

The basic dogma of this form of thinking is that acquired characteristics will not be carried over through heredity into following generations. However, studies carried on in recent years seem to indicate that certain chemical substances can bring about changes in the chromosomal pattern. Equally, certain types of radiation are found to be capable of influencing and changing the chromosomal pattern. Whether we call these changes mutations or simply changed chromosomal patterns is irrelevant. The facts and results are the same. The question, therefore, presents itself immediately—is this influence upon chromosomes limited to certain chemical substances only drawn in a rather narrow scope, or can chemical substances and perhaps even radiation possibly influence, in principle, chromosomes and, therefore, bring about changes in hereditary patterns? And, can influence range from infinitesimal to exceedingly strong?

On the other hand, many psychiatrists are convinced that it is the environment and all its influences from infancy on which form the personality pattern of the individual, attitudes toward life, and, therefore, also emotional and mental disturbances.

When we realize that these extreme positions are held by some psychiatrists—the bulk of psychiatrists taking in-between viewpoints—and when we realize that ultimately every psychiatrist has his own standards and yardsticks in evaluating a patient and his condition, we will not be surprised to find that some psychiatrists and clinics are more inclined to call a condition in a patient, for instance, a psychoneurosis, whereas other psychiatrists may call the same condition at the same time psychotic.

The *Diagnostic and Statistical Manual* of the American Psychiatric Association gives the following definition of psychotic disorders: "The disorders are characterized by a varying degree of personality disintegration and failure to test and evaluate correctly external reality in various spheres. In addition, individuals with such disorders fail in their ability to relate themselves effectively to other people or to their own work." We see, therefore, that an essential part of a psychotic mental condition is the inability of the individual to be realistic.

Very frequently, one of the characteristics of disturbed reality appreciation is a delusion. What is the definition of a delusion? Louis Sim, M.D., defines delusion in *Comprehensive Textbook of Psychiatry,* edited by Freedman and Kaplan (1967), as "a false belief that is maintained more or less unshakably and fixedly in the face of reason. Furthermore, the belief held is not one ordinarily shared by other members of the patient's sociocultural and educational group; for example, it is not a commonly believed superstition or a religious or political conviction. Delusions are pathognomonic of the psychoses. They occur most frequently in schizophrenia, but they can be observed in all psychotic states, including those of organic origin." Several rather startling conclusions can be drawn from this definition. I shall try to illustrate this with a few examples:

> 1) If early Polynesians, for instance, held that the scorn of the firegod of the volcano Mauna-loa could be appeased by a virgin sacrificially jumping down its crater, this was not a delusion (supposedly) since this belief was shared by many other members of the group.

> 2) When Semmelweis first maintained that childbed fever was caused by the administering physicians themselves who assisted in deliveries with unclean, germ-infected hands, he was ostracized and his mental condition seriously questioned. A similar case can be made for Galileo and innumerable other pathfinders who disagreed with established thought processes. We see how dangerous it can be to bring forth new ideations because, by their very nature, they challenge the adjustment of the majority.

We see also that however obtrusive and unrealistic an attitude may be, as long as it goes as religious belief and is shared by many other individuals, it passes as mentally healthy! I certainly will not have to cite many examples to illustrate this most obvious and universal attitude. They range from the obolus, which the ancient Greeks put into the mouth of the deceased so that he could pay Charon for his travel over the river Styx, to the bonfires lighted by stoneage men at the time of the winter solstice to help the sinking sun to come up higher again over the horizon. Whether circumcision, sacredness of cows, or lighting of candles has a more realistic influence on events to come, I will have to leave up to the reader to decide.

The deeper question, however, arises as to why such a blanket exception has to be made with regard to religious beliefs? Is a certain degree of human unreality unavoidable or actually characteristic of mankind and we pass only as long as we more or less conform or are able to gain sooner or later enough followers to our attitude? Is unreality less delusion when it is held by many or all? Is delusion not characteristic of mental disease or insanity and psychosis, and is the human race less insane because the condition is shared by all? And then, of course, what is the origin of this universal need of unreality? The animal kingdom, certainly the animals in their free habitat, unencumbered by human beings, seem, as far as we can observe, realistic—they react to danger directly and appropriately within the scope of their natural endowment. The antelope and gazelle flee before the hungry predator. But the hunted animal will expend its energies only to the degree and as long as necessary to escape the danger. Once the danger is over and the fearsome dread has passed, we see the potential prey close to the feared predator who, at this moment at least, is no threat. This consideration will deserve closer discussion in the chapter on Psychophysiological Reaction.

We see that in the definition of delusion, a strong point is made in favor of conformity. The dialogue between the individual and his rights and society and its requirements is an ancient one. Aristotle already described a human being as *zoon politikon,* a herd animal. The requirement of each herd is the acceptance of the rules of the herd by its individual members. This is, of course, tantamount to conformity. If any difficulties arise in the animal kingdom, the herd deals with the offender effectively. Some strong, powerful individuals may successfully absentee themselves from the herd and live a rogue existence. In human affairs, this situation is more complicated. The human desire to feel as an individual may collide with society's requirements. A narrow line will at times exist between what society can and will tolerate.

It can be said that the happier the reception was which the infant found on his arrival in this world, the happier the experiences were which surrounded his development, the more benign will be his perception of the world as a whole. He will find no great stress in identifying with and conforming to existing attitudes. On the other hand, unhappy, painful, and even hostile environmental experiences will create horror and revulsion in the child in his formative years from the very beginning. These malignant influences cannot help but have a decisive influence upon him as much as he consciously or unconsciously detests them.

The role of the psychiatrist is a two-fold one. He tries to bring about the patient's understanding of himself, and helps him to become objective about the influences which formed him and thus ultimately to realize he could not have turned out differently than he did. He was ultimately only an adjustment reaction. Once this self-knowledge is achieved and, please mark well that I speak of ideal psychiatric conditions, the patient, who is now better named the individual, can free himself from earlier patterns which have proven not only useless but at times outright disastrous to his life and pursuit of happiness.

But we see also that the psychiatrist has to keep the requirements of the society in mind and to that degree it is true that he is viewed as a guardian if not warden of the herd. Since the requirements of various societies change tremendously at times, one can see great discrepancies in the attitudes of psychiatrists under various conditions. A point in question is the accommodation, if not at times even enthusiasm, which psychiatrists showed in Nazi Germany to the changed cultural mores. It can be said not only that their own survival necessitated their adjustment to new attitudes but that, by the very definition of social adjustability, a certain degree of conformity was expected. If we disregard those who had no choice in the matter and in their fate and those who were economically and otherwise independent enough that they could choose to leave a country whose philosophy they abhorred, the average German was only true to the concept of conformity to his own group and shared by the overwhelming number of psychiatrists in his own country.

chapter 2

BASIC ANXIETY

In this chapter, I do not wish to concern myself with the inevitable degree of psychosis, which is characteristic of mankind but with the causes which specifically determine the degree to which this basic psychosis manifests itself. We are all, by necessity, disturbed, unrealistic, and psychotic, but why are some individuals more psychotic than others?

All great thinkers in modern psychiatry have perceived anxiety as being of critical importance in the etiology of disturbed neurotic or psychotic symptomatology. Freud at first felt that undischarged libido energy accounted for human anxiety, causing emotional and mental disturbances. Later, he abandoned this concept, considering it only peripheral. In 1926, in his monograph, "The Problem of Anxiety," he developed his "signal theory" in which he connected anxiety with traumatic and danger situations. Anxiety became a signal of danger. Freud considered anxiety a biologically inherited and needed form of reaction, necessary for survival. But, in the same paper, he expressed his own dissatisfaction with his theory and concept. Neither Adler nor Jung made any contributions to the better understanding of anxiety. Rank emphasized later the so-called importance of birth trauma, Horney the cultural factors, and Sullivan the interpersonal relationship factor in causing anxiety. Fromm also emphasizes the latter two factors. Their contributions are doubtless very valuable but, as Zetzel pointed out in an important paper, psychoanalysis has made no further advance from Freud's days in the quest for an explanation of anxiety. An "existential anxiety," caused by the actual frailty and transience of human existence, has been postulated by more recent observers, but its relevance to the specific clinical problem of neurosis and psychosis remains problematic.

When I wrote my book, *Basic Anxiety, a New Psycho-Biological Concept,* in 1962, I thought I had coined a new phrase. It was only later that I learned that Karen Horney had previously used the same expression, although in a different sense. She referred to the cultural influences causing anxiety. I feel that this differentiation should be kept in mind lest the reader stumble over this coincidence.

Basic anxiety, as I use the term, is the anxiety which the infant must feel unavoidably (but which varies in degree for each child) when he senses that, even under the most favorable circumstances, his birth and presence are not an unmitigated source of joy and pleasure to his mother. The more the infant and child senses that his existence is not only not a joy and pleasure but also an outright inconvenience and imposition on the mother, to that degree he will, only subconsciously of course, sense that his life is in danger and that he is threatened by his mother. It is the most logical thing that anything which is an incumbrance or imposition to us we would just as well be rid of. Of course, the mother will feel that she is in a terrific bind. In one way, her maternal instincts will make her feel normal only to the degree that she enjoys her own offspring, or, at least, is able to fulfill her maternal requirements without excessive stress. On the other hand, we cannot criticize the mother who resents her own child, if only we are fully aware of all the circumstances that brought about her pregnancy. The fact, however, remains that regardless of the circumstances which accounted for the attitude of the mother, the infant senses only the degree of her rejection. And this rejection is sensed by the infant as a threat to his own existence and as a fear for his own life. This definite appropriate fear, experienced by the infant and child from the moment of his birth through his formative years and beyond, I have called "Basic Anxiety." It is a rational and realistic response on an emotional level to the threat to his life which is sensed by the infant. We see, therefore, it is not an hereditary and biological characteristic of man, but a very definite acquired fear reactivity experienced in the formative stages from the very beginning. In human affairs, pregnancy, delivery, and the raising of an infant and child can never, even under the most optimal circumstances, be a totally joyful experience. If nothing else, the fear for her own life and the hardship and deprivation which a potential and actual mother must accept in order to be satisfactory to the infant, makes the experience not totally delightful. Obviously, I speak here with tongue in cheek. We all realize how often and to what high degree a child is an imposition, if not an outright hardship, to his mother. Every bit of maternal impatience is proof of this fact and if patience results only from an intellectual reasoning effort, the receptivity of the child cannot be fooled. Impatience, shown or suppressed, is only a measure of the infant's unwelcomeness.

Before I go on focusing on the maternal significance in creating basic anxiety in her offspring, we have to evaluate the role of the father of the child. The mother has to expend her energies for the infant, and her maternal responsibilities will only be experienced as joy if she, in turn, gets all the human emotional support she needs from her husband or companion. To the same degree the husband is enthralled that his wife brought forth a new human being, his offspring, the mother will not feel abused and resentful, but joyful. This emotion will transmit itself to the infant and he will develop in a most happy and joyfully healthy way.

I realize that all this description sounds like an ideal condition that is impossible in reality. This is quite so, but we at least have a clue as to what it would take, hypothetically, to bring forth happy, healthy, and self-accepting human beings. We must allow for the fact that this ideal situation may never be reached, but we can postulate that the closer a situation approximates this ideal, the better the results which will be manifested in the development of the child. On the other hand, we can state that the less these ideal conditions prevail, or, to put it differently, the worse the prevailing conditions are, the worse the adjustment of the child will be.

Let us think of some examples—how can we expect joy from a mother if she became pregnant without her knowledge or against her outspoken wish, and now finds herself stuck with an unwanted child. If the mother consented to pregnancy only to achieve other goals, for instance, to get away from her own home, we can postulate that this child only served the mother as an object to achieve her own ends. What mother would dare to tell her child that it was only born because pregnancy had already progressed beyond the stage that abortion could still be safely performed? And how can we expect a mother to enjoy her child if the husband resents the pregnancy—the consequence of his intercourse? The mother would expect her mate to enjoy not only the intercourse but the consequences of it, if there are any. These are the conditions prevailing in the animal kingdom in the free habitat. The female, after some form or other of courtship, copulates, gets pregnant, and carries through her biologically conditioned assignment. Copulation only takes place when the female is in heat. No male would dare to approach her sexually unless she was receptive. The male will fulfill his biologically conditioned expectations, depending on the requirements of each individual species.

In human affairs basic biology is subjected to cultural requirements. We can postulate that the human male originally, similar to his anthropoid relatives, was polygamous. If one female of his harem was pregnant or in the nursing stage, he had other females available to satisfy his sex urges. Aculturation complicated this simple biological situation. In order to permit the offspring to develop all the skills necessary for a higher degree of aculturation, he had to be taken care of over a prolonged period of time before he was able to fend for himself successfully. In most of the higher mammals, the raising of the young takes one or two seasons. The female mostly will teach them all that is required by the species to survive. After the cubs have adequately matured, they will find themselves on their own. The female is ready to get in heat again. The same cycle will repeat itself. Only in the anthropoids does one find some indication of the overlapping of cub generations, the one- and two-year-old cubs still depending on the mother while she nurses her newborn. Biologists will have to elaborate on these facts in more detail. For practical purposes, however, we can state that only under human conditions, due to the prolonged periods of time required to permit adequate aculturation, do we find a situation where a mother might find herself with several children of various ages, perhaps one infant still in the nursing stage, and perhaps pregnant to boot.

In order for these offspring to all receive adequate time to develop to the necessary level of human civilization, the male is required to limit his economic and emotional contribution to one household, so to speak. His biological, basically polygamous drive, therefore, has to be curtailed and satisfied by the same female. A great insoluble contradiction arises, therefore, which can never be totally resolved to the complete satisfaction of all concerned. The male has an ongoing drive and striving for a sexual and emotionally satisfactory outlet; the female is not prepared biologically to have subsequent pregnancies followed by exhausting child-raising requirements, certainly not in short successions. To satisfy the sexual requirements of the mate, she has to accommodate him long before she is physically or emotionally ready to prepare herself for a new pregnancy. Indeed, if we rightly postulate that a six-month nursing period is biologically the norm, then intercourse before this period of time will not only interfere with lactogenic hormonal production, which interferes with the infant's development, but will stimulate ovulation preparatory to new pregnancy for which the female is not biologically or emotionally ready. Still, the wife wants and has to keep her husband and certainly does not wish to see him hopelessly frustrated or drifting away from her. She, therefore, has to accommodate herself to his sexual requirements, permitting him to have intercourse only a few weeks after a recent delivery. (Modern gynecology, as a rule, will consent to intercourse after about six weeks after delivery. This is a practical accommodation considering the overall situation.) The price for aculturation, however, has to be paid. Let us assume that an early conception will take place. Emotionally and biologically, the female will find herself in a practically unsolvable situation. She is given to the requirement of her infant and all her body physiology, at the same time, changes to the new coexisting pregnancy. There is no totally satisfactory answer to these divergent requirements. If, in addition, the case is complicated by the existence of several other children, each demanding, loudly or muffled, his own rights, we can see what is required of the human female. Even when contraceptive methods are used, thus eliminating fear of further pregnancies, a newly delivered woman may be psychologically and physiologically unprepared for intercourse which has a deleterious effect on her hormonal balance.

Now, when we realize that the mother herself had only inadequate emotional reception in her own infancy and childhood, we see that human emotional deficit is carried from generation to generation. The entire situation is, if not compounded, then complemented by the equal amount of emotional deficit from the side of the husband. This emotional adjustment is every bit as important to the development of the child as the mother is, but it takes a child a few years to find this out, if he ever does, because as an infant he dealt primarily with his mother.

Another point comes up again and again. When one deals with parents of disturbed children they will invariably point out that they have several children, and, although the rest of them seem to be all right, only this one child in question seems to show disturbances. Are they not the same parents to all their children? No, they are not, as little as they may realize it. Each child is conceived and received under different emotional conditions. The first pregnancy may be eagerly anticipated or it may be the most dreaded one; a boy may have been expected and a girl came, or vice versa; the husband may have revealed himself not as a hero but as a weak individual who had to borrow strength from alcohol or whose unreliability came through glaringly in the hours of emotional need. The possibilities and diversifications are innumerable. The wife may have found herself pregnant again long before she was ready, and, if we at first wanted a boy, we now want a girl, regardless of all conscious protestations that we only care that the child be healthy, etc., etc. In addition, if we have found a scapegoat among our children on whom we heap all our own anguish, frustration, impatience, and outright hate, we can treat the other children more patiently. Interestingly enough, the rest of the children will then develop an invested interest that the scapegoat in their family remain what he seems ordained to be—the scapegoat—which permits them to enjoy a better place in the pecking order.

In this sense, we can even speak of the importance of the mentally sick to the functioning of the so-called mentally healthy, or, to put it more mildly, the contribution of the handicapped individual to the apparent successful functioning of the more fortunate one.

The viewpoint of the infant and child deserves close understanding to show how the reception and acceptance that he finds in his formative years victimize him and ultimately determine his functioning or non-functioning level in life. The child only reacts to the environmental circumstances he finds. The infant senses clearly that his very existence depends almost exclusively on his mother. Mother is life itself—she has breasts containing milk, milk is food, food is life. Any deviation from this biological fact is only substitution. The child will go to any lengths to stay in favor with this all-powerful person. These reactions do not take place on a conscious level, of course. To the degree he senses his mother would be better off without him and is burdened by his existence, reactions will take place which will tend to lead to his own self-destruction. Projective mechanisms, which we call "somatizations," will account for many of his physical diseases.

In addition, as he senses the mother's anger and exasperation with him, and since Mother cannot be wrong, the basic human vanity dictates that he is no good, it is all his own fault. Here we get to the extreme of non-acceptance. As we sense that we are not accepted, we feel acceptance by the key person, our mother, can only be gained by non-existence. The death wish, which Freud described, can also be seen as an expression of fulfilling the implied wish of our mother—namely, that we should not exist. To the degree that we were not accepted, we don't accept ourselves. Only to the degree that we were accepted, do we feel we should exist, that we have value, and that we are justified in living. Since, however, we all have the striving for self-preservation on a deeper level, we have to come to grips with the implied threat to our existence also. As much as Mother represents life itself, she represents also the destroyer. To the degree that we sense she longs for our non-existence, our striving for self-preservation can only be satisfied by the destruction of the threat. We, therefore, all harbor, to a certain degree at least, the destructive impulse against our mother. From the mildest form of resistance to the extremes of the Orestes syndrome, we can see the scale. The Oedipus syndrome is well discussed in literature. I call the Orestes syndrome the destructive deadly hate which Orestes felt for his mother, Clytemnestra. Whether or not some basic homosexual connotation is implied in this fear of the opposite sex is speculative. The female offspring's destructive self-protective hate against her mother could be equated to an Electra complex—the daughter avenges the father on the faithless mother.

The mother, on the other hand, is pictured as the source of all that is good and noble. How can we harbor ill-will against her? We must be insane to feel hostile against her. We most assuredly are entrapped in a most entangled tragic constellation. We cannot believe even that we are the natural children of our parents and our mother, in particular. We must be adopted or somehow not belong because no natural mother could feel toward her offspring as we perceive her to feel toward us. And again, it has to be re-emphasized that only the degree differs from case to case, from the mildest form to the most devasting degree. We might be somewhat aware of our feelings, or they might be totally repressed. As a rule of thumb, we can generalize that the higher the degree of the disturbance, the less we are able to face up to its reality, the more defensive we will be, and, therefore, the less chance exists for an insightful recovery by facing the facts as they are.

The next two chapters will deal with the forms in which the manifestation of these disturbances can take place.

The entire situation is, furthermore, tremendously complicated by the very fact of natural heterosexual attraction present in the formative years. We consider it normal, and, indeed, very cute if the four-year-old son tells his mother that when he grows up he will marry her. His mother, if well balanced, will smile at this statement but reply that she belongs to Daddy and he, the son, when he grows up, will marry someone like Mommy. Similarly, the four-year-old girl will tell her Daddy that she will marry him once she is grown up and the father will reply in the same fashion as the mother did to her son. A certain jealousy of the parent of the same sex is, therefore, unavoidable even under optimum conditions. How disastrous this constellation gets under less than optimal conditions or particularly if the overall situation has been deplorable to start with! How can we dare to realize that the very person to whom we are sexually attracted signifies to us, at the same time, death and destruction? Little wonder that we may consider ourselves insane and yearn only for an end to this torture or try to resolve it in any way that promises relief, absurd as the attempt may be. Innumerable examples come to mind to illustrate these facts, but I will leave it to the intelligent reader to use the storehouse of his own memories to fill them in.

Here is the key to human insanity. What is biologically natural receives a frightening connotation of aberration. None of us is completely free from some touch of this disturbance. Realization of it and acceptance of its unavoidability is the best we can hope for.

And, if all this were not yet enough, there is still superimposed the culturally conditioned tabu of incest dread. The animal, in its natural habitat, has no way or reason to reject, nor to particularly seek, copulations with opposite-sex mature members of his family eligible for such reproductive activity. Cultural requirements, well discussed by Freud in *Totem and Taboo,* bring forth a deadly dread of incestual activity. No erudite speculation satisfactorily supports the thesis that primitive people wanted to avoid the possible unfortunate consequences of inbreeding. In ancient Egypt, it was only the Pharoah who was permitted to marry his own sister. We see a kaleidoscope of disturbing influences affecting normal biological drives in Mankind. That successful reproduction does take place, considering all the adverse constellations, gives proof of the tremendous adaptability and elasticity of men. Only under disastrous conditions will the entire mechanism break down. It is, however, conceded that we all function way below our potential. Although, ideally, life could be a delightful experience, instead it is mostly experienced as a duty, if not an outright disaster.

I conclude this chapter with an assumption which will need a certain degree of imagination, but which will go a long way in explaining the mechanics of human disturbances. On the one side, let us assume the optimal conditions imaginable under which a human being is born and raised—two parents who love each other, cherishing parents, delighted with each other and overjoyed at having the good fortune to bring forth a new generation. The child will feel easily that he is able to give joy to his mother, that "I am somebody." No problem. Now, let us measure the discrepancy from this ideal state to the actual existing reality, varying as the case may be. Certainly, not on a conscious level but factually, the child will sense and react to this deprivation of his naturally endowed rights. He is expected to act and function according to such an ideal endowment and reality has dealt with him bitterly. What stressful attitudes must prevail and play havoc with his available energies? Or, what disastrous hate for the entire world situation will develop where destruction of such monstrous injustice seems a good deed? Little can we expect each individual to visualize that, although victimized, he is only subject to the natural law of selection of the fittest. It is difficult to perceive this as a world ruled by justice in the face of being the cast-off. The basic human vanity will revolt against this concept.

chapter 3

A HOLISTIC APPROACH TO THE HUMAN PERSONALITY

We can clearly discern four elements in the mature animal which are indispensible for its own existence and survival and for fulfilling the highest law of nature and life, the preservation of the species. It should be clearly understood that when I speak of animals, I refer to them only in their natural habitat, undisturbed and uninfluenced by human beings. Exposure to men and certainly domestication changes their entire reaction pattern and we subsequently can notice deviant behavior and adaptation far different from their development in the wild. These four basic elements are: (1) Physical health. (2) Adequate orientation to the environment in which it lives, which includes appropriate approach to members of its own species and members of other animal species and even man, if necessary. (3) Economic self-sustaining self-reliance. Almost nowhere in the animal kingdom do we observe animals that are fed or supported by other members of their species after they reach maturity. Perhaps exceptions can be made for drone bees and the higher anthropoids who sometimes care for their sick or injured mates. (4) Reproductivity—no mature animal of its own choice practices celibacy. Its very existence is subservient to the uppermost law of life itself—the preservation of the species.

Now, let us examine how these four elements present in the animal kingdom compare to the human requirements:

(1) We can postulate that the element of physical health or physical sickness in human beings is equivalent to that in animals.

(2) What we called adequate orientation to their environment in animals can rightfully be compared to socio-mental health or sickness in human beings. This encompasses the individual's adequate orientation on this earth and his relationship to his fellow human beings and the world at large.

(3) We expect the mature, well-balanced, healthy human being to be self-sustaining and not to rely on the economic support of others. This basic desire to be economically independent is an indispensable characteristic of maturity and we feel that only exceptional circumstances like serious war injuries will justify later dependency on the support of others.

(4) The last element human beings share with the animal kingdom is the drive toward procreation, the preservation of the species. No reasoning, as high-sounding as it may be, can deny the fact that without procreation the human race would not preserve itself. We can, of course, always rationalize our own attitude if we do not participate in the reproductive

process by pointing out there are others who do participate and that there is, furthermore, a population explosion going on. We can even go so far as to feel very satisfied with ourselves because we do not contribute to overpopulation. This attitude has many followers under many different guises. We certainly find it difficult to argue with couples who already have children in their desire to limit the number of them according to their own physical, emotional, and economic capabilities. Suffice it to say that in the animal kingdom, in its natural habitat, deliberate celibacy or sexual abstinence and deviant sexual behavior to avoid reproductivity are unthinkable. If over-productivity takes place, the forces of nature, which we like to call ecology, will come into play until the proper balance is restored. True survival of the fittest takes place and the laws of nature are well served. This free play of natural forces is highly interfered with in human affairs. I am well aware that no easy recommendation can be made but the facts at least should be recognized for what they are. I shall not hesitate to state that abstinence from the reproductive process in maturity is a deviation from the laws of nature. It is well understandable sometimes, and, since perfection is impossible in human affairs, some allowance has to be made, but the allowance is a compromise and this has to be kept in mind.

In human affairs, there is a fifth element, completely absent in the animal kingdom. It is the specific aspect which actually distinguishes us from other animals. It is the human factor of self-awareness. This is the feeling which at times is identified as "I am somebody," a feeling of being worthwhile and of value, self-respect, etc. As I pointed out previously, under ideal conditions (note well that these can never exist but only be approximated at best) no difficulties would arise. The child would sense the joy which his mere presence gives his mother; he would feel, "I am able to give joy to my mother, I am somebody, I am worthwhile." Unfortunately, this ideal condition is only a fantasy. Reality will always fall short. If we only occasionally feel that our mother is able to enjoy us, we have been very fortunate. Unluckily, the opposite is mostly the case. We feel we are a burden, an unwelcome imposition on our mother, and that she would be better off without us. But we depend on her and our striving for survival is very strong.

In order to be able to feel that we are somebody, we now have to derive some strength from any of the other four previously discussed biological aspects or from any combination thereof. Obviously, some curtailment of the involved requirements will take place and this curtailment again can vary from a comparatively mild form, under fortunate circumstances, to outright disaster. A few examples seem indicated here:

Again and again we hear that people of a high creativity level, perhaps a happily married parent of several children, gets sick and dies of an incurable disease while still young. Why? Is it that their natural emotional endowment is depleted and that physical illness results out of this imbalance? Again and again we hear of cases where an individual functions well as long as he is not reproductive, but as the additional stressful responsibility of childbirth takes place, mental or physical breakdown results. Again and again we hear of cases where an individual enjoys good health as long as no civic or economic expectations are forced on him, but as soon as he is expected to become self-supporting or to serve the needs of his country, illness befalls him.

In my many years of psychiatric practice, I have not infrequently noted an occurrence which, of course, is open to different interpretations. Some may consider it mere coincidence; however, this occurrence seemed more than an accidental or unrelated coincidence to me. My observation has been, and I hope other psychiatrists will be able to confirm it, that patients that were usually in good contact, but perhaps with basic paranoid personality features, had physical breakdowns of a not serious, temporary nature, when suddenly faced with a firm, unyielding situation where no manipulations of any kind seemed feasible. Skin erruptions, low-grade fever reaction reminiscent of influenza, sore throats, vomiting spells, etc., seem to act as a vicarious tension release safety valve. This is mentioned to point out that mental disturbances can be converted to physical disturbances and vice versa. It is noteworthy that with cortisone or ACTH therapy, some patients suffering from various physical ailments such as rheumatoid arthritis, asthma, etc., show improvement of their physical condition only to develop outright psychotic reactions. The common interpretation that the biochemical action of the hormones attacks neurological structures does not seem satisfactory. The point which I wish to make is that the balance between the four basic aspects of biological requirements is not necessarily unchangeable, and deficit in one aspect is partially or totally convertible into one or any combination of the other aspects. The less the specific human factor, self-awareness, is developed, the more primitive we are, the less we have evolved from the animal kingdom. This statement is not a slur but should be taken literally.

The optimum adjustment which I feel a human being can make is a realistic self-appraisal, realizing and accepting his own deficits; however, this self-acceptance seems unjustified unless it has been preceded by a total effort of self-knowledge. The best wish we can have for a human individual is that he be born into a family in which the overall emotional climate between his parents was predominantly benign. We can postulate that all intellectual striving for understanding is basically nothing but to free man from the aberration resulting from his splitting off from the animal kingdom. We must, however, keep in mind that we can never speak of the failure of parents to provide their offspring with the desirable degree of warmth. All parents, in a way, do the best they know how, depending on the emotional acceptance and investment they received in their turn and so forth. We can only speak of cause, not of fault, and even this differentiation implies a voluntary attitude—that parents could have been different. The best they can do may be, and most of the time is, most deplorable, but they, too, were children in their time.

Actually, this holistic concept of the human personality is a most logical one. We cannot departmentalize the human being to the point where we think economic efforts have no bearing on the physical health or mental adjustment of an individual and vice versa. The same certainly can be said about sexual life and attitudes.

The next chapter will be totally devoted to the relationship between physical and mental health and sickness. The high personality development, which is the necessary aim of man, once he has split off from the animal kingdom, takes a heavy toll on his basic system. What I have tried to show in this chapter is the interrelationship of the four basic aspects of life upon which is superimposed in *Homo sapiens* the specific human striving to feel one's own individuality. It is easy to be physically healthy and reproductive if one is ruthless in the pursuit of one's own ends at the expense of others. The only stress such individuals will experience is the uncertainty of how soon the others will catch up with them. This chapter is devoted to the concept that no human being can be properly evaluated unless we see him in his totality.

chapter 4

THE PSYCHOPHYSIOLOGICAL REACTION

The familiar term "psychosomatic reaction" is usually employed in a broad sense, encompassing emotional reactions accompanying any illness, regardless of how little repressed emotions had any part in its etiology. Here, for instance, I think of illnesses resulting from pure accidents, inflicted upon the individual without any knowledge whatsoever. In addition, "psychosomatic" also covers conversion neurosis or hysterical neurosis in which unconscious conflict is expressed as disguised and symbolic somatic symptomatology. Here, as an example, I would think of "globus hystericus," a feeling of a mass in the throat accompanied by inability to swallow. In the conversion neurosis the sensorimotor system furnishes the innervation and it functions by symbolic somatization. Psychophysiological reaction encompasses all ailments and disturbances of organs innervated by the autonomic nervous system which is not under voluntary control. Excellent books are available on these subjects.

I will try, not so much to reiterate the well-known facts of the emotional influence on body function and disease, but rather to focus on how far this influence can go and whether it is justified to speak of strictly organic diseases per se at all, unless under exceptional circumstances as pure accident or strictly hereditary—congenital conditions or noxious factors beyond our own emotional reactivity. The time-honored division of somatic illnesses into organic and functional seems not quite satisfactory anymore. Those conditions were termed functional in which no organic pathological changes could be demonstrated or in which no irreversible organic changes seemed to occur. With the advent of more refined instruments such as the electron microscope and refined biochemical techniques, pathological changes could be demonstrated on a far subtler level than previously. Intracellular changes could be observed in functional disturbances which definitely classified these disturbances as organic, although not yet observable on a more conventional level and in the absence of gross pathology. These changes have an accumulative effect and can lead to demonstrable gross pathology. On the other hand, gross pathology at times, for reasons only poorly understood, seemed to have resolved itself and a self-healing process took place. The autonomic nervous system is the physical transmitter of human emotions. We live and die by our own autonomic nervous system. I will not review here the anatomy and functioning of the autonomic nervous system. The reader who is not thoroughly familiar with its functioning should certainly acquaint himself with it by using one of the excellent books on this topic.

Suffice it to say that each event in our life, each thought, has some implication for us. This implication may be so insignificant that no discernable reaction takes place. On the other hand, the emotional reaction may be extremely noticeable. Each event, each thought, may be pleasing and predominantly welcome to us, or it may imply a serious threat to our existence and, therefore, be accompanied by a severe reaction of displeasure, fear, anger, and hate.

In my chapter on Basic Anxiety, I formulated the concept that each infant, even under optimum conditions, will sense a threat to his very existence in response to the fact that he is not totally welcomed and accepted by his mother. Much more frequently, the infant senses a serious, if not disastrous, degree of rejection by his mother. This rejection is perceived as a threat to his own existence. Fearing for his life is an appropriate reaction.

I postulate now that this threat to his life may be perceived in three different forms and the reaction pattern of the child will, therefore, vary accordingly. The infant may sense that his mother would like to be rid of him by outright destruction; I postulate that the physiological defense reactivity to outright aggression is, in the sense of Cannon's Law, "fight or flight reaction."

Let us point out here the fact that it matters little whether the mother is consciously aware of her destructive urges against the infant or whether their realization is suppressed unconsciously. The fact of her destructive hostile feelings toward the infant remains and the infant reacts to it in his system. Obviously, this is a spontaneous reactivity and, since it takes place in his earliest formative stage, no memory whatsoever will remain. A reaction pattern is formed which later will be a decisive factor in the personality pattern and physical development but the roots cannot be traced back.

The fight or flight response comes through the sympathetic part of the autonomic nervous system. It is easily perceivable that if an infant grows up with the recurrent or persistent reaction to surmised threat to his life, an over-stimulation of the end organs of the sympathetic nervous system will take place. In addition, a personality pattern will develop which, even after infancy and childhood, will sense life-threatening attacks even if in reality few or no such threats exist. Psychiatrically, we will easily recognize this as a paranoid personality development which is constantly alert against dangers and attacks. Just as the infant surmises such threats to his existence where realistically there are none, we overreact completely out of proportion.

The terminology of sympatotonic personality has been coined for such a pattern, and by constant overstimulation the physiological normal response to a threat is repeated excessively and continuously and final pathological anatomical changes will take place which can be recognized readily as specific disease entities. We have now only to remember the innervation pattern of the sympathetic branch of the involuntary nervous system. In a general way, the functions of the sympathetic are catabolic in nature. It serves the organism physiologically when rapid readjustments to the environment are necessary. It serves as a rapid mobilizer in situations of fear, anger, or fight or flight, whether physical or emotional. Our early imprint determines how secure we feel in this world. We can, of course, take refuge in the delusional psychotic adjustment that we are perfectly safe and that nothing can happen to us. There is comfort in insanity. As long as we are realistic, we pay the price and basic insecurity can be converted into physical symptomatology.

If we review the innervation pattern of the sympathetic branches of the nervous system, we can see physiological reactions under attack or assumed threat. Among these are: pupillary dilatation for greater visual perception; increased heart rate; increased blood pressure; increased blood sugar levels in response to increased adrenalin secretion; increased heat production; more perspiration to keep body temperature down; and decreased gastro-intestinal activity and concomitant increased tonus of the sphincters. If these reactions take place with inordinate frequency, corresponding organic changes will result which will go under different terms of morbidity and eventually irreversible pathology.

The second form in which the infant may feel his life threatened by his mother is a more passive one; namely, that his mother on whom his life so totally depends in the early stages may abandon him. Little does an infant know that other people might appear to rescue and feed him and prevent him from starving. To the infant, abandonment by the mother means death by starvation. (I wish to remind the reader of the pathetic crying of newborn birds and the pitiful squeaks emanating from newborn puppies or kittens, if their respective mothers do not return to them or are prevented from returning to them. Death occurs slowly.)

I postulate now that when starvation takes place, a desperate physiological reaction pattern occurs to stimulate and mobilize all body resources subservient to the life-sustaining, digestive process. It is the parasympathetic portion, the vagus division, which is the part of the autonomic nervous system physiologically charged with this activity of the organs and glands. Under the constant and recurring threat to our life by starvation, we develop a predisposition which has been called vagototonic. Vagus hyperactivity develops and subsequently a disease pattern will develop which corresponds to parasympathetic overstimulation. In general, the parasympathetic functions are anabolic, building up reserves. This reaction pattern is more predominant at night during the time of rest, which, incidentally, also accounts for the fact that the majority of deliveries take place at night. The vagus part activates the musculature concerned in emptying the hollow abdominal and pelvic viscera. Interestingly enough, the various parts of the parasympathetic system are more capable of separate action than the sympathetic division which tends to function in a more collective manner.

There is a third way in which the infant may react to the perceived threat to his life resulting from the unsatisfactory maternal attitude. The infant is helpless against threats from the outside. There are innumerable examples of the female coming to the defense of her cubs against any odds, if need be, and she does not hesitate for one moment to risk or give her very life in defense of her cubs. I postulate that the infant needs to have the same feelings of security, to sense that his mother will protect him to the fullest, even at the risk of her own life. To the degree an infant senses that he is not totally welcomed by his mother, that he is not a source of total joy for her, a reaction pattern takes place that makes him feel insecure, unprotected against external dangers. Dangers are perceived out of proportion.

Hypersensitivity to dangers and irritating situations will develop. Hypersensitivity, which is nothing but our allergic reactivity, will develop. Under emotional stress, this hypersensitivity is more likely to manifest itself.

It is easy to enumerate the various conditions which are thought to be due to a hypersensitive reaction. As long as we try to identify each specific agent incriminated as causing a certain allergic reaction without getting to the core of what causes the hypersensitivity in the first place, we can be compared to fighters against malaria, chasing down each individual *Anopheles* mosquito instead of destroying their breeding grounds and breeding pattern.

We see, therefore, that the maternal attitude, due to its emotional connotations, will ultimately determine the disease pattern and the severity of the diseases we develop. Indeed, we have a yardstick by the severity of the disease to measure the degree of rejection which surrounded us in infancy and childhood.

Outright destruction at the hands of our mother would cause immediate death. Starvation has a gradually fatal pattern. In the case of fear of lack of adequate protection against external dangers, this is only a hypothetical assumption because such a life-threatening situation might actually never arise. Perhaps we can draw from this a parallel to the severity and immediacy of corresponding diseases. It is noteworthy that in allergic reaction adrenalin and related drugs are remedial. Adrenalin is the sympathetic hormone of the supra-adrenal glands. It is exactly this hormone, mobilized for fight or flight, which we need to overcome allergic symptomatology. It strengthens the body for the fight against the excessive danger hypersensitivity has bestowed upon us.

It is not my purpose in this chapter to reiterate the excellent discussions on or about psychophysiological reactions and subsequent organ disease patterns. I rather wish to point the way to new insights and explanations of facts which so far are not well understood. I shall not go into a discussion of the long list of disturbances but rather will discuss only a few entities which can be considered typical. Neurological diseases deserve special attention.

Several theories have been offered for the development of multiple sclerosis; none has been definitely accepted in the face of exhausting studies. I wish to submit my own theoretical consideration which probably can be similarly applied to several other conditions. In some individuals an inordinate disproportion exists between the emotional endowment which the infant and child received and the expected level of his performance. We see that individuals afflicted with this disturbance have a high level of drive and determination quite inadequately supported by endowed emotional strength. This discrepancy creates excessive stress on the nerve cells themselves and a breakdown follows. In the case of multiple sclerosis, the breakdown is a degenerative one, specifically demyelinization of the neuro-axons. This obviously diminishes the functioning of the individual and, in the face of his collossal drive, reduces him to the level of functioning which corresponds to his original emotional endowment, which might be minimal or actually negative. Temporary remissions, so characteristic of this disease, are in a way nothing but relapses into new attempts to function again on a higher level of standards and productivity than the original emotional endowment justified. It is recognized that in spite of almost innumerable treatment approaches, emotional encouragement and reassurances are the most useful form of treatment. This emotional substitutional support lessens the degree of basic emotional deficit. Perhaps it can be reemphasized here that all other treatment approaches, although not realistic in themselves, yet have value inasmuch as the administering physican by his own enthusiastic belief in the value of his administration transfers encouragement and emotional support to the patient as long as the physician's enthusiastic belief prevails. Osler's old dictum comes to mind: "Give the medication the first six months after its release; this is the time it will work." How far and to how many diseases does this principle apply? I would answer to the degree the etiology of a disturbance was based on basic emotional deficit.

I wish to discuss here two more examples: First of all, there is the well-known case of infantile paralysis which for practical purposes has disappeared with appropriate preventive immunization against the virus identified as the etiological cause. Before I draw certain conclusions, I wish again to point out that it was proverbial that it was precisely the very active, perhaps overactive, children who in the past seemed particularly susceptible to infantile paralysis and particularly vulnerable after excessive stressful activities. It was also impressive that many afflicted women were pregnant and as they partially recovered they carried out their duties with incredible determination even from an iron lung. The point I wish to make is that again an overexerted motor neuron became fatigued, exhausted, and open to the attack of the virus which destroyed its function. The difference between this disease and multiple sclerosis is the specific vulnerability of the motor nerve cell and its attack by well-identified viruses. Another point, however, deserves consideration, although this point is only speculative and no proof whatsoever can be presented at this time—the individuals who, in the past, before the advent of the immunization process, were potential victims of the disease, seem at this time sure to escape infantile paralysis, but is it not highly logical to assume that their basic emotional deficit remained unchanged and that they now become victims of other diseases and disturbances, perhaps in the behavioral socio-mental category? Is it not possible that a certain amount of juvenile acting-out individuals, including drug users, would in earlier days have shown their vulnerability by developing infantile paralysis? To illustrate my point, I wish to remind the reader of the metaphor presented earlier.

Let us visualize a room with a plastic tarp firmly attached at its edges on the floor. Let us assume there is an air bubble in one place. If we push the air bubble down, it will only reappear in a different spot. By pushing it down, we have only displaced it—we have not removed it. I see the temporary relief of many symptoms in this way. Furthermore, if an individual develops an acute disease and he is cured of it, he is not actually cured because his basic vulnerability remains and will manifest itself sooner or later with the same or another form of symptomatology. None of us will remain invulnerable forever, but it makes quite a bit of difference whether we get a cold every few years or practically every two or three months. The examples are unlimited, of course.

Now I wish to discuss a very important proposition concerning cancer and malignant diseases.

Twelve years ago in my book, *Basic Anxiety,* I expressed the conviction that ultimately a virus would be linked to cancer etiology. Today this concept is on the threshold of universal acceptance. Again I wish to establish a link between the emotions (including altered allergic activity) and the deadly affliction of malignancy by intercession of viruses. I cannot speak for virologists and their findings. At the same time, I cannot overlook the present state of cancer research and all well-justified findings. It seems an established fact that the development of a tumor, benign or malignant, is the result of an interplay of many extrinsic and intrinsic factors. Among intrinsic factors, the most frequently mentioned are heredity, race, age, sex, and hormones. Among the extrinsic factors are a long list of physical agents, chemical agents, and living agents. An interesting statement once considered valid—that cancer is a disease of civilization—had to be corrected as our knowledge of more primitive races increased. This statement cannot be accepted at face value anymore, but it still carries a considerable amount of weight.

Only recently do we see the emotional factor discussed as an intrinsic etiological factor. I use the example of viruses as an extrinsic factor since they seem to play an ever-increasing role in the development of malignancies. But ultimately, even if other agents are recognized as playing an important role in the development of a neoplasm, I wish to emphasize the predisposition created by the emotional situation. When we speak of a higher susceptibility of one individual compared to another, I feel the emotional personality pattern is decisively influencing their physical reactivity. I also feel that not enough differentiation is made between hereditary and familial diseases. Hereditary diseases are based on disturbed chomosomal pattern; familial diseases are based on my dictum that sick people raise sick people. This does not imply that the same disturbance has to follow the same disturbance pattern. Emotionally deprived parents, functioning at a low grade of social acceptability, may at times produce offspring who are most impressive as persons and in their contributions; however, we do not know yet how the emotional deficit may manifest itself finally in the sense of the previously discussed holistic approach.

I postulate that viruses are omnipresent, perhaps specific, perhaps convertible into various modes of attack, depending on changing situations. I now postulate that an individual who functions in a very rigid framework of emotional adjustment and who is totally frustrated in expressing any anger in any form whatsoever will, organically speaking, break out of this total frustration with a wild all-pervading immature cell productivity which finally becomes all-pervasive and life-destroying. Several factors have to come together to bring about such a development. First and foremost is the deficit of the basic emotional endowment. This has to be followed by exceedingly high standards of socio-mental functioning unable to be balanced by adequacy of the emotional availability. Third comes an exceedingly rigid attitude which does not permit minor, yet adequate, pressure releases. This situation produces an intolerable combination of acts to which we would normally react with hate and anger but for which, however, no outlet is provided. Now the self-destructive process sets in and the viruses are the catalyst, so to speak.

As mentioned above, it is possible that other agents besides viruses may also be involved as catalysts. It certainly can easily be understood that continuous cell irritation of one type or another may greatly increase this predisposition to the point that in extreme long-lasting irritations, as, for example, the lip cancer of pipe smokers, the irritations alone seem sufficient to bring forth the malignancy. Cancer is predominantly a disease of the aged. Perhaps the cumulative effect of frustration through many long years of life is a contributing factor in the development of malignancy. Yet it cannot be questioned that the same degree of irritation will not necessarily bring forth the same response in different individuals. In animal experiments, this factor of variability becomes negligible.

chapter 5

THE ABHORRENCE OF MENTAL SICKNESS

In the herd animal, a conformity to the rules and requirements of the herd is essential. The welfare and survival of the herd and, therefore, of the species supersedes the survival of the individual member. The examples which rightfully can be quoted to confirm this dictim are innumerable. If a herd animal does not live up to its requirements, it will be dealt with effectively and decisively by the other members. In certain species watch animals are posted to alert the herd of impending danger. If the watch animal fails in its duty, the herd will turn on him and destroy him. Ostracism is the least punishment which a failure in performance causes. Ostracism for most herd animals is tantamount to a death sentence. The survival instinct of any herd animal predicates strict observance of herd rules and requirements. This basic instinct to conformity is well represented in the human species. To be "normal" seems to be of highest concern to human beings. Little do they realize that there is a world of difference between the concept of "average" and normal. Average, of course, is the cross-section in the behavior pattern or appearance of a number of human beings. I shall try to illustrate this fact with some examples. The average IQ is 100. To qualify for successful college studies, an above-average IQ—perhaps between 110 and 120—is necessary.

Even if 90% or more of all mothers use the bottle-feeding method and this method, therefore, represents the average, it can never be considered normal. This method will not be normal if 100% of all mothers use this method. Innumerable examples could be mentioned to show that normal, although not perfect, is the optimum condition in human affairs. Average, obviously, is only a cross-section, taking all highs and lows into account. As long as human beings feel they are "normal" or are thought to be "normal," they are satisfied and accept their fate as well as their situation. Indeed, we could postulate that, if there were a remote area on this earth inhabited by people having six fingers or a big birthmark on the face, everybody living there would wish to be "normal" and would wish to bear identical markings. Indeed, a sense of beauty and desirability is highly conditioned by similar circumstances.

An admission of one's own abnormality would, by implication, incriminate the formative forces responsible for our pattern formation. The mother, of course, is to the infant the overwhelming personality upon whom his very existence hinges. It is not so much that she carried us for nine months and gave birth to us (although even this factor deserves the closest study), but the very fact that our existence depended on food, and milk was our natural first food and it was contained in the breasts of the mother. Any other form of early feeding, by bottle or wetnurse, was only substitution for the real thing. If, therefore, we received a pattern, whatever it might be, we received it through the attitude of our mother. If we subsequently came to the conclusion that we are abnormal, by implication we would say that our mother was abnormal; since, however, we see her as the very basis of life—if not outright life itself for us—how could we consider anything abnormal which in reality was our only experience? From the viewpoint of the infant and child, it is much more logical to consider the entire world abnormal than to doubt one's own mother.

I am fully aware that, on the surface at least, many people later try to dissociate themselves from their mothers and become critical, if not rejecting, of her. But this is only surface appearance. We may think we have outgrown her and become independent of her, but, in reality, we may turn out exactly like her, or like the imprint she conveyed upon us. Only deep, searching, and analytical study can reveal that the more we disapprove of a person, the more we may identify with him or her. Implied in all this is the subconscious feeling that we would lose life if we dissociate ourselves from what we perceived as life itself at first. We, therefore, are frozen in a vicious, almost self-destructive pattern. We have to uphold a personality pattern imprinted and programmed upon us in the formative stage, although this pattern may prove to be not only not useful, but outright disastrous. We are blind and unable to be objective about ourselves. The admonition that we should see ourselves as we really are is nothing but a pious wish, unable to be fulfilled. The words of wisdom throughout the ages were always: "Know thyself." Human beings will go to any length to keep functioning along their own pattern formation. They will put up with the greatest hardships, from clashes with society with possible dire consequences, to illnesses, physical or mental, and maladjustments of any variety, to keep functioning or apparently functioning, at least, according to the pattern programmed upon them. Theoretically at least, it would be the simplest of the solutions if an individual, realizing his own unfortunate pattern, would freely come for a review of it and gradually gain a revised, more favorable, and successful pattern formation. It is realized this is only a wishful concept. Our pattern formation is organically conditioned into the synaptic neuron associations in our central nervous system, which is just as organic as the reflex arch of the knee jerk or pupillary reflex.

chapter 6

GRIEF, SADNESS, AND DEPRESSION: A REVISED VIEWPOINT

"Melancholia" has been known as far back as written history records. King Saul suffered from it. Hippocrates (400 B.C.) blamed "black bile" for melancholia, which is only a translation of it. Aretaeus, a Roman physician 500 years later, said that flatulence as well as anger, grief, and dejection of the mind were to be blamed for melancholia. He also noted some connections between melancholia and mania and said that these disturbances do not affect the intellect. Galen, in Rome about A.D. 150, felt the study of the brain would provide the answer to the disturbance. Not until as late as Adolph Meyer (1866–1950) was the word melancholia replaced by the term "depression." Mood-swings are commonplace in all men. Only if they reach unusual depth or persist excessively long can they be called pathological "depression." Depressions are characterized by deep sadness and despair, but frequent concomitant physical symptomatology such as excessive fatigue, listlessness, impotence, inability to concentrate, slowness in doing one's work, sleep disturbances, loss of appetite, etc., many times prompts a mistaken diagnosis of "exhaustion state."

We always look for the apparent cause of grief. The more real it is, the better the prognosis. These cases fall into the category of "reactive depression." The patient will look desperately for a reason for his depression and if no reason is readily apparent, he will come up with minor infractions, perhaps committed decades previously, to salvage the causal relationship of his depression and thus appear logical to himself. The "unpardonable sin" may be nothing but that twenty years before he took a dime from a pay telephone. Almost all depressions have physiological equivalents and loss of the sexual drive is frequently the first to come and last to go. Suicide is a great danger, particularly if the physiological symptomatology predominates and causes what is termed a "latent" or "masked depression." In depression, a feeling of worthlessness and a sense of being a burden to the world and to one's family is frequent. Indeed, he feels the family would be better off without him. In addition, obsessive thoughts of an obscene nature occur, especially in over-conscientious people. Depressions usually disappear spontaneously, even without treatment. Of course, without therapy it can take months and even years. However, prevention of suicide remains critical. Depressions do recur not infrequently.

Many classifications of depressions are in existence but this is not my concern at this time. After a very serious suicide attempt, which is frustrated, the patient often shows surprising improvement and no tendency to repeat the act. However, this statement has its exceptions. The feeling of hostility against the family and the world at large is easily noted in most suicides.

"Now they will be sorry they acted so to me!" Indeed, it has been postulated that suicide only disguises the original murderous attitude inasmuch as under no conditions do we wish to become murderers, and, since we have little faith in our own strength of inhibition and self-control, we have to immobilize ourselves for good. *Mord* and *Selbstmord* are the German equivalents for murder and suicide.

Freud clearly recognized the kinship between mourning and depression. Both are usually caused by the loss of an object or person. The mourner at the appropriate time will detach the cathexis, which was invested in the lost love object, and reattach it to other objects, persons, or interests. Freud discerned the ambivalence present in all human relationships and, therefore, at the loss guilt feelings arise.

Cultural influences have to be mentioned. Kraepelin already stated that depressions are rare among primitive people. In higher civilized countries, depressions are rarer among the lower classes than in the higher classes. We speak also of an involutional depression, if there is no history of previous depression until middle age.

We come now to the essential part of this chapter. Freud spoke of the work of mourning inasmuch as he postulated that, at the loss of an object or person into which an individual had invested cathectic ties, an individual may be overwhelmed by the sudden release of all libidinal attachments and the resulting grief may overwhelm the individual. Freud then postulated that only a gradual loosening of attachment to the lost object takes place. Every mourner builds up a kind of substitute object within himself. Freud postulated that mourning becomes complicated and sometimes even pathological if the relationship of the mourner to the lost object was very ambivalent. The incorporation then not only represents an attempt to preserve the loved object but also an attempt to destroy the hated object.

Fenichel stresses the role of the superego in depressions. It represents a protective and punitive power. In depressions, an attempt is made to restore the self-esteem that has been damaged.

Rado clarified the connections between depression and self-esteem. He also believes that the manic/depressive periodicity can be explained on a basis of transgression and expiation. Incidentally, we should mention that apparently many depressions develop during psychotherapy or psychoanalysis which was undertaken to relieve other symptoms. The dynamics which could barely be foretold become clear when the person becomes depressed. It is generally believed that depressions usually develop in persons with a rigid, obsessive, serious, anxious, worrisome, pre-morbid personality pattern.

I wish to offer my own concept as to the etiology of grief, sadness, and depression—the basic vanity of mankind represented in each of us does not permit certain individuals in whom this vanity is excessively strong to accept the concept of their own helplessness. As previously pointed out, a mechanism had to be found, unrealistic though it was, to maintain the psychotic sense of grandeur. If the loss of an object or person, cathectically tied to the individual in question, occurs, a feeling of anger and fury arises which is essentially directed against the person or object that left us, or against the forces which caused or at least did not prevent their loss. I postulate that a child whose parent dies will, in spite of all explanations offered, basically hate the parent who abandoned him and rewarded his love with absence. It will take every persuasion to cover up this primitive hurt and hate and supersede it with all readily obtainable rationalizations. If sickness kills a parent, the point can be made that, to the degree we have an overriding purpose in life, the love for a child, disease might not take the upper hand. From this viewpoint, the child may be right in feeling that, if his parent loved him enough, he would not have become sick and left him. This is a daring assumption and no proof of its validity can be given at this time, but this concept has some appealing qualities. Indelible emotional damage is done to the developing personality of the child. This damage may not be overt later on; time does not heal but rather covers up. Nevertheless, the question can always be raised as to what degree the child would have viewed the world in which he lives as a happier place than the world he experienced with this loss. Incidentally, the short tangential remark may be permitted that our personality pattern basically is a reaction adjustment to the happy or unhappy events which make up our life experiences and environmental climate.

To return to the main concept—we are totally frustrated in the fury and hate against the object or person who left us. If we are more primitive, we may raise our fists against heaven to indicate our scorn. In ancient days, it was not unusual to punish the gods for surmised injustices. Victims withheld sacrifices or switched their loyalty to other deities. This sometimes worked in reverse. The Greeks, for example, in one of their ancient myths, tell how Poseidon and Pallas Athena vied for the devotion of the Athenians. The citizens decided they would worship the deity who gave them the greater gift. Poseidon gave man the horse and Athena, the olive tree. The olive tree was judged the better gift and the city was named Athens in honor of the Goddess.

Grief is most openly displayed among more primitive societies. Rending of garments, ashes sprinkled on the head, loud wailing, tearing of hair, beating one's chest, are all accepted expressions of grief in societies where display of emotions is not frowned upon. The more a society prides itself on dignified restraint, the more the mourner is expected to refrain from display of grief. A furtive tear is the limit of permissible display. But the fury against the forces which permitted such a painful event to take place, completely disregarding and inconsiderate of our feelings, is overwhelming. Hand in hand goes serious doubt about the prevailing universal justice. We become disillusioned and from believers, we turn into cynics. Established religion has the most difficulty in conveying to the mourner at such time the concept of infinite goodness of the deity. If nothing else, the explanation is given that our faith is being tested.

Reactive depressions are the milder forms of the disturbance since a realistic cause for the depressed mood is present. Depressions, on the other hand, do occur when no discernible cause-and-effect relationship is evident. We have then to look for deeper personality patterns predisposing to the disturbance. If our attitude is basically one of great self-pride (which, of course, had its origin in that we were not adequately received with joyful love in our infancy and childhood but more likely a decent, dutiful attitude prevailed), our basic human vanity is just as much offended by any degree of disrespect, real or imagined, to which we were subjected.

There is, in addition, an aggregating mechanism also present which in time makes small irritations grow to an unbearable degree. We become filled with fury and hate but we are completely frustrated in their open release. Our increased intelligence tells us that we cannot really whip God; our rigid, self-priding attitude prevents us from an early release of anger; economic or other pressures force us to display a cheerful attitude inconsistent with our repressed feelings. In such predicaments, we finally turn the hate and fury on ourselves, at least in superficial appearance. We withdraw from contact with other people on an emotional plane, not involving our intelligence but developing a listlessness about playing ball, being part of the proceedings, and could just as well die from anger and implied resentment and implied punishment to others. "Look what you have done, you lousy God—you permitted all this injustice to be heaped upon me; you lousy parents who cared so little for me; you lousy husband who only uses me for your own self-satisfaction; you lousy wife who uses me only as a beast of burden; you lousy children for whom I sacrificed all my life and now you go off and get married and live your own life."

We have to be able to put ourselves in the framework of thinking like another person in order to understand him. The very word "understand" implies this. To know ourselves implies to fully realize every feature within ourselves and only then, if we achieve this lofty goal, do we find every feature represented within ourselves and through empathy we become truly understanding of the feelings of other people. The training analysis of psychoanalysts has this as the implied goal. However, it is an artificially designed mechanism. It is not so much motivated by the sincere resolution of one's own disturbance but by the desire to qualify for a cherished profession. It is, therefore, an act of faith and religion rather than sincere self-healing motivation. The finally-arrived-at tenets are exactly that—articles of faith instead of expressions of empathetic warmth and identification.

Not without a certain degree of pride, I wish to point out that once the concept of basic human vanity and unreality is clearly perceived, a clue is obtained which sheds light on problems which previously were only dimly explained. Fun is only an inadequate substitute for joy and joy itself is only open if objectivity of the highest degree is reached —objectivity about ourselves, and, therefore, objectivity about others and the world at large.

There is an additional point which deserves discussion. Inasmuch as there is always some gain in a disturbance, the painful experience of a depression cannot be minimized. However, is it not true that something within ourselves imposes this suffering on us? To write it off simply by calling it a masochistic principle does not explain the dynamics of the situation. Pain tries to convey a certain message, implying that the pain has served its purpose and would cease to exist if only we would heed its lesson. Is it not true that so many of our patients come to us not so much because we bring about an alteration in their living conditions, but rather because we help them to resolve their perplexity and to understand "why" things turn out the way they do, most unhappily? The answer to this question is obvious to the astute observer. If depression is caused by the discrepancy between our unrealistic vanity and self-love and occurrences which befall us which we experience as an unbearable affront to our self-image, the solution lies in perceiving ourselves realistically. We are nothing but part and parcel of the infinite universe, and no force makes particular accommodations to our feelings. From infancy on, we are recipients of all the formative imprints working upon us, and we are nothing but the result of this adjustment reaction. If we become realistic enough to perceive ourselves in this light, we will enjoy pleasant occurrences, but our vanity will not get smashed if untoward events befall us. No force in nature plots to do us in; no force in nature goes out of its way to spare us bruises and sledge hammer blows. The more useful our early pattern formation was, the better we will be able to judge and calculate the risks which the pursuit of life and happiness daily forces us to face up to appropriately and realistically.

Here again, the law of the survival of the fittest can be noted. In this sense, the fittest is the one who sees life most realistically. He is also the one who, by the strength of his appropriate judgment, is more likely to make consistently successful decisions, who will shun avoidable frictions, and who, therefore, is more likely to lead what is generally called a happy and well-adjusted life.

chapter 7

THE ROLE OF THE PARENTS IN CHILD AND ADOLESCENT PSYCHIATRY

Each child is the product of his parents. This seems a redundant statement and more than self-evident but, nevertheless, when a psychiatrist or therapist is engaged in child or adolescent psychiatric practice, he cannot help but note very soon how little parents are aware of this fact at times. Nor are they prepared to face up to this fact. The reader who has carefully followed my thesis so far will realize that each parent, according to the imprint he received himself, will do the best he can, inadequate or even as disastrous as this may be. Our sense of vanity, of course, revolts against the thought that we could not have done better. Therefore, the parent may have a consciously—or even unconsciously—perceived guilt feeling. This feeling of guilt is an intolerable human emotion. We will go to any lengths to free ourselves from this gnawing, self-derisive emotion. Religion has recognized this for a long time. Penitence and atonement seem to be institutions primarily designed to make the individual feel purified again. It is proverbial that the criminal who has served his time in a penal institution feels that he has paid his debt to society and now should be accepted on his merits. Equally, the child who has been punished will feel it greatly unjust if subsequently he is not considered completely forgiven.

But, as far as the parent is concerned, one of the most frequent devices to avoid the painful feeling of guilt for having caused a disturbance in one's own child is, of course, to blame outside circumstances for the disturbance. Most often parents will maintain that their child was a wonderful person until he or she got involved with bad company. Nothing seems more face-saving to parents than to be able to blame it all on bad influences. Little does it occur to these parents to ask themselves the question: What was it in their offspring that attracted him or her to this so-called bad company? In addition, there is quite a difference between the normal curiosity which makes an individual interested enough to wish to see what this forbidden territory is all about, and acting like this forbidden territory is actually the promised land and embracing this frowned-upon life-style most thoroughly. Certain elements can be recognized in these differing attitudes.

First of all, we feel attracted to and perhaps actually taste the forbidden life-style—whether it is drug experimentation or participation in unlawful behavior of one kind or another. Then let us disabuse ourselves of the notion that such behavior has never occurred at any time and any place in the past. Our fathers were found smoking and drinking alcoholic beverages in young years and indulging in rebellious behavior just as every other generation did in the past. We can recognize in this attitude the element of defiance and perhaps rebellion in addition to innocent curiosity. To the degree our need to establish a feeling of personality and individuality was neglected, not respected, or outright repressed, this emotional quest for feeling "we are somebody" will determine our attitude. I am tempted to say—what we don't get by hook, we get by crook.

Of course, the person who is most likely to be blamed for what we perceive as undesirable attitudes in our children is our mate. It is a time-honored statement that "all good qualities in the children come from me—all undesirable features come from you and your family." Even if this were so, we are forced to ask why we felt attracted to and actually married a person who later on turns out to be so deficient. The least we have to admit is that we lacked good judgment at the time of decision. We might blame it on the inexperience of our youth but it will not occur to us to see the reason was an inadequate home environment, even when we ourselves could not wait to escape. In a way, we actually abused our potential mate when we used him only to presumptively improve our own living conditions. Little recognized at times is the fact that children unknowingly act out the unconscious wishes, temptations, and desires of their parents. The children sense the presence of these temptations in their parents and, completely subconsciously, sense that they will win the approval of their parents on an emotional level, even if the words contradict or deny it. As I pointed out earlier, this total dependency of the infant on his mother cannot be overemphasized. As we get older, its recollection wanes or sinks into the subconscious inasmuch as we need the illusion of freedom of will. Before birth, it is literally through the umbilical cord that life is sustained in the fetus. At birth, the factual umbilical cord is severed but in the mammals the mother will remain the life-sustaining force. We can say that the child is completely fixated on the mother in an almost hypnotic state of dependency. Even in his attempt to be independent at the toddler stage, the child follows only the unspoken desire of mother, who, to a certain degree at least, wants the independence of her offspring.

We see this relationship clearly in the animal kingdom. The immediate response of cubs to special sounds of their mother is instantaneous. The cub senses that its very existence depends on its immediate compliance to maternal signals. Even in adult life, we will totally adjust ourselves to the wishes of another person as long as we feel our life depends on his good will. I will use an example which was brought to my attention recently and which seems almost a paradox. A person who has been kidnapped and whose life is totally dependent from second to second on another person will go so far to please and endear himself to the kidnapper that he will point out any flaws which may exist in his plans to obtain the ransom. It is only if we are prepared to die for an issue or a person that we will put up resistance in the face of annihilation. Subconsciously we may feel we will live on in the issue or the other person. We thusly feel we will not die.

Children will like the persons whom their mothers like and dislike the persons whom their mothers dislike. To the degree the child senses his mother's approval of her mate, the child is permitted to indulge in his own biological urges with regard to the father. To this degree, the boy will feel free to identify with his father, accept his example, and strive to be like him. On the other hand, ultimately the mother did choose her mate probably for reasons of which she herself is completely unaware. If this mate subsequently turns out to be unacceptable to the mother, he only lives up to the unconscious expectations of the mother. The boy will take this unacceptable imprint from him because the mother actually wanted the father to turn out to be unacceptable. This seems complicated but it is not. A woman who is patterned so that she actually hates and fears men will fall in love and mate, if and when she does, only with a partner whom subconsciously she senses would eventually justify her hate. Did not her own mother convey to her this attitude? The mother cannot be wrong. The same, of course, is true for the man who will only fall in love and mate with a woman who ultimately will live up to and justify the expectations planted into him by his own mother. We have to consider a rather paradoxical situation. What creates a situation where the child actually turns on his mother, rebels against her, and finally rejects her or hates her? Several points come into play. To a degree, the growing child feels that the mother actually interferes with the development of his biological goals. The boy innately has the drive to emulate the male example in his life, the father. To the degree the mother, so to speak, vetoes this, the boy will obey and follow mother's veto. But, on an unconscious level, he will hate her for interfering with his biological destiny. This maternal veto can, of course, come in any degree—from the mildest form of disapproval of her mate to catastrophic hate and total rejection of her husband. Whether or not parents remain married or get divorced is not necessarily decisive. No greater disaster can be visualized than two people spending their lives together united in deadly hate. The maternal veto of the mate will also have its disastrous effect on the female child but perhaps in a subtler form, the results of which may become overt only much later, perhaps only at the time she becomes biologically mature. The emotional relationship the girl is permitted to form with her father will determine her later emotional relationship to the opposite sex and, therefore, to her potential and eventual mate. The courtship game, which takes place in the animal kingdom, serving the selection of the fittest and thus giving the survival of the species the best chance, is modified in human affairs to a selection of the potential mate who will best satisfy our own emotional needs. If we are basically afraid of the opposite sex (and who is not to a certain degree at least?), we will only feel attracted to (we call it: fall in love with) a potential mate who, we sense on a subconscious level, will live up to this emotional need of ours eventually. What we fear, we hate. The degree of fear of the opposite sex will vary from individual to individual. It does us little good to recoil from the word hate. Hate by any other name is still hate.

We come now to the very subtle problem of the child rejecting the mother and even outright hating her. We have in this case to postulate that the mother not only, subconsciously at least, invites this rejection but outright expects and needs it. The child in this case fulfills only the spirit of the mother, although on the surface the appearance may be totally different. To the degree a mother feels she is not worthwhile, she has to bring about a situation in which she reaps what she feels she deserves. This feeling of being rejected by one's own children has, of course, a great compensatory mechanism. One certainly can indulge in a great deal of self-pity which is only another form of self-love and vanity. "What cruel fate befalls me," we can feel—"I who have always sacrificed so diligently for my child." Little does such a mother realize that no child wishes to hear that his upbringing involved sacrifices by his mother. Was he not meant to be a joy to her? Was it a sacrifice for her to indulge in intercourse which resulted in his birth? Was she forced into it? What motivated her to consent to it? Was she herself so dependent that at the price of sex she secured a mate? The child, future adult, is not likely to ask these questions bluntly when he deals with his own mother, but subconsciously these questions are present whether we become aware of them or not.

I feel the scene is now set for closing in on the overt topic of this chapter. Let us assume a child does not develop well or satisfactorily and is brought to the attention of a well-qualified therapist. What avenues are open? Obviously, three all-important variables determine the approach—the age, the type of disturbance, and the degree of the disturbance. The degree of the disturbance is likely to be the most critical consideration. We can assume that a child who shows serious disturbances in very young years must come from an emotionally forbidding home environment. (Some recent studies implicate neurological damage in illnesses such as autism, but I feel these psychiatrists overlook the distinction between real warmth [for which there is no psychological test] and correct behavior. Because a family appears "ideal," it need not be so in fact.) I like to use the word warmth in preference to the much misused word love when we wish to describe the emotional climate which an infant and child finds or is deprived of. At no time should intellectual acceptance from the mother be confused with warmth. Just as she herself will not feel enriched if her own husband remembers every one of her birthdays and important holidays, and assiduously makes sure not to default, but only from a sense of duty, her offspring will be deprived of the enriching experience of warmth if she only—even most dutifully but coldly—administers to its needs. We have seen the sickest children coming from such an emotionally barren background. Leo Kanner has described these children and their background most accurately and called them autistic, withdrawn into themselves in very young years. Let us ask ourselves the most obvious question. When does any creature withdraw? When it is afraid it may get hurt. This point cannot be emphasized too much if we want to understand children and human beings altogether. Indeed, this thought can be followed much further if we are so disposed. Otologists have assured us that much of the development of deafness has emotional conditioning elements, at least at first. Is this not also a subconscious withdrawal inasmuch as it protects the individual from hearing offensive auditory noise? Severe, recurrent physical abuse will also bring about a withdrawal from reality which functions as a protective mechanism. We know that severe persistent pain is intolerable to individuals and shock and ultimately death is nature's normal way of dealing with an unbearable situation.

What can be done for such seriously disturbed children? The best we can do, most likely, is to free them from this forbidding home environment. This approach will simultaneously give the parents relief from the burden of the child, as much as they might deny it, and switches the burden of raising the child to other people, or society at large. Even under optimum substitute conditions, no approximation to a development can be expected which takes place under a reasonably healthy emotional climate. The parents will be much too defensive themselves and not be prepared to see themselves in the deplorably emotionally deprived state in which they are functioning. They might have made every conscientious effort to be adequate and dutiful to their child. They feel this was love and cannot perceive it as only a desperate dedication to preserve self-respect.

If the disturbance of the child is of a milder degree, the situation is already much more favorable. In young years, attention extended to the child, which he perceives as pleasant, will improve his outlook and attitude toward life. Ultimately, the entire question boils down to whether the child and later the adult perceives this life as predominantly pleasant or not, whether one should protect oneself against it since nothing good is expected to come anyhow, to withdraw from it to a lesser or higher degree, or to take refuge in fantastic assumptions—unrealistic as they may be.

Strictly speaking, the development of every individual is only an adjustment reaction. To the limits our endowment permits, we adjust ourselves to the conditions to which we become exposed. We can postulate that the emotional home environment is much more benign if the disturbance of the child is only minor. In this case, the defensiveness of the parents will not be excessive. An objective psychiatrist will be able to involve these parents in the therapeutic approach. If the therapist, in addition, has gained the objectivity to clearly perceive the difference between cause and fault, he will be able to overcome any defensiveness which may still linger on in the parents. Ultimately, the question boils down to making the parents realize that they themselves have arrived at a crossroad in their life. What is more important—their subconscious loyalty to their own parents (and their mother, in particular) or their loyalty to the future generation represented by their children? The less frightening their own parents were to them when they themselves were young, the easier they will find it to become objective about them and thus to win their own emancipation. They first have to become emotionally independent of their own parents, to grow up and mature, so to speak, until they in their turn become emotionally adequate parents to their own children. If such a desirable development takes place, we can truly say that we never know what good can come from bad. Again and again, I have observed that in such favorable cases parents have become much closer to each other and communication is established between them which had been nonexistant for a long time. Each child dreams and wishes that his parents are close to each other, feel comfortable with each other and enjoy each other. I remember the young girl, whose case I shall present here as fairly typical, asking me as she was hospitalized, "Can you help my parents?" Children in their confused vanity feel that they are actually the cause of parental discord and everything would be fine for the parents if they themselves did not exist. This feeling, of course, conflicts with the biological drive for self-preservation.

The case of the young girl, which I shall present in great detail, has many interesting features and certainly could be discussed from several viewpoints. The electroencephalographic findings done by the highest authority in this field reveal what is termed minimal brain dysfunction (MBD) syndrome, so frequently mentioned in the literature in recent years. I shall dwell on this subject for a while because I feel the supposedly organic changes demonstrated in the electroencephalogram influence many psychiatrists to emphasize the cellular organic origin of the emotional disturbance. They, therefore, feel more inclined to treat such children by chemotherapy, with some improvement, it is admitted. However, they neglect to come to the core of the etiology of the disturbance, which is of emotional origin. Although they can show some improvement with their therapeutic approach, they fail to obtain possible optimal results. A comparison could be made with a surgeon operating on an injured hand, who obtains healing but at the price of lessened function of the fingers which a more perspicacious surgeon may have obtained.

(Incidentally, at this point I wish to mention that an emotionally desirable environment does not only encompass warmth of the mother, but firmness as well—love is never weakness; firmness is never harshness. Only to the degree we feel sure of our love for our child or any other person do we feel we can afford to be firm. A child will not be able to deter us from our decision by saying, "I hate you, I don't want to see you anymore." If we are sure of our love, we will say, "I am sorry that you feel this way, but the answer is still 'No.' " Eventually, the child will recognize that we had his welfare at heart and appreciate us all the more. Actually a child, like a duckling or any cub, needs and wants adequate guidance in this life and we can easily sense his confusion when he has to strike out on his own if proper guidance is not forthcoming. The ultimate goal of a well-balanced mother is not so much to aim to be loved by her children, but to lead them into this life so they in turn in their own good time can take their rightful place on this earth. Love and appreciation for work well done will follow.)

This 17-year-old, pleasant-looking, rather gentle-appearing girl I will call Susie was first seen by me in my office, accompanied by her parents. The history revealed that she suffered from severe depression and that she heard voices at times, and was quite withdrawn. She had been under the care of another psychiatrist for several months previously and had been hospitalized by him for two months in the psychiatric department of a general hospital after she took a heavy overdose of phenobarbital tablets in an admitted suicide attempt.

After she was discharged from the hospital and had been back home for three weeks, she again had suicidal ideations. At this point her psychiatrist apparently became frightened and she was committed to a state hospital. Here she signed herself out after two weeks against the advice of the hospital physicians and staff. Her parents were thoroughly frightened and desperately sought help. They placed all their faith and hope in me.

At this initial interview, the girl was in good contact, spoke coherently, answered questions relevantly, and seemed cooperative on the surface. I suggested rehospitalization under my care and outlined concurrent family therapy with her parents. The parents readily consented but Susie objected strenuously to rehospitalization, promising cooperation on an out-patient basis. I explained to the parents that unless I had adequate control, I could not undertake the therapy. I also felt somewhat that Susie had, in a way, always been able to manipulate her surroundings in the past. This most undesirable situation frequently arises when the mother feels unequipped to be firm with a child when firmness is indicated. The parents took her to the hospital after Susie was convinced that I would not hesitate to bring about court action to ask for her commitment.

After her hospitalization, I asked for psychological testing, which I always order in adolescent cases, not so much because I wish to gain additional information but rather to involve the parents in the therapeutic endeavor. My psychologist always makes it a special point to interview the parents of an adolescent thoroughly prior to his testing the youngster. I always give a separate copy of the finished report to each of the parents, requesting them to review the report independently and comment on their reaction at the next interview. I favor independent review by each parent to get the individual separate, uninfluenced, first-hand reaction. The complete psychological report reads as follows:

Reason for Referral: The patient (a 17-year-old girl) was referred for psychological evaluation because of severe depression, hearing voices, feelings of depersonalization, and withdrawn behavior. She was hospitalized during the months of March and April of 1974. This was because of a suicide attempt. While at school she had ingested ninety to ninety-five tablets of barbiturate. In addition she had taken half a bottle of Darvan and also numerous aspirins. After her discharge, she was home for about three weeks. During this time she was in psychiatric treatment. It was found during treatment that she was again fantasizing suicide ideations. She was committed to a state hospital. On June 7th, she signed herself out. This was against the advice and recommendation of the hospital and the psychiatrist.

The psychological examination was specifically requested in order to assess the underlying dynamics of her personality and behavior relative to the causes for the depression and suicidal ideations.

Tests Used: Wechsler Adult Intelligence Scale (WAIS) (Short Form)

Verbal IQ: *112*
Full-Scale IQ: *111*
Performance IQ: *108*
Classification: *Bright/Normal*

House-Tree-Person; Post Drawing Interrogation; Bender Gestalt Visual Motor Test; Rorschach Ink Blot; Incomplete Sentence Blank.

Interview With Parents: The mother said that her pregnancy and delivery had been normal and without complications or problems. Walking, talking, toilet training, and other milestones of development were accomplished in logical developmental sequence and without any problems. When Susie was 12 years of age she developed a "strep throat." The mother related that since that time she has had "aches in her joints," and "pains in her chest." A culture hinted at the possibility that Susie may have a predisposition toward the development of rheumatic fever. Her tonsils were removed when she was 12. Aside from this, there was no history of any unusual illnesses, injuries, high fevers, or head traumas.

Susie was described as a very bright, alert, and inquisitive young child. She had a very vivid imagination. She was always in a world of imaginary dolls and friends. There was an impression on the part of the parents that she "always held back her own feelings." In this respect she was considered more of a "loner." She seemed to be somewhat withdrawn, would hide her feelings, was extremely patient, never exhibited any display of temper, and would always give in to the needs of others. She was described as being "almost too good." However, this was not necessarily true when she dealt with her friends.

She had always enjoyed school friends and had been an honor student, receiving almost straight A's throughout her school career. Her desire was to become a teacher. Presently her desires are to become a missionary nun and a doctor.

There are two younger female siblings in the home, 16 and 14 years of age. There was no unusual sibling rivalry among Susie and her sisters.

Her father is the oldest in a sibship of four. He has one sister and two brothers. His parents are divorced. This occurred when he was in the first year of high school. Since that time his father has remarried. His sister is presently hospitalized because of "severe mental strain." She has suffered a series and succession of surgeries and operations, including kidney problems, hysterectomy, removal of skin cancer, and a problem due to injury of her leg. As a result, she has suffered seizures and convulsions. It was during one of these convulsions that she slipped and received a head injury. Since that time the seizures have been occurring with greater frequency. There is no diagnosis of her condition, nor has the cause of the seizures been determined. He further related that his brother's wife is a schizophrenic. His father has suffered some back problems. He himself also has difficulty with severe migraine headaches. Occasionally, he must be confined to bed.

Susie's mother is the only child in her family. Both parents are deceased. Her father died of pneumonia when she was in the fifth grade. Her mother died of cancer of the breasts when she was in the eighth grade. With regard to her own health there are no serious difficulties or problems.

No marital difficulties were related. No angers, hostilities, or underlying tones of tension were noted. Generally, they are in agreement with regard to the handling of Susie and her sisters.

Susie had recently related to them that during the time of her prior hospitalizations she had been hearing at least five voices. The reason that she did not tell her parents at the time was because she was afraid they would not understand. On one occasion, she seemed to feel that she was another person. The father related that he saw his daughter change in that she "braced her shoulders" and seemed to straighten up; her eyes were wide open and this other personality came out. At that point Susie was of the opinion that this person was from another world. It could only be discovered who this other person was when Susie died. The parents related that this was probably the first time that they had ever seen their daughter express herself in a very determined voice. The second time was recently at the psychiatrist's office when she refused to be hospitalized.

Interview With Susie: She appeared to be somewhat withdrawn, confused, and depressed during the initial interview. Her eyes would fill with tears from time to time. There was much anxiety, timidness, and hesitancy. There was definitely a problem with regard to overall affect. She presented a picture of dejection and helplessness. Preoccupation was with her concerns and hospitalization.

With regard to her verbalizations throughout, she expressed feelings of inferiority, guilt, and disappointing her parents. She related, much as she did to her parents, her hearing of voices, the presence of another person within her, and her own fear of hurting people. It was basically this fear of hurting people, mostly verbally, that caused her initial depression and attempt at suicide. She has always subjugated her own feelings for the benefit and welfare of others. In this respect she stated that she never wants to go against her parents and this has caused her to "give up her own feelings." Although there was much anger and resentment, there was a tendency for Susie to deny the intensity of her anger. Primarily she was concerned that she had let her parents down. During her first hospitalization in March and April her parents had planned a vacation when she became ill. Presently they are again planning a vacation and once again she is letting them down by being hospitalized.

Susie saw her parents as being rather strict. However, she never has or will disobey them. Primarily, she felt that she got along rather well with her parents. She did state, however, "I do not have much to give them; the only thing I can give them is good grades." She had insight that she never asserts herself, gives in primarily to the needs of others, and never under any condition does she wish or have the need to raise her voice. Nevertheless, it was noted that there was much ambivalence. This was with regard to "being by myself," yet "being with my parents." Primarily, emphasis was upon her attempt to express her love of people. She stated frequently, as if to reassure herself, "I like people," "I love people," and "I must help people." There was also emphasis upon God, her belief in God, and her need for righteousness.

She recalls that even as a child there appeared to be a strong "force" which seemed to impel her on the right track and to do "the right thing." This was so she should not stray or commit any sins or acts of disobedience. She related several novels that she had been writing. From the description of the perils of the hero and the heroine there was some hint that she may be projecting herself into these novels. The stories generally concerned capture, escape, guilt, fear, terror, and self-punishment as well as hurt to the heroine.

There was no doubt that Susie had difficulty and was making a concerted effort to "hold herself together" and to "integrate her ego." There was a hint of some disorientation in her thinking and also the possibility of intense preoccupation with fantasy and a tenuous hold on reality. Occasionally her defenses would weaken and her associations would become loose, slipping into her fantasy preoccupations.

Test Results: During the interview it was apparent by Susie's use of words and rhetorical expressions that her IQ was extremely high. The related facts that she is an honor student, her ability to undertake writing novels, and expressions and recitations of poetry all tended to fortify the hypothesis that she does indeed possess a brilliant intelligence. Nevertheless, it was surprising to find that she struggled with the formal intelligence testing. The anxiety, depression, confusion, and disorganization were factors that interfered with her score. She missed some of the easy items but was able to answer correctly some of the more difficult items at the upper end of the scale. This indicated disturbance in her thinking and her thought processes as well as strong internalized underlying anxiety factors. There was also some interference with regard to common sense, judgment, and reasoning. Nevertheless, despite this, her verbal IQ score was found to be 112.

On the performance IQ her score was 108. There was no indication of a problem with visual-motor coordination. There was no hint of organic behavior. The full scale IQ of 111 places her within the bright normal range. However, there was, as stated, evidence that her IQ is within the superior level of intelligence. There is no doubt that the underlying emotional problems are very severe and pervasive and they are presently spilling over and interfering with achievement and potential.

On the Bender-Gestalt her drawings were extremely miniscule. This was indicative of withdrawn, contracted, and possibly severely inhibited behavior.

The results of the projectives presented a picture of Susie as having strong feelings of inferiority, insecurity, and inadequacy. These feelings appear to pervade every area of her being and personality. In addition, she was seen as being very immature, childish, and naive. There is also a problem with regard to this naivete at the conscious level. It is as if she is surprised at herself and her poor judgment on occasion.

Other findings tended to show a problem with fears. These fears are intense and pervasive. Generally they are concerned with her own hostile impulses. There is a fear of her acting out her hostility and hurting someone, and this terrifies her. In addition, numerous guilt feelings were also noted. The guilt is because of the intensity of her hostile, aggressive, and destructive feelings. As a result there is self-blame for whatever happens. This would seem to involve what is happening to her aunt and any problems in the family and it is spilling over into all of the problems of mankind. Susie appears to be rather masochistic in that she feels responsible for everyone's unhappiness and misfortunes. It is as if she is carrying the cross for the entire world.

The most important findings were with regard to anger and rage. Susie harbors severe feelings of rage and anger which terrify her. At all costs she must repress, suppress, and remove from consciousness the awareness of the intensity of this anger and rage. She therefore has developed a reaction-formation against her intolerable impulses. She is really terrified, fearful, and angry at people. Her defenses, however, are with regard to love, trust, and acceptance. This is a defense against her intense anger and the tremendous amount of rage that she has toward them. It is as if her needs have not been met. She is unable to direct any of her rage or anger into any proper socially accepted channel. There is no avenue for her to funnel off any of this rage. As a result, it is turned inward and directed toward herself. Her withdrawn behavior is a protection against this rage breaking loose and her fear of hurting others or herself. There is the conscious awareness that she may hurt others and since she feels she has little control she is terrified of the thought of damaging or harming her family or herself.

Further, Susie was seen as being very lonely, unhappy, and extremely depressed. Efforts are constant to escape from her loneliness and depression. Since she has always been overwhelmed with her fears, her only escape has been to fantasy preoccupations. An analysis of her fantasy world indicates that this has possibly been present since early childhood. She has not been able to resolve or work out these fantasies at appropriate stages because of tension and anxiety. Therefore, she has learned to resort to the use of autism and fantasy as a respository for many of her feelings.

Other feelings are rejection, desperation, and deprivation. She has an insatiable need for succor and acceptance. She seems to have an extremely rigid ego. In this respect she is concerned with justification, doing the right thing, and never straying into sin. It is as if Susie has a fear of the world. For her the world is a very hostile place in which to live. She is terrified of herself and is fearful of people to the point of suspicion, mistrust, and paranoid ideations. She has intense feelings of worthlessness, has a very poor self-concept, and is constantly terrified that she will be led down paths of destruction and punished for her bad thoughts and ideas. Susie is very ambivalent and frustrated, and this compounds her problems. On the one hand, she has severe rage and anger toward her parents. On the other hand, she has intense feelings of love and admiration. She cannot please herself or others and sees herself as constantly "letting them down." She wants to be with them, yet wants to run from them. She has a fear that she will harm them and is generally terrified and fantasizes terrible things happening, including the loss of her family. Preoccupations are with hell, death, and destruction. She is fearful of doom, impending disaster, and being absorbed and destroyed by creatures from another world.

Her thinking is definitely idiosyncratic and symbolic and there is also regression. The regression is severe and it is to a very primitive stage in all development. The problem is mainly one of separation anxiety. There is a hint that her attachment to her mother borders on the "symbiotic."

Despite her denial of preoccupation with suicide, there was a hint that there are suicidal fantasies. The intensity of her rage and anger, with no proper social outlet, fortifies the danger of self-destruction. She has a very unstable sense of self-identity and a low self-esteem. It would appear that every new situation is a threat, a strain which easily disrupts her weak ego and defenses. The constant feeling of emptiness, a sense of void as well as panic, offers no escape from reality or from her fantasy. There is a tremendous sense of disappointment, resentfulness due to parental overprotection, and yet insecurity and unsureness of her own ability. Susie has difficulty dealing with reality effectively. Some feelings of persecution, ideas of reference, and other symbolic thinking were noted.

Summary and Recommendations: The results of the present psychological test indicate that Susie has potential for functioning within the superior level of intelligence. For the most part, she has been able to function close to her level of intelligence. However, presently her emotional difficulties are severe and incapacitating and are spilling over into and interfering with her intellectual ability. She has very intense feelings about herself which include inferiority and insecurity. She is very frightened, fearful, and immature and is concerned with her own thoughts and ideas. She was further seen as being suspicious and mistrusting. This is because of her fear of the hostile world and of the people in it. As a result she is lonely, unhappy, and depressed as well as withdrawn. The purpose of her withdrawn behavior is in defense against acting out some of her hostile impulses. She fantasizes that she may hurt others and this terrifies her. Her idosyncratic behavior indicates a tenuous and rather unstable hold on reality. She is definitely subject to delusions and hallucinations because of her weak defenses.

An analysis of her fantasy indicates fears regarding her hostility, anger, destruction, and homicidal ideations. She feels helpless and rejected, and has severe guilt. Every new situation is very threatening and strains her already brittle ego.

Her parents appear to be realistic, concerned, and understanding. Nevertheless, there was some hint of overprotection. There is worry and anxiety about Susie and her condition. There is some hint in the background with regard to preoccupation with illnesses. The parents may be communicating some of their fears and anxieties to Susie. Her mother indicated that when she was Susie's age, she was also very concerned and had deep religious beliefs in God much as Susie has had recently. There is also the subtle hint by the mother concerning her own preoccupations that "schizophrenia is inherited." This may have been in reference to the aunt's difficulties. There is also some unconscious message being communicated to Susie regarding the mother's overconcern with her daughter's health.

It was not possible to determine whether there were any unusual marital difficulties, problems, tensions, or anxieties in the home. Generally, the kind of condition and illness that Susie seems to be suffering from occurs in a home where there is tension, anxiety, and conflict. Although this was not elicited, there is every indication that her defenses are poorly developed. As stated, there is only the hint that her mother is overanxious and overprotective and this may have been the source of Susie's tensions and anxieties.

There was also some hint that the home situation is one in which there is repression of feelings and a problem with self-assertion or expression. Susie's attitude regarding separation and her breaking down at a crucial time prior to the family vacation are also significant. Her withdrawn behavior, feelings of hopelessness and helplessness, and intense guilt have made her more depressed. Her feelings that her needs have not been met has caused intense rage. Giving in to others, never being able to assert herself, and refusing to accept as well as denying her rage and anger has further upset and caused Susie to be frustrated and depressed.

Regarding the religious aspect, there seems to be a displacement of her repressed wishes onto God. One problem is with regard to identification with her parents. She obtains conscious and unconscious gratification by her religious beliefs. Identifying herself with the God figure is a means of protecting herself from the dangers and fears of her own hostile and destructive fantasies and impulses. She is projecting her conflicts outward and seeking a strong force to prevent her from acting out or from complete loss of contact with reality.

One of the problems that may have contributed to her condition is, of course, the illness of the aunt. Susie was very close to this aunt and she is probably upset and under tension because of the aunt's seizures and convulsions. The mother recalled that when Susie was in the eighth grade (and occasionally since then) on several occasions her daughter "hyperventilated." Susie feels responsible for her aunt's behavior because of her self-blame and intense guilt. The primary problem is the severe rage and anger. It appears that there is no avenue of escape for her. She is fearful of the world and frightened of the people in it, yet has no recourse in that even her own fantasies are full of hostile and destructive ideations. The intense feelings of worthlessness, the need to be punished, and the impending fear that something bad will happen to her are, of course, compounding her difficulties and problems. There is definitely suicidal fantasy and no indication of properly funneling off her rage and anger into any socially acceptable channels.

In view of the findings, Susie is in need of continued hospitalization and treatment in an in-patient setting. She is still in a deep, disturbing, incapacitating emotional state. Intense rage, self-punishment, and self-destructive tendencies all point to active suicidal fantasies and ideations. Hospitalization would also provide Susie with a separation experience and possibly an opportunity to break what seems to be a symbiotic bind. In treatment with Susie, it is necessary to strengthen her brittle ego so that she is able to tolerate stress since there is the possibility that in the future, whenever she is threatened or whenever there is severe anxiety, she may again break down, necessitating other periods of hospitalization. With regard to the parents, there were some subtle hints regarding separation anxiety, communications of anxieties, and (especially for the mother) struggling with the inheritance of mental illness, all indicating overconcern as well as overprotection. It may be these forces that are causing tension and anxiety and precipitating Susie's problems. It is, therefore, necessary to involve the parents in group and individual psychiatric treatment so they can cope with some of their own feelings and can be helped to understand Susie and her problems better.

There is every indication that Susie suffered from a "schizophrenic reaction." Susie seems to have numerous strengths which can be used and capitalized on in treatment with her. The fact that she had a determined voice and resisted hospitalization would seem to indicate that she is headed in the direction of asserting herself and possibly this could be a means of funneling off some of the intensity of her anger towards herself. There is a need to have her ventilate some of her feelings, face her angers and repressions, as well as help her through her ambivalence, intense fears, and anxieties. Primarily, the need is to bolster her defenses, help her tolerate future stress, have her grow and mature, become more independent of her family and her parents, and help her to assert her feelings and to express them adequately and appropriately. It is necessary to reinforce to the parents that Susie must continue to be hospitalized and that, despite her objections to the contrary and her denial of suicidal intention, they must not give in to her and that she should continue to be a patient until the psychiatrist and the staff at the hospital are thoroughly convinced that she is ready for discharge. Even at the end of her hospitalization there is a need for Susie and her parents to continue in psychiatric treatment on an out-patient basis.

—end of psychological report.

The following is the electroencephalographic findings in regard to Susie:

"The patient has 14- and 6-per-second positive-spike seizure discharges. As you know, we believe that these suggest a thalamic or hypothalamic focus of seizure activity. The cause, however, is not indicated; the most common is trauma and encephalitis is next. There is usually no structural damage. In fact, if the injury is severe, this form of abnormality does not occur; instead spikes or spike and slow wave activity are likely to appear. Fourteen- and six-per-second positive spikes are a minimal, highly reversible form of disorder.

Convulsions may occur in persons with this type of discharge but headaches, attacks of dizziness, and "black-out" spells are more common. If episodic symptoms are present they can usually be eliminated with moderate doses of Dilantin and phenobarbital, Dilantin and Mysoline or Dilantin and Mesantoin."

—end of electroencephalograph report.

Susie was to some degree impressed by my firm yet gentle approach. After the first days of hospitalization, she developed a psychophysiological reaction manifested in persistent vomiting. Proper medication given parenterally and the prospect of intravenously administered fluids, if necessary, had a very beneficial effect and the vomiting soon stopped.

The parents were seen in regular weekly sessions. After having first received permission from the parents to ask deep-going penetrating questions, I discussed with them their marital and sexual adjustment to each other in great detail. I learned that sexual relations took place only twice a month and were engaged in upon the command and order of the husband since the wife agreed she owed him that degree of consideration. She fellated him and he used cunnilingus on her.

I learned that in earlier years he had slapped his wife on two occasions and forced her to accept his mother into the household to live with them because it was his mother to whom he turned for funds to buy a home which his wife dearly desired. Incidentally, when the time came to repay the loan, it required all his funds to reimburse his mother and he subsequently declared bankruptcy.

I further learned that his wife had been totally orphaned in early life and had been taken in by Catholic nuns, although she was Protestant. She had identified with these new surroundings to such a degree that she asked to be accepted into the Catholic faith. She joined the church and became very religious.

After about three weeks of regular family psychiatric interviews, I was informed that Susie's father had been suffering of late a recurrence of a severe muscular pain in his neck. He was very promptly hospitalized by his orthopedic surgeon, traction was applied, and I was told he was to remain in traction for about ten days. After a few days, he supposedly felt much better, but when the time came to leave the hospital and return home he experienced an apparent reversal. Surgery was resorted to and a cervical fusion operation was performed to alleviate his symptomatology which was the apparent result, according to X-ray studies, of cervical arthritis.

The mother kept seeing me on a weekly basis in my office in the meantime. I saw Susie herself three times each week for extended interviews at the hospital. As mentioned before, she had a psychophysiological reaction in the first few days of her hospitalization. After this reaction was controlled, the psychological tests were taken and her parents were permitted to visit her. At one time the patient vomited again immediately after her parents started to argue and she complained of headaches before they arrived. She expressed quite freely to me her fear that she caused the disturbances between her parents.

At a later date she realized for the first time that she was very angry. She then said she liked it at the hospital and felt that she belonged there. She related that she still did not wish to live but did not feel like covering up anymore. She said that she knew how to block out things but did not wish to do it any longer. She added that she had suffered from frightful and weird nightmares for a long period of time in which she bloodily and bestially hurt her parents. At times the patient seemed to have setbacks. She spoke of the voices which bothered her more and more and which told her that she would give in to them again. If she did not, the voices threatened, they would hurt her sister.

At this stage, I became gradually more and more sure that Susie was not suffering from a true schizophrenic process but rather exhibited a strong hysterical element in order to get people excited. In the next few sessions it became almost enjoyable to talk to Susie. She impressed me at that time as a sweet young girl to whom one easily could extend considerable warmth. At one time she related that she always froze up premenstrually, but that she also had fewer nightmares. She told me that in her nightmares she either killed her parents or set them against each other. She had above all the thought of hurting her parents and wanted to get away from them. During one nightmare, she related she saw the Devil's eyes staring at her from all sides. It was at this time that her mother had told Susie that perhaps it would have been better if she had committed suicide after the death of her own parents, so that all these complications would never have arisen.

After approximately a month of hospitalization, Susie was permitted to return home for week-end visits. During one such home visit, her younger sister caused some disturbance. Apparently the sister did not wish to lose the center stage completely; the mother, however, remarked that such disturbances only took place when Susie was home. When I heard of this incident which caused a setback in Susie's progress, I discussed the various aspects of the remark in great detail with the mother who subsequently obtained a more objective perspective.

When the day of her father's operation arrived, Susie wanted to be with her mother to give her moral support. She reiterated, however, her previous beliefs that she had three forms—Susie, Annie, and Pauline, that she came from another world, and that she had been offered the assignment of coming to this world to help someone else. She also related at that time that she usually had good control over everything, but that recently another person had gained more power over her and this scared her. She could not identify this other person.

She said two months previously she had seen a monk-like figure walk to her father's bed, and that later he wanted to throw her into the fire. The night before, she said, she had had similar sensations again. She concluded by saying that perhaps she became scared too easily.

At the next session, Susie was at her best. She was pleasant and easy to talk to and I was hopeful that good progress was being made. Susie and I parted with great friendship and warmly shook hands.

When I arrived at the hospital two days later, the nurses called me aside and informed me that Susie had definitely told someone that the next weekend on her visit home, she would kill herself. I felt that in view of our recent good understanding, Susie's remarks had to be taken as a challenge and definite provocation. I felt I could not take chances. I ordered her to be transferred from the general psychiatric ward to a highly supervised intensive treatment unit of the hospital. I rescinded all her privileges, phone, visitors, etc., and, of course, cancelled the weekend pass.

I sensed that Susie had a overriding hysterical desire to excite people and shock them and thus gain their attention. When I saw her again, she apologized for her behavior. She agreed that it was true that she wanted to shock people, a mechanism which had apparently brought her attention from the mother in early years. She agreed with my statement that it is understandable that a human being wishes to gain his goals by hook or by crook.

At another session she admitted that she was not yet ready to return home even after the beginning of the new school year and wondered whether she could attend classes while hospitalized. I assured her that this could be done. She further worried about what alternative she had to suicide if she returned home. I pointed out to her that within one year she would graduate from high school and that she had always been a good student, and she certainly could become self-supporting. In addition, she would continue to receive supportive outpatient treatment after her release from the hospital. Susie related that previous therapists had also mentioned such possibilities to her but it was only now that she felt strong enough to contemplate such a course. Up to now for various reasons, about which she was not too clear herself, she had rejected such possibilities as unacceptable solutions. She indicated that she and her girlfriend had considered applying for a scholarship. At no time had it occurred to her that she could live away from home.

She recalled at the same time how her mother had tried to prove to her in early childhood that her father was an unfaithful husband; she added that her mother returned every gift her father ever gave her. She thought this rude and inconsiderate of her mother. Now she finally admitted that she hated her mother. She also told me that boys in school would confide their troubles to her, but that she had never been out on a date so far. This came about when I honestly told her that if I were 50 years younger I would ask her for a date myself. It was obvious that she opened up like a blossom when she experienced, probably for the first time, a clear warmth from her therapist. Incidentally, it was about this time Susie first dreamed that she was a bride and had boyfriends. Susie agreed with me that in a way she accomplished her goal of scaring the heck out of her parents.

There was no longer any doubt in my mind that in time Susie would be able to leave the hospital. Her parents by that time would have widened the scope of their own perceptions and finally an adequate home adjustment would be obtained, acceptable and satisfactory to all concerned.

I have chosen this case, which was truly difficult to handle, as an example to illustrate that intensive parental participation in child and adult psychotherapy is the single most important point without which no adequate solution can be obtained. It is admitted that the less the parents make themselves available for participation in the therapeutic endeavor, the less benign is the prognosis and ultimate outcome. On the other hand, there is the broad spectrum of parents who would be open to a widened scope of insight if their potential readiness were adequately utilized. It should be added that, for reasons of their own, sometimes parents default on staying in therapy. Many reasons can account for this. They may feel emotional stress on themselves.

The implication is that the children were used primarily to serve their own emotional needs, whereas the parents should primarily serve their children's emotional needs. We see then, not infrequently, the children, who have done progressively better while the parents were under concomitant therapy, apparently having recurrences. This permits the parents to place the child under the care of another therapist, thus saving face. If the child or patient subsequently seems to improve decisively, the second therapist may think it is because of his own administration that this spectacular improvement has been achieved, little realizing he is only the beneficiary of the abuse taken out on the earlier therapist. Thusly, unbeknownst to themselves, the parents set the scene to discharge repressed hate and resentment on the first therapist, who, performing his best, involuntarily but unavoidably becomes the scapegoat, and, on an emotional basis at least, serves as the sacrificial lamb for the disturbed. The principle of scapegoat and sacrifice of the innocent has a long history in human development and delusional thinking.

In religion, the reality of the therapist is replaced by an imaginary god-figure. Depending on the individual circumstances, the unconscious hate and anger, although buried in each of us to a varying degree, is the rage within us for the inadequate emotional reception which we all received at the early stages of our lives from our parents and specifically our mothers. This is the basic, unacceptable truth. The mother—the life sustainer—is also the destroyer, at least from the individual's viewpoint, and this imprint remains indelibly programmed into our brains. The more empathetic, the better the psychiatrist, the more likely he is to be hurt.

chapter 8

THE ILLUSION OF FREEDOM OF WILL

Human interrelationships and social intercourse are founded on the concept of freedom of will. We assume that we and other people, after deliberation, come to conclusions freely and independently and base our decisions and actions accordingly. If we think this concept through to its logical conclusion, each act in itself is, therefore, unpredictable and mankind can be compared to an aggregation of molecules or atoms in which each individual molecule reacts on the spur of the moment in a totally unpredictable way. Firm objects for no outward reasons whatsoever might decompose into particles and disintegrate or, for no noticeable reason, congregate into unpredictable forms. The particles would not behave in any predictable manner and, therefore, no law of nature could be visualized or deduced.

We know that on an atomic level, modern physics has postulated a law of the unpredictability of atomic behavior; however, I think this law can be interpreted as a human attempt to explain reactions which, so far, have escaped our observation. The entire concept of action and reaction would otherwise have to be reformulated.

Philosophers have at times questioned the concept of freedom of will and suggested a philosophical determinism. It can be stated with certainty that no human being is responsible for his heredity and genetic endowment. By implication, all psychiatrists and physicians who feel that genetic endowment is of overriding importance in human life deny freedom of will to the degree that they see genetic endowment as an inescapable imprint.

Equally, human beings are not responsible for the environment into which they were born. There is no doubt but that in the formative years an imprinting or programming of the individual takes place which, after a pattern has been formed, in summary will later be considered the personality. The factors which are most important in this early imprinting were, of course, the factors on which the infant's life primarily depended, or at least as far as the infant himself could discern. I refer here to the previous chapter on basic anxiety and my thesis, in general—suffice it to say that the infant in reality only reacts to the environmental condition he finds. A reactive, conditioned reflex pattern is stamped into his brain cortex which, strictly speaking, forms a definite neuro-anatomical synaptic pathway which will show definite reactive-conditioned reflex responses upon certain stimuli. Like a computer which is programmed, the human brain will come up with an answer; that is, a response anytime a problem is presented to it. No computer can come up with the right answer unless it was properly programmed. The human brain must review all data at its disposal before coming up with a response. The time which it takes to thoroughly review all determining factors we can call thinking or deliberation. At no time should this deliberation be confused with freedom of will. No factors can be introduced into this deliberative effort which were not previously part of the experience of the individual. Any new information given to the individual at the time of his deliberation is only an additional factor to be added to the total store of considerations.

The daily experiences of an infant are so vast that only a complete motion picture, as previously mentioned, taken from the very moment of birth on through every second of the formative years, would give a complete record of all programming and, therefore, an understanding of his personality pattern. Once the personality pattern has been formed, it will react in an almost predictable way to new situations which the individual meets, and the reaction is only unpredictable because of the circumstance that, even under optimal conditions, one can have only a superficial knowledge of the tremendous diversification which went into the personality pattern formation in the first place.

Let me digress here for a moment to the most interesting and frequently quoted example of identical twins. I postulate that their identical, or more precisely, similar life cycle is not so much conditioned by the fact of equal genetic endowment, but that they received identical receptions by the overwhelmingly important person in their formative years, namely, by their mother. Differentiation in their life-style came about because sooner or later the mother must have learned to differentiate between them and one infant, by necessity and even with the best will of the mother, at times will feel less readily attended to than the other, and at the same time, the other twin will feel preferred. This attitude, in itself, will have its feedback on the mother and some differentiation will follow.

Human vanity does not permit human beings to see themselves realistically—that they are nothing but reactors to the sum total of determining influences, whatever these might be. Human vanity needs the unrealistic, and, therefore, delusional assumption of one's own power and grandeur. Because of this misconception, we deal with other human beings and declare them responsible for their actions and even for their thoughts. So far, at least, we have not held anyone responsible for his dreams—perhaps because we have no way of knowing them or interpreting them correctly.

For ourselves, we will always have excuses for our misactions or misdeeds by citing all the factors which we feel were responsible for leading us into faulty reactivity. As the skilled lawyer in defense of his client, we go to any length to plead, if not innocence, then at least limited culpability, by citing all extenuating, if not explaining, circumstances which led to the formation of the personality pattern of the accused. The adverse home conditions under which a defendant grew up will play a major role in the defense of the accused. This certainly becomes most obvious in capital cases when the death penalty is under consideration. The lawyer will reason correctly that his client could not have developed into a different human being considering the environmental influences.

It should be kept in mind that once a personality pattern has been formed, the individual will seek friends and companions who are, in his opinion, congenial and compatible persons. It is, therefore, not the "bad" environment or the "bad" friends with whom an individual associated himself in later life that changed his behavior pattern, but rather the need to find compatible surroundings and companions that attracted him to other individuals of similar personality pattern. *Similis simile gaudet* is an ancient Latin proverb. As cripple marries cripple, birds of a feather flock together as well.

Human delusional grandeur comes through again, of course, in the fact that humans, alone of all forms of creation, reserve the right of freedom of will to themselves. The hedgehog, which in early spring sticks his nose carefully out of his hole to survey weather conditions and the presence or absence of enemies, is, of course, only acting by instinct, the same as a lowly quail that tries to lead her covey back to the safe roadside, noticing the oncoming car. If, however, human beings review a given situation and come to the same conclusion, this is called thinking, and freedom of will is surmised.

The fallacy of this assumption of freedom of will permits us to feel righteous when we deal sternly with, or at least attempt to deal sternly with, individuals whose pattern formations do not work in conformity to established rules of behavior. The entire criminal code is based on the concept of freedom of will and upon the concept of one's responsibility for one's actions. It is quite possible that the deterring influences which pattern an individual against antisocial acts were not effective or were used inappropriately to permit the formation of what is generally considered criminal or sociopathic. Once such a development has taken place, however, we would perhaps be much more realistic and, therefore, constructive by not confronting such an individual in a primitive way, but simply by stating that his pattern formation, and, therefore, his character, was incompatible with the life, liberty, and the pursuit of happiness of the society at large. He must, therefore, be restrained from acting destructively against members of the herd, since, obviously, the herd or society does not seek its own destruction. If this understanding would go hand in hand with a firm but not vindictive attitude, the individual in question would find it much easier to perceive this benign firmness as a new but constructive experience in his life and adjustment of his personality pattern would much more readily take place in a socially acceptable way.

I realize that this book is not written as a panacea for human ills, but an attempt to find facts and appreciate reality. Even if at first these concepts appear to be only theoretically significant, they will always be beneficial in the long run because human beings can only react realistically once the objective facts are known to them. Practical application will always follow theoretical considerations of fact.

Determinism and fatalistic attitudes deserve clear distinction. Determinism takes into account the effort of the individual to strive for the optimum achievable results. Fatalism, on the other hand, seems to imply the absence of personal effort. A simple example will serve: parents of a sick child will do everything in their power, seeking out expert help in order to bring about a happy outcome. Encompassing all their efforts, the outcome is determined. In fatalism, parents sit back and make no effort to attempt to influence the outcome.

chapter 9

THE BATTLE OF THE SEXES

(Or Whose Programming Will Be Dominant)

The battle of the sexes is an ancient expression. Goethe put the question in the mouth of Mephistopheles who tells Faust not to waste his time meditating about infinity, but rather to concern himself with why men and women have such a hard time with each other. The literature is replete with examples of human ecstasy when two lovers find each other and a love story never fails to give us vicarious delight. Fairy tales conclude promisingly: "And so, they lived happily ever after." Unfortunately, these are only fairy tales.

Scientific research has, to my knowledge, never devoted much time to identifying the causes of prevalent human heterosexual discord. Of course, it is assumed that clashes do occur because each partner, by necessity, comes from different backgrounds, similar as they appear to be at times. While this may only be an assurance that they stick it out with each other, at no time does this guarantee that coexistence is only slightly better than quiet despair.

I am impressed by the fact that many patients who consult psychiatrists because they find themselves in difficulties, ask not so much to overcome these difficulties, but rather state that they would be satisfied if only they could understand why. The human factor in us apparently seeks above all the understanding of the mechanics of a situation. We apparently feel a situation much more tolerable and acceptable if we perceive the causes of its existence. The reader who has followed me so far through this book will notice that my concept of human pattern programming in the formative years, superimposed later by the specific vanity that we have the freedom of will of decision, is the key to the understanding of human reactivity. This is exactly the critical point. We react to presenting circumstances—we have no choice in determining the course of events as much as our vanity revolts at this concept.

In a later chapter, I define the term "falling in love" as a trance-like state where we mobilize all elements within us to such a degree that we appear attractive and lovable to a potential mate upon whom we have designs. It is basically a self-serving mechanism. It is true that in the animal kingdom birds preen themselves constantly for courtship; they sing their most beautiful songs and develop their most beautiful colors; mammals also strut their stuff—sending forth the most exciting odors, bringing the most delightful morsels of food to the one they court.

In animal affairs, copulation follows and each species follows its own pattern. Where promiscuity of the male is a pattern, the female will almost exclusively take charge of raising the cubs. At times, the male function will be restricted to preserving the territory, no mean task in itself. The role of drones in the beehive is, of course, an exceptional one, as is the role of the queen bee. Mammals have come a long way in their development from the insects and we had better limit ourselves to comparing humans to their nearest relatives—the higher mammals—otherwise we get lost in the comparison.

Suffice it to say that it seems characteristic for the human species to find, consciously or subconsciously, discord after copulation. It is true that only in human affairs do we find that the male has to forfeit his biological urge to promiscuity for monogamistic adjustment to serve the requirements of acculturation of his cubs. It is also true that monthly periods based on ovarian cycles keeping the female in a short-term recurring state of possible impregnation is to my knowledge a human specialty. This condition, subserviant to acculturation, will bring forth the human situation where a mother has children following each other in short succession, long before the formative requirements of one generation are satisfied. These are all complicating factors and only prove that a high price is exacted for human acculturation.

We have learned that what we consider human personality is nothing but the programming and imprinting the infant and child received in the formative years. This, of course, holds true for both potential partners. Imprinting can never be identical. We deal, therefore, after union has become a fact, with two differently programmed computers who are expected to come up with answers to problems satisfying both. The very best that can be hoped for is compromise. On one occasion, your answer is accepted; on another, my answer is accepted. In the courtship days, the trance-like state assists in relegating the programming of our mother to second place. We adapt ourselves, temporarily at least, to the surmised requirements of the love object. But once the goal is accomplished a change of pattern gradually takes place once again and our original imprint comes to the fore. We are once more our old selves, for better or for worse. When this pattern becomes disturbing to the mate, clash occurs; tears may flow; a temporary rekindling of courtship attitudes takes place and reconciliation occurs in bed. This pattern, of course, loses its effectiveness as time progresses. The sexual factor becomes less pressing and approval of our personality pattern cannot be satisfied by occasional sexual excitation any longer. A mutual compromise is, however, much more likely if it involves only the coexistence of the two mates. The situation becomes much more complicated when the pattern formation, the programming of offspring, becomes reality. The clashes about the raising of children become the battleground of many marriages. Both partners have the programming of their own mother and parents. This imprint, which has sustained them so far through life, is in addition the post-hypnotic command, so to speak, received in their formative stages. The more maturity our programming permitted and the less we remain emotionally tied to our parents, the more we will have the emotional resources available for the necessary investment in our offspring. If, on the other hand, we have been imprinted in such a way that we remain emotionally tied to our parents and our mother in particular, we cannot, try as we may, free ourselves from this crippling immaturity. We will be most inadequate in our emotional availabilities to satisfy the emotional needs of the partner. The partner, of course, is in no condition to be objective about his own mate and will harbor, consciously or subconsciously, fury at the surmised insensitivity and indifference of the mate. The ensuing battle will be fought noisily or coldly, openly or surreptitiously, depending on the pattern present in the involved mates.

However, it can be said that there is one unfailing battleground where the fight will always culminate. Obviously, I refer to the bed, even if the battle does not get to the bed. How can we best, on an emotional level, smash our mate to smithereens and still feel innocent about it? Frigidity and impotence, revulsion at the thought of sexual contact, and perhaps even miscarriages after pregnancy has developed are, after all, the emotional responses to anger at the mate. We punish the mate, so to speak, taking out our hostility and frustration on the partner. Instead of mutual synchronistic efforts, we find dissonance and diverging results. All these attitudes come, of course, in every degree. Frigidity and impotence are autonomic nervous system reflex responses to subconscious feelings.

Here we have an excellent example to lead us to the understanding of body language. If a person starts to vomit uncontrollably each time he sits down for dinner at the table of his mother-in-law, the message becomes quite clear to everybody concerned very soon. At the same time, the son-in-law may think of himself as very dedicated to his mother-in-law, particularly if he senses his wife may take a dim view if he did not show such dedication. The emotions manifested through the autonomic nervous system provide the answer to his real feelings.

I postulate that in each case of involuntary nervous system reaction, whether temporary reaction or permanent organic changes, one has to ask oneself the question—What is the motivation of the individual if he knowingly and deliberately brings forth the same symptomatology? To a great extent sickness serves a purpose and the gain implicit in the cases of conversion hysteria is well recognized. I do, however, feel that this limitation to conversion hysteria is far too narrow. I feel that the demarcation line between conversion hysteria, psychophysiological reaction, and many other ailments, which traditionally are considered primarily organic, is rather artificial. The emotional goal, that is, gain, is common to the total spectrum; however, they differ as to the potential degree of destruction in the organism.

The more rigid the basic pattern formation, the more devastating will be the results of the emotionally conditioned reaction. Nobody dies from an hysterical aphonia. People do die from ruptured stomach ulcers, heart attacks, and strokes. The emotional influence or the etiology of these organic disturbances is clearly perceived by some observers and greatly questioned by others.

Let us return to the battle of the sexes. One mate might have a pattern of dependency, the need to relegate leadership to the other. On the other hand, the mate may have a need to assert his masculinity or a woman may be unable to entrust herself to the leadership of a man. Indeed, the female may be inclined to desire leadership in her own right and men can be just as dependent as women are supposed to be, if they wish to be reproductive and serve their offspring.

Suppose the following situation is present: a woman with two or three children does not get adequate emotional support from her husband, who himself feels strained by the responsibilities which came about because of his own need to assert his maleness, what avenues are available (obviously, however, only on a subconscious level)?

She can develop a sickness which would even lead to death; she can leave her husband, even though burdened with her children and at the same time perhaps feel guilty since she has been patterned to believe that children need their father. In addition, her own dependency on her husband patterned the children to look up to their father, above all, so to speak, following the example of their mother. She may feel unable to function, lose her appetite, become restless, lack re-energizing sleep, become depressed and imbued with the wish to die. If she can seek and obtain the helping support of an understanding and capable physician, she, the husband, and the children are very fortunate. The structure of the family is preserved. The husband also receives indirect support, although he may feel sorry for himself because all the bills have to be met by him. If, however, the condition of the mother is more serious or persists for a long time, more drastic measures may have to be taken. Hospitalization for a more or less extended period of time may become a necessity. This in itself may finally awaken the husband to his shortcomings—for which, in reality, of course, he was as little responsible as his wife was for her shortcomings.

Sometimes, the disturbance is so severe and the desire of the mother to return to her children is so great that shortcuts have to be employed such as electroshock treatments. The basic dependency need of the wife will not permit her to cut her tie to her husband because she feels incapable of functioning adequately on her own. Basically, on a subconscious level, she harbors great resentment and hate for her husband. However, since she is so dependent, she is not equipped to realize this resentment and hate consciously, and turns these emotions upon herself self-destructively. Also implied, of course, is the punishment of the husband, much as a child, angry at his parents, visualizes himself deceased and at the same time, from above, watches the grief of his parents with a certain glee.

The battle of the sexes goes on, although outwardly the family exists in totality. Whose imprint will prevail now on the children? I would be hard pressed to make the decision. On the surface, we may assume that in this case the attitude of the male remained dominant over the female, since the female got sick and needed treatment which means help. On the other hand, the female had her way—by hook or crook, health or sickness—since she proved the inadequacy of the male because he failed to give her, the mother, the adequate and necessary emotional support. Whose imprint will prevail on the children? Probably both—modified, of course, by such variables as sex, age, sequence of birth, original reception by the mother, etc.

In order not to appear partial, let us turn the tables:

(Case of an alcoholic): A male child grew up in a forbidding emotional climate. He wanted to feel like a man in the worst way. His father was an inadequate example, being completely submissive to his wife for the privilege of being permitted to have intercourse with her when she felt that she preferred his lovemaking to the licking of a dog. Unable to take the treatment he received at the hands of his wife, he developed a disease. Eventu-

ally he became a permanent invalid, thus being cared for perhaps in an institution, at the same time forcing the mother to exert herself as the leader of the family and to pride herself on her efficiency, if not strength. The father may have been very dedicated and tried to be responsible beyond his natural emotional endowment and finally had to depart permanently when the discrepancy between emotional stress and innate resources became disastrous. In any case, in similar situations, the mother seems to function as the Rock of Gibraltar, whereas the male remains a victim on the battlefield. On the surface the child will feel how strong his mother was since she took care of him when the father faltered. We would assume that this would be the determining factor in pattern formation; however, there is more to it, perhaps less consciously perceived. Was it not the attitude and requirements of the mother which the father could not satisfy which led to his destruction? Could a boy, for instance, not develop an attitude that it would be wiser for him not to deliver himself into the hands of what he may perceive subconsciously as the deadly clutches of a female? Might a daughter not deeply resent the mother who destroyed her beloved father and might she not grow up with the subconscious fear that as a female she may grow up to be like her mother and thus be disastrous to men? Would it not be logical to refrain from heterosexual contacts to a greater or lesser degree in order not to feel she is an annihilating force? Or will the attitude of the father—who never, even at the price of self-destruction, openly revolted against their mother—prevail?

Perhaps we can also take a look at the relationship which may prevail if alcoholism is present, since this is a very frequent condition: No single factor has been clearly identified that accounts for a tendency toward alcoholism. Alcohol has been called an escape, one that is readily available. Even though this is true, we can postulate that an alcoholic considers the situation around him to be so unpleasant, that it becomes desirable, if not mandatory, to get away from it. A situation may be unbearable because by its very nature it exceeds the adaptive ability of the best integrated individual. Nobody can resist determined and persistently applied torture for any extended period of time. If the victim is totally dedicated to his convictions, shock and cardiovascular death ultimately result. There is a pain tolerance level in every individual. On the other hand, a sensitized person may have a lowered pain threshhold and find irritations unbearable which seem tolerable to less sensitized persons.

In order to become sensitized an individual must have had particularly unfavorable exposures and experiences in the formative years. Once a conditioned reflex pattern is formed—for example, we do not expect anything favorable to come our way, or, even worse, feel that surrounding forces if not the world at large are out to hurt us—we live in a continuous state of emotional alertness and defensive aggressiveness. From a psychiatric viewpoint, such an attitude can readily be described as paranoid.

A feature which is recurrent in alcoholics is their need to drink in order to be sociable and find human companionship. The feeling of being alone is unbearable to these individuals. In addition, as time goes on the performance of daily routine and work becomes less possible. The alcoholic wishes to function as a "normal" human being and will do anything to maintain this functioning as much as his basically paranoid nature will permit. He will only seek help when he has completely failed in getting results from his own self-administered form of medication—alcohol. Self-administration has another apparent attraction. It preserves, for the time being at least, the illusion of his own power and independence. The very fact that alcoholics at times need alcohol intake to be sexually aroused gives a good clue to their basic attitude toward the opposite sex. On the one hand, he abhors any homosexual connotation and he wishes to prove his own so-called normality, his own masculinity (or her own femininity); on the other hand, there exists, subconsciously of course, a deep fear and hatred of, and therefore destructive impulses against, the opposite sex. Here is perhaps one common specific clue to all alcoholics which can be traced back quite clearly to their formative years. It is found again and again that alcoholics come from a home environment where the parents resented and rejected each other. The hate a woman feels at becoming pregnant by an individual whom she loathes has to be transferred to her offspring. If the mother critically says to the child, "You are like your father," and the child knows how deeply the mother hates the father, the child senses the true feelings of the mother toward himself. In the case of a girl, the beloved father, her model for later sexual adjustment, becomes forbidden territory. The alcoholic needs sex to prove his normality and he hates sex and wishes to destroy the sex partner in an ill-conceived striving for self-preservation.

The alcoholic, on the other hand, does not rank at the very end of the human scale of sociopathy. It is characteristic of the alcoholic that he wishes to function constructively and makes almost heroic efforts to be a useful member of human society. I am fully aware that to a great extent these statements represent generalizations and that each case has its own individual shadings. But, no textbook description of appendicitis would be possible, if the common factors were not stressed.

Let me repeat once more, even if it seems redundant, that the parents of the future alcoholic do not in any way deliberately cause the disturbance in their offspring. They do the best they know how, inadequate as it is. A generation before, they were only children and received their pattern formation at the hands of their parents in turn and so forth. Unless we have this point clearly in mind, we miss the concept. It is not, of course, a question of fault. Many patients will resist deeper psychiatric insight for the simple reason that they do not wish to incriminate or ultimately hate their own mothers, for reasons which I have previously pointed out. Only the highest degree of objectivity and the acknowledgment that their mothers did the best which their formative circumstances permitted will free these individuals from the devastating influences which patterned their formation. I single out the alcoholic as an example of the divergent and ambivalent emotions which surround each child in the formative stage. The intensity of the ambivalent love-hate relationship of the parents to each other will vary from the mildest degree to outright destruction of the mate. Equally, the form of manifestation will vary from wild outbursts and physical abuse to subtle innuendoes, infidelities, frigidity, impotence, dyspareunia, desertion, unhappiness, sickness, etc.

This is the human scene into which every one of us was born. This is the price we have to pay for having climbed out of the trees and having developed the delusion of self-vanity. Was it worth it? This is not an appropriate question anymore. We all share the fate of mankind now. *Ala jacta est!* The die is cast and we have to follow the fate of mankind to its bitter end even if it is only a glorious failure of nature. But in nature, as far as we can see, everything takes its course on the universal level, if nowhere else. As long as life persists, the action goes on. Goethe said in his *Faust,* "To exist is a duty, be it only for the time of an eye blink." I would like to say existence can be a joy, be it only for the time of an eye blink. If possible, not a moment of this potentially pleasurable time ought to be wasted. I do not preach, because I know to do so is useless. I only point out the potentials.

In modern times, the problem of divorce has gained great prominence. In the Western world, the great majority of divorce actions are, legally at least, initiated by the woman. There is no question that changed social conditions were instrumental in this development. Less than a century ago the female was almost totally dependent on the financial support which her husband provided. Like it or not, the female had little choice but to look out for her survival by becoming a wife and homemaker.

The statistics of every insurance company indicate that the man was likely to survive his wife, who was apt to die in childbirth or as the result of repeated pregnancies. It was exceedingly common for him to remarry in order to provide a step-mother who could raise his children.

The sociological changes of the last century have combined to remove the pressure of the "meal-ticket" attitude from the woman. She can earn her own living, perhaps not as well yet as she likes, but quite well if she is so inclined. The various contraceptive measures which have come into general use permit her to get sexual gratification without the ensuing responsibility of pregnancy and child raising. Most impressive is the deep-going alteration in longevity expectations which accompanied all these changes. Today it is almost assumed that the husband will depart from this life before his wife. Every insurance company can furnish ample substantiation for this fact.

Perhaps we are justified in saying that the onus and stress of marriage which for so many centuries, if not millenia, rested on the female have switched in recent times to the male sex. If the generalization is permissible, it can be said that unless the male is a source of pleasure to the female, she no longer feels compelled to put up with him.

How do the children come out in this interplay? We know that it is the pipe dream of every child, consciously or subconsciously, that he has been wanted, that he is a pleasure and a joy to his mother, and that his parents deeply like and approve of each other. This happy state of affairs would safeguard and provide him not only with all physical and emotional requirements but also provide him with the sense of security and self-acceptance which is the epitome of human development.

When a divorce takes place, how are the children affected? The mother overtly finds the husband unacceptable and expendable. I do not, however, imply that sticking it out with a hated mate is a healthier solution, nor do I imply that adultery, as practiced widely in certain countries and more recently also in the United States, is the lesser of two evils. In either case the deficient emotional climate will have its impact. The divorce, however, has the devastating effect of finality. But even this statement deserves further clarification.

A divorce is only a legal document in itself. It dissolves the partnership of marriage. It permits remarriage and only in this vital respect it supersedes legal separation. Strictly speaking, in separation, legal or otherwise, the child is not burdened with the confusion of considering a substitute parent as his real one. Perhaps a woman who finds it intolerable to share table and bed with her mate and has severed this relationship without, however, being immature enough to consider her own wish fulfillment above all (that is, obtaining a divorce to open the door for subsequent legally accepted sex activities), is less emotionally deficient than the individual who feels she has been deprived of all her pleasures and above all considers her own gratification.

Usually, in a court order visitation rights are safeguarded for the father, but here again the situation varies from the indifferent father who fails to exercise his rights to the father who ultimately forfeits this right because he senses that his ex-wife, set on vilifying him in the eyes of the children, implicitly or directly sets the children against him. Thus, his visits seem to contribute to the disturbance of the children. If the children were aware of what happens to them, they would say to their father: "You were unable to prevent the divorce; if you love us now, don't disturb us further. Our mother would rather destroy us than make adjustments." Of course, from the viewpoint of the mother the entire situation looks different. Her husband imposed the children on her. Perhaps she only wanted to prove that she had a will of her own in marrying him. He was not satisfied with what she was; he wanted something from her which she was not equipped to provide, so he became unbearable.

Few, if any, are the cases where a father after he has been divorced by his wife will not by biological and emotional necessity sooner or later drift into the arms of a new companion. As much as he may live up to his court-stipulated financial contributions, as soon as his emotional ties go in a different direction, the emotional deprivation to the children is unavoidable.

The idea that substitute parents can successfully take the emotional place of the natural parents is wishful thinking. It is self-serving to the degree that it permits us to seek the satisfaction of our own emotional needs and desires without adequate consideration for the innate needs of our own offspring. Confusion is created by these modern remarriages where children are brought from one marriage into a new one after a divorce. In addition, there may be children from an earlier marriage of the new mate. Little wonder that children at times long for the moment when they can get out of this entanglement. What marriage partners and parents will they make themselves when their own primary motivation for marriage was escape from an intolerable situation? And what other happier adjustment is open to these offspring short of forfeiting sex and reproductivity totally in order to salvage self-respect?

I have known of only one case where the father, although pushed out of the marriage and frustrated in his visitation rights, did not persist in enforcing his rights because he feared destroying his children. By that time they had totally come under the control of their mother, but he persisted throughout all the years of their childhood in living up to and even exceeding his economic requirements, thus permitting the children to feel his influence, although mostly indirectly. In this respect the emotional damage to the children was minimized and kept within tolerable limits. Obviously this father could never indulge in fulfilling his own emotional needs first. Thus his love for his children became the moving force mobilizing every emotional resource within him.

Divorce in such cases is nothing but the trump card in the battle between the programming received by either parent. The degree of emotional immaturity can be measured by the emotional dependency on the mother, alive or dead, long after this dependency has outlived itself biologically. The mother, so to speak, needing the emotional dependency of the child to compensate her for her own emotional deficit, never did and never could afford to release the child from this emotional tie. When new requests which put a strain on the subconscious commitment to the mother are placed upon such a child when, physically at least, she has grown up, the basically immature person will hold fast to her emotional commitment to her mother and sell short her marriage and the emotional needs of her own children.

Figuratively, we can say that to these immature individuals the past generation is more important than the future generation, their own children. The disturbance is thus carried over from generation to generation in an almost endless succession. If we have the opportunity to go into the environmental history of the parents of our patients and even into the history of the grandparents and so forth, this statement will find ample justification. Unfortunately, complete family histories only rarely are obtainable in human affairs. A complete family history, if properly taken, would demonstrate the disturbances occurring in the various members of the family—some direct victims, some indirect through transmission of deficits to offspring. The deficit does not necessarily manifest itself in the same way in each generation, but may vary in appearance, thus blurring the original of the basic common deficit. We can speak of the familial origin of disturbances but have to keep strictly in mind the difference between hereditary disturbances transferred by chromosomal deviations and these emotionally transmitted disturbances.

Sick people raise sick people—only that which is generally considered sickness is debatable. We can even go a step further and say that cripple marries cripple. Here again, it may be debatable what constitutes a cripple. A beautiful woman pushing the wheelchair of her husband whom she met and married in this condition and the man who marries a divorcee with two children may have something in common. Basically, they may both be afraid of the opposite sex. The vulnerability of their prospective mates, on the other hand, may have been precisely the critical ingredient which neutralized this fear and so this person became attractive to them. I postulate that this mechanism is mostly subconscious.

There are endless examples which can be brought forth to back up this point. Right or wrong, at times certain groups of people consider themselves superior to others and vice versa. It was not uncommon after the Second World War to see American GIs marry Japanese girls. I grant these Japanese girls were beautiful, but they were also Japanese. At that time, at least, the GI felt superior to them. He may have felt ill-equipped to face up to an American female, but that fear of the opposite sex faded away when he dealt with a member of a race to which he felt superior. Other racial and religious intermarriages frequently have the same connotations. Unless two human beings of the opposite sex are so completely free from any considerations of religion, race, etc., that they become truly indifferent to what group the prospective partner belongs, any intermarriage has a factor of surmised superiority implicitly built in.

In spite of all protestation of insignificance of religious teachings, once children arrive, a strong attempt to influence their religious outlook is made. The Jewish father who consented to have his children raised as Catholics will still make his viewpoint felt by not attending church with the family on Sunday. The mother may have acquiesced up to this point but now she feels that her endeavor to raise the children may ultimately be frustrated after all. Perhaps she married the Jewish husband above all to demonstrate her own will and independence from her mother, but she did not mean to have the situation get out of hand and end up with Jewish children. On the other hand, this example cannot be generalized. Some women want to free themselves totally from parental domination and, therefore, totally accept the religion and racial patterns of their husbands. All these examples, of course, can be made in reverse also. It is exceedingly common that a husband is absorbed into the life-style of his wife and her family and is submerged into submissiveness. To the degree that a mate knowingly or subconsciously submits his imprinting to the imprinting of his mate, the children will receive this programming. Ideally speaking, two emotionally mature mates will find it possible to make compromises in their own programming to satisfy the emotional needs of each other. This statement is well contained in the old words: "Give and take." The more rigid the programming in each individual is, the more he or she will become eligible only to an equally rigid individual or, on the other hand, to a completely dependent individual. Clashes will occur or total submission will have to follow. In either case, the result is disastrous. The clashes may lead to divorce, catastrophes, and innumerable other complications. Those who submit totally may end up in mental institutions, taking electroshock treatments, or with physical disturbances of an endless variety.

chapter 10

RELIGION: THE SOCIALLY ACCEPTED FORM OF INSANITY

Before reading this chapter, it would be highly desirable for the reader, if he has not already done so, to read *The Golden Bough* by Frazier. Let me remind you that the word religion has its origin in the Latin word *ligare. Religare* means to tie together firmly into a cohesive group. Strictly speaking, the original sense is group formation and exclusivity, rather than the universality which many established creeds wish to propagate. However, all these creeds with implied universality clearly state: "Universality, yes, but on our terms," which means nothing but "we are superior and better; we have the real truth; we are glad to impart our truth to you—you, of course, must see that your truth was not the real truth—only we have it."

All through history we see that when a tribe or nation is defeated in war, they surmised that their own god was not as good as the god of the victorious army. Let us therefore, they reasoned, accept the religion which prevailed in battle. We might easily think this attitude went out with antiquity, or, at least, with the Thirty Years' War, but let us take a second look. After the Second World War, Emperor Hirohito seriously considered accepting Christianity. If nothing else, the American life-style certainly conquered Japan. For a considerable period, the dialogue of this century between capitalism, religious nations, and communistic, non-God-fearing nations was seen as the issue of our times. First of all, we have to disabuse ourselves of the concept that the narrow interpretation of religion in relation to an assumed supranatural deity or deities is the only concept applicable. In a wider sense, all rigid fanatical beliefs qualify as religions also. The belief in the state and the righteousness of the state, as it seems to be propounded in modern communistic societies, can also be called a religion. The pilgrimage places of mausoleums and the catechism of modern communism are well known. In all historical honesty, God-fearing capitalism felt very justified in trying to crush, or at least to contain, the foreign religion of godless communism for as long as possible.

We see a remarkable development at this time. To the extent that the Western God-fearing capitalistic world has been unable to dispose of the new upstart religions of the USSR and Maoism, an accommodation, perhaps, to a degree, a mutual accommodation, takes place. This accommodation, incidentally, reaches far into the emotional field. Acupuncture, for instance, which certainly would have taken the prize for faith healing or charlatanism as little as a decade ago, now receives face-saving studies by Western wisemen who will ultimately find some pseudoscientific explanation in order to bless its acceptance, which they could not obviate in the first place. Similarly, gurus and Eastern religious sects and foreign creeds abound now in the United States, not because they have won on the battle field, but because they sense the void created by the weakening of established creeds. The maxim "Nature abhors a vaccum" can be enlarged from the physical world to the emotional one. Human beings emotionally need to lean on a crutch and little does it matter whether this crutch is unrealistic and, therefore, psychotic.

I will first deal in this chapter, however, with the traditional interpretation of religion in the sense of the time-honored interpretation of man's relationship to his gods, or supranatural forces in general. Later we will enlarge the thoughts to all other rigidly and fanatically held beliefs.

Obviously, here again a thorough knowledge of the earliest traces of logical thinking and later religious attitude becomes desirable. At this point, I have to refer the reader again to my thesis. No eyewitness account is available of these early days of the development of man. We are only permitted to draw justified conclusions based on the findings available to us. There are persons who are not even convinced in the face of the Colorado Canyon that the river cut the gorge through the mountain over millions of years. If this evidence is not convincing, we have to go on and ignore these individuals who lack every bit of confidence in their own powers of observation.

I postulate, and this is the central theme, that our earliest ancestors—call them *Pithecanthropus erectus* or any other proper name—over millenia or perhaps even longer periods of time—gradually developed an understanding of cause and effect when they dislodged, accidentally at first, purposely subsequently, rocks and boulders to stop persecuting predators.

I also postulate that a similar cause and effect was observed when boughs and branches of trees were broken off, first accidentally, to slay the predators; later and gradually, boughs were purposefully used as weapons. Much later, of course, these two parts were put together to form a stoneaxe, a formidable weapon. Be that as it may, superiority over the other animals, even the dangerous ones, was gained and, incidentally, the tool-making destiny of man started. And this was the crucial moment of mankind. Little does it matter whether this moment was only a flash in the mind of these early ancestors or whether, more likely, it took millenia or more to bring about the emotional concomitant counterpart to this new-found sense of power and superiority. I postulate a sense of grandeur gradually pervading these early ancestors. It is as if they were strutting about, so to speak, with blown-out chests, as if to say, "See, what a mighty grandiose being I am!" This new-found feeling of power might have almost, like wine, gone to their heads and, once obtained, this feeling will not be abandoned. But then, this newly formed grandiose creature was confronted by the forces of nature with all her destructive vehemence. Floods, earthquakes, fires, lightning, eruptions of volcanos, hurricanes, tornados, meteors, droughts with famine, and starvation, etc., confronted these self-glorious individuals. How could early man reconcile this intoxicating new-found sense of grandeur with the helpless dependency on these overwhelmingly powerful and frightening forces of nature over which, apparently, they had no control? To preserve this feeling of grandiosity, a mechanism had to develop, unrealistic as it was, to give him the delusion, at least, that in one way or another he could control these external forces of nature. In an anthropormorphic fashion, he projected extensions of himself on to all these forces. Man created not one god in his image, but each tribe created their own, almost by the thousands at first, I dare say. Each tree, each mountain had its god or spirit. One could talk to them and bring them gifts. One could even go so far as punish them as Darius did only 2,500 years ago when he whipped the unfriendly sea. Certainly one could withhold sacrifices, etc. By all these means, primitive man tried to influence forces of nature over which in reality he had no control.

Nobody can doubt that this attitude is a delusion and, therefore, unrealistically psychotic. As time went on, out of myriads of gods and spirits, a concentration of power into fewer hands took place. Perhaps the most familiar examples occur in ancient Greek mythology. Even the gods did not get along well with each other. One had to be headmaster. The entire Trojan War came about only because Eris, Goddess of Discord, had her fun. Western religions finally settled on one God. The principle, of course, remained the same: follow certain dogma, bring sacrifices, pray, try to find favor in the eyes of God, and maybe eventually the good things will come to you. The emotional comfort gained by this attitude is paid for by one's own abandonment of objective, realistic thinking. It is conceded that the realities of this life are frightening at best and man has to see himself without delusion in his infinitesimal unimportance. Every vestige of the sense of grandeur has to disappear. Humility in the truest sense of the word is the realistic attitude.

In addition, since the days of Moses and Zoroaster, commandments of behavior meant to preserve the cohesion and coexistence of the tribe, or men in general, were felt to be laws indispensable in protecting the weak and safeguarding what passed for peace.

This book is only meant to be a fact-finding study. It is not intended to come up with a panacea. The thought has to be considered, however, that self-respect may be the highest good, and once one has partaken of it, one cannot go without it anymore.

The less secure we are, the more we need absolute security which, of course, is unrealistic in this frightfully insecure world. What reality does not give, fantasy has to provide.

chapter 11

THE NON-RELIGIOUS FAITH HEALERS: THE TWILIGHT ZONE OF PSYCHIATRY

Since the dawn of mankind, religion and medicine have been closely allied. Indeed, it is more likely than not that the healing arts were totally entrusted to and carried out by priests of Chaldea, Babylonia, Assyria, Egypt, Greece, and Rome. It was the outstanding exception rather than the rule which gave birth to a Hippocrates and a Galen.

Philosophers like Aristotle made their imprint on medicine with their concept of the four elements and medical phenomena were divided accordingly into four compartments known as the four humors—blood, phlegm, black bile, and yellow bile. At any age of the ancient tribes or empires, there were varieties of cults and healing practices employed about which our most extensive studies do not give a complete picture. I refer the reader to the many excellent works on magic, faith healing, and human gullibility. Libraries can be filled with works on quackery, nostrums, and scientifically endorsed practices which ultimately had nothing in common with objective healing results but the belief which was invested into their efficacy. But, since this participation of faith is such a recurring theme in the healing arts, it should be subject to scientific investigation. If, as I have pointed out, human beings are not primarily rational but, at least to an equal degree, irrational and psychotic animals, this unrealistic, insane part of the personality must also be satisfied if healing is to be accomplished. Science in itself becomes, then, a faith and belief and it requires subtlety to discern the objective values against the emotionally conditioned benefit. Belief in the efficacy of vitamin administration in quantities by far exceeding scientifically established usefulness has such connotations. Sometimes vitamins, such as vitamin E, are employed in the absence of any proven efficacy. The administration of hormones plays at times a similar role in the hand of a shrewd physician. Parenteral administration of medication has come into wide use partially because the public expects particular effectiveness from injections versus oral administrations. There is, of course, a second point which contributes to their aura. Whereas in oral administration the hospitalized patient has a say as to whether he wishes to swallow a pill or not, he can be forced to receive an injection by restraint. Thus, emotionally at least, he recognizes the superiority of the physician which adds to his healing power. We must always feel that the therapist knows more about the disease and life itself than we do if he is to impress us and become established as an authority. To what degree the child-parent relationship is again involved is open to discussion. A regression into a child-like dependency state is certainly present to a high degree and the feeling of being safe and protected has a considerable influence on this relationship. It is proverbial that the patient must have confidence in his physician. How he obtained this confidence is irrelevant at this point. The very origin of the word "doctor" in Latin *docere*—"to teach"—implies that the practitioner is equipped to teach, which implies the recipient of the administration has to learn. In general medicine, it is exceedingly difficult to draw a clear line between objective physical findings which are symptom-producing and symptomatology which is primarily due to emotional manifestations through the autonomic nervous system. The question is further complicated to the degree that the development of outright organic pathology could be prevented by adequate early neutralization of noxious autonomic nervous system impulses. Emotional stress factors in many diseases are accepted even by the average physician who can, in a sense, be considered the high priest of chemistry and scalpel. From emotional stress to peptic ulcer formation and possible malignant degeneration is only a continuous line of succession. Fight-or-flight predisposition, hypertension, cardiovascular stress, and premature degenerative changes and death are a continuum.

A 72-year-old spinster showed signs of depression, anxiety, and high irritability. Her history indicated a lifetime of borderline emotional adjustment. She had never been married and lived with her sister. They were both semi-recluses all their lives and apparently neither of them had ever had any heterosexual contacts or experiences. After short-term hospitalization, she returned home. Two years later she was again brought to my attention since her condition had worsened. Adequate neurological testing now revealed a space-occupying lesion in the brain. Two years previously the same tests had been negative. What is noteworthy in this case is that a lifetime of emotional maladjustment finally culminated in tumor formation. It may, of course, be argued by some that the tumor formation was entirely independent of the emotional background and may have developed even in an individual whose emotional maladjustment was less obvious. It has been said that one only finds what one looks for. The researcher who is basically an organicist will not note nor look for the emotional component as the basic factor in outright pathology.

The vulnerability to bacterial and viral infections under stress conditions deserves much further investigation. Emotional debilitation opens up the organism to noxious attacks which we call diseases but which are attempts of nature to eliminate individuals not properly equipped. Overgeneralizations along these lines can be very misleading but this caution should not prevent us from focusing on the reality inherent in these observations.

Stress, of course, can be temporary or chronic and life long. What do we actually expect if we discern that an individual functions under permanent stress? An adjustment reaction to this stress will ensue which will manifest itself, according to the holistic approach, in one of the four aspects of life or in any combination thereof, as previously discussed. With the advent of the period which is usually called the Enlightenment, a division took place in medicine that separated the physical aspects of the healing arts from the emotional, mental ones. No sharp line of demarcation was ever successfully drawn nor is such clean separation ever likely to come about. The body and the emotions are indivisible from each other. Whatever is helpful to one will have beneficial effects on the other. Body and mind have a somewhat parasitic existence; one can thrive at the expense of the other. We see at times physically powerful individuals whose minds are approximately nonexistent and, on the other hand, we see individuals with serious physical injuries whose brain function is of the highest order.

The psychiatrist-physician with adequate grounding in the physical aspects of diseases has been entrusted with the care and healing of the mental and emotional aspects of the disturbed individual. Lately, he has also been called on to administer to social maladjustments.

Two variables became immediately discernible. One is the quality of the psychiatrist—that is, the degree to which his education and experience are founded on self-awareness and self-knowledge. The second is the receptivity of the patient or individual to his administration and approach. What good is the most accomplished psychotherapist if a reluctant individual does not wish to avail himself of his attention? But how tragic is the opposite situation when a potential resolution of a disturbance in an individual is not accomplished because the insight and necessary width of comprehension are lacking in the therapist. In such a case the therapist in reality prevents the potential recovery of a patient because of his own limitations.

This concept of limited help deserves further exploration. The quality of the surgeon who treats the lacerated hand of an injured workman is estimated by the optimal results obtained. Amputations, when preservation of the hand or finger was potentially possible, and partial or total immobility of fingers, when total or at least better functioning could have been obtained, reveal, conversely, the deficiencies of the surgeon. It is conceded that no two cases are alike, and that some form of healing, although with reduced functioning, may result from different forms of treatment. In addition, there is a great self-healing propensity in the living organism which may permit the physician to take credit for favorable results, which, strictly speaking, are not due to him.

In the lecture hall of the Vienna Medical School, there is a Latin admonition to the budding disciples of the art: *Primum non nocere*—"Above all, do no harm." In surgery, at least, an objective observation is possible. In psychotherapy, no objective yardstick is available. The patient who complains about his therapist may receive the best treatment while the patient who likes his therapist may not receive the best or even adequate treatment. Penetrating, expressive, and interpretive psychotherapy is painful but it has healing propensities; supportive psychotherapy is soothing but, if ill applied, may fall short of optimal reachable insights and the resolution of the disturbance.

What yardsticks exist to measure the quality of the therapist? Title and education are important yardsticks. Education can be viewed as an obstacle course of some length which tests the stamina and emotional dedication of the participants. It is not, however, an absolute indicator of quality. Persistence and learned education cannot compensate for wisdom and personal humanity. On the other hand, shortcuts in the educational process may give rise to foreboding about the human qualifications of a therapist. It is conceded that the economic environment greatly determines the degree to which education can be pursued. Specialization and self-limitation have become accepted practice in modern medicine. The average physician is not expected to overstep the boundaries of his competency. Dependent on location and circumstances, the threshold level of this surmised competency is variable.

What is the situation in psychiatry? There admittedly exists a shortage of well-qualified psychiatrists. In addition, the personal qualifications of some therapists possessing all the titles and even honors of this world are highly debatable. The public which in large measure expected miraculous cures from psychiatrists has learned not to be too impressed by high-sounding titles. Common sense, whatever this term may mean, has been found wanting in many high-titled therapists. A general feeling not to be denied holds that psychiatrists by and large are basically quite an emotionally disturbed group of people who perhaps, through a desperate attempt to become the judges of mental health and illness, escape scrutiny themselves. This thought deserves a wider follow-up. On a more primitive level, many psychiatric aides and even nurses may seek employment in state mental hospitals or similar institutions, not so much for material benefits but to give themselves the illusion of mental and emotional adequacy by administering to the needs of the mentally disturbed. In this sense, they use the mentally disturbed for their own ends instead of serving their needs. This principle applies not only to the lowly aides, but also to the great majority of the mental health team, from the psychiatrist downwards.

Just as the do-gooder needs the sinner to shine and glorify himself, psychiatrists, psychologists, and psychiatric social workers need the mentally and emotionally disturbed, not only to procure a reasonably good living but to have the illusion of superiority and mental competency and health. The victim who gets entangled in such constellations needs great wisdom and great emotional balance to free himself once he is caught in such a spiderweb.

How can the emotionally disturbed therapist recognize the emotional adequacy of the patient? To a large degree, the yardstick a psychiatrist uses to determine a patient's mental health is the absence of violent tendencies. If a person is considered nonviolent, he is likely to be deemed acceptable. The psychiatrist has thus become largely the warden and protector of modern society.

The need to believe in the supranatural which corresponds to the basic vanity of being able to manipulate natural forces beyond our control has apparently found an interesting expression in modern Soviet society which shuns a religious tradition. The study of the occult has gained respectability. Parapsychology is taken seriously and complements the drab, emotionally unsatisfying religion of the all-powerful state. The supranatural connotation is an emotional necessity for the more subtle mind which needs fulfillment on a transcendental plane. Psychokinetic experiments are validated; mind over matter is the issue. Telepathic and similar experiments are carried on continuously and given scientific and pseudoscientific approval. The official Soviet hierarchy looks with much favor on such studies. I refer the reader to *Psychic Discoveries Behind the Iron Curtain,* by Sheila Ostrander and Lynn Schroedler. Extrasensory perception, mind over matter, eyeless sight, dowsing, pictures of the aura, telepathy, acupuncture, suggestology, parapsychology in general, psychotronics, reincarnation research, astrological birth control, and hypnosis are only a very inadequate sampling of topics studied. Similar studies on the university level go on in practically all Communist countries.

The emotional irrationality of man cannot permit him to function for any length of time on a rational basis. The theistic concept has been almost totally rejected by the ruling class of Soviet society. As soon as the immediate physical struggle for survival was taken care of, the emotional needs made themselves felt. Under a scientific disguise, irrationality became the accepted form of Soviet society when going to Lenin's tomb no longer answered emotional needs. The Soviet citizen may shake his head when he sees Western man hurrying to Sunday worship with the same disbelief as Western man shows at Soviet dedication to the occult. Both attitudes seem diametrically opposed to each other, but, in reality, they have a common principle: The unrealistic belief and wish to influence transcendental forces in order to maintain the self-idolatrous glorification of man. Insanity is again at work.

An all-powerful Church in the Middle Ages and even later easily dealt with splinter groups and apostates. Witches knew what fate they could expect. Established churches have never been known for their tolerance toward other churches unless their own vulnerability dictated keeping the claws withdrawn. The theistic churches are in no position to argue with the atheistic, pseudoscientific, newly emerging religions of Communist society. During the French Revolution, a new goddess of Reason was also deified but she soon came into disrepute. How long will parapsychology last? That human perception is quite limited is a well-accepted fact. If we learn to widen the scope of our receptivity, much additional knowledge can be gained. When we overstep our boundaries, we reach into the area of psychosis.

Modern scientific ideas have given all these concepts a modicum of justification. Each cell which consists of molecules and atoms has an electromagnetic field. It is argued that aggregations of cells into living organisms have a sizeable field which can be registered and has an effect on proper receptors. Many discoveries in animal physiology have encouraged a belief that nothing is impossible. Some animals have been found to have sensory organs of such refinement or of such unheard-of capability that traditional concepts have to be reviewed. After an exceedingly fine and precisely functioning radar system had been discovered in bats, new experimentations seem to prove that certain owls have infra-red light perception which not only permits night vision but also the recognition of warm-blooded prey, such as mice. Minimal amounts of specific scented substances will attract certain eels over vast stretches of water. When these established facts are considered, nothing seems impossible to the unstable mind which seeks absolute security in a most insecure universe when faith in traditional religion has been shaken.

When I pointed out the degree to which parapsychology at large seems to have become almost the state religion of Soviet society, the degree to which psychological preoccupations (such as movement groups, massage experiences, truth groups, alternate life-style labs, psychological karate, human potential groups, confrontation groups, self-management groups, humanistic psychotherapy, Zen, Yoga, Transcendental Meditation, Tai Chi, T-groups, graphic groups, etc.) have taken a foothold in Western culture should not be overlooked.

The appeal of the various forms of group therapy (such as sensitivity training groups, recovery groups, Alcoholics Anonymous, Gestalt groups, Weight Watchers, bio-energetic groups, Synanon, psychodrama, transactional analysis, nude encounter groups, sensory awareness groups, inquiry groups, psychosynthesis, meditation, and life planning labs), which have taken hold of considerable sections of the population in the United States, is impressive. These group sessions cover a large range—from recovery group sessions, which are only social meeting places for patients who perhaps had previously been hospitalized in mental institutions but who still felt the need for some sort of group therapy meetings where no deep-going probing was entertained, on up. Whether the group leaders realize it or not, they provide a setting from which the participants derive a certain degree of support but deep-going insights can never be expected in group settings. In addition, it is highly questionable whether the group leaders themselves are equipped to tolerate objectivity to a larger extent. The question has to be asked: What were the motivating forces which prompted individuals with some leaning toward psychology (perhaps having themselves had only slight exposure to psychiatry to gain an adequate adjustment to carry on their own lives and without ever gaining deeper insight into objectivity toward themselves) into these psychiatric fringe activities? If I completely disregard economic deliberations, I have to come to the conclusion that it is a feeling of importance and influence which conveys a feeling of value. The followers, in a way, serve the emotional needs of their leaders and thus the leaders use their disciples for their own emotional needs.

The similarity to priests, religious leaders, medicine men, and shamans is obvious. The more convincing and self-assured the potential leader sounds, the more rigid and eloquently high-sounding, the more likely he is to amass followers who, in a trance-like herd instinct, follow the leader. Of course, there are some leaders who impress potential followers not only by waving their fingers and making noisy gesticulations, but by their affected meekness and apparent self-effacement, mild manners and affected humbleness. No attitude reeks more of self-glory than the attitude of supreme meekness.

Much attention has recently been given to Oriental customs and attitudes found particularly among the younger generation. What role is played by rebellion and vindictiveness against their parents when reasonably well-educated and economically privileged children of Western culture dress themselves up in saffron robes and shave their heads? So the emotional gain in many bizarre attitudes of customs and clothing styles not only increases attention, but it creates shock and challenge.

There is no limit to the panorama of fringe groups which pass before the observing eye. This line reaches into the most distant past and is well represented, to say the least, at the present time and will most likely extend into the distant future until the end of mankind.

As long as the abberation is not destructive to the highest degree and the cult is not incompatible with the existence of society, great tolerance is shown at times. Anthropology is replete with examples of odd customs and tribal exercise serving occult and spiritual ends. The psychotic animal is certainly an appropriate description of man.

As for psychiatry, which I call the attempt toward a rational approach to human personality, it cannot quite free itself from irrationality since even, at best, the practitioners of psychiatry themselves are human beings and only able to reach a variable measure of objectivity about themselves. Freud delved deeply into himself to establish self-value, perhaps because he was surrounded by a society where he had to see his beloved father step off the sidewalk to make way for an insignificant member of the dominant Gentile population. The extent to which this imprinted feeling of inferiority was unbearable to him (to the point that he dedicated his entire adult life to overcoming this feeling and arriving at a point of self-acceptance) must be clearly understood. What he found most painstakingly within himself to a high degree became the creed of a later generation.

We see in recent psychiatry a back-door renaissance of traditional religion. What influence priests, ministers, and rabbis may have lost in the pulpit and before the altar, they try to win again by trying to associate themselves with psychiatric institutions and approaches. They do not wait until disturbed individuals seek them out on their own initiatives, but practically force their presence on the disturbed individuals. Partially, psychiatrists themselves have never been able to become objective about religion; partially, psychiatrists have to put up with the power of the representatives of the various churches in order to avoid a contest against overwhelming odds.

In addition, it has to be mentioned that a large number of the population feel that psychiatry is only for the mentally sick and, therefore, they would rather seek out counselors, such as priests, ministers, rabbis, marriage sociologists, general physicians, or social workers. Still, psychiatrists themselves use face-saving excuses to avoid coming to grips with their real problem, because they dare not challenge the existing powers. Soothing salve is preferred to the healing knife.

chapter 12

THE MISFITS

Criminals, sociopaths, homosexuals, perverts, alcoholics, addicts, fanatics, minorities, and other victims of Nature's law of the selection of the fittest, including all of us to a certain degree

Who is a fit person? Who is a misfit? By what measure do we apply our yardstick? Was Helen Keller a misfit because she was so cruelly handicapped? Was Beethoven a misfit because he was not very gregarious and ultimately became deaf? Is it not true that the ancient Greeks liked to depict their wisest men and seers as old and blind like Tiresias? Does history not tell us that the great Byzantine hero "Narses" had to be carried onto the battlefield on a stretcher? Did Demosthenes, the great orator, not overcome his speech impediment by placing pebbles in his mouth and trying to outshout the seas? Don't we see every so often spectacular mountain climbing feats or ski performances by amputees?

Is a misfit perhaps only someone who considers himself a misfit and only to the degree that he considers himself thusly? We know, of course, by now that no human being is responsible for the programming and imprinting he received in his formative years. Strictly speaking, we can therefore blame nobody for a final attitude toward other people no matter how disastrous and destructive such an attitude turns out to be. This does not imply that society has to sit back and let destructive persons act out all their venom. To the degree society and other human beings feel justified in their own existence, they will stop such destructive individuals and contain them as long as their destructive attitude prevails, for a lifetime if need be. It is precisely ill-conceived permissiveness, which ultimately leads only to self-destruction, which permits angry individuals or basically ruthless individuals to act out their frustration on society or on certain people in particular.

How deep does this instinct of frustrated hate go in all of us? It can be noted that entire religious concepts are built on the scapegoat principle literally or figuratively. An innocent victim is found—whether a goat or other animal or a virgin or other human sacrifice—and in principle we are freed by venting our frustration on it. This principle is clearly a projection and, therefore, unrealistic, and we know by now that unrealistic equals psychotic. Passive self-sacrifice is limited in effectiveness when its application must serve a constructive effort. When, under the leadership of Gandhi, Indians placed themselves across railroad trestles to halt transportation. It worked because the British engineers could not bring themselves to move the engines over their bodies. No such self-sacrifice would have availed against the Hitlerian paranoic sense of almightiness. Theoretically speaking, the population of the entire world would have to sacrifice itself before a person of such paranoic dimensions as Hitler would finally perceive the fallacy of his attitude. As sole survivor over three billion corpses, Hitler might have perceived his lonesomeness.

Crimes are traditionally classified into violent and nonviolent ones. Violent crimes are viewed more seriously in general since they involve people while nonviolent ones involve property. The magnitude of the crimes varies, of course. The criminal, or the person whom we call a criminal, has a poor identification with other human beings at large if they don't belong to his own group. Perhaps the group or gang substitutes for a very deficient family structure in the formative years. We find group integration and absorption under different auspices but for similar reasons. This partly explains the complete absorption into a religious society or into the more loosely knit communes of today. Some branches of the military services have always prided themselves on asking the total dedication of the volunteer. Many similar examples could be cited. We can surmise that the individual who develops an anti-social attitude must have received early approval of such tendencies and, to a high degree, followed examples. The basic attitude is such that the individual gains stature and personality value to the degree that he can demonstrate his "superiority" over other human beings by taking advantage of them or even physically dominating or destroying them. It is clear, of course, that basically a feeling of insecurity and inadequacy must pervade the offender. The criminal mind will always try to outsmart or bully the prospective victim. In order to win, one has to have the better position whether with the gun or by better application of the laws. One has to prove one's superiority but, at the same time, one has to demonstrate the opponent's inferiority. As long as we are able to do this, the sense of mental adequacy is preserved. This self-centered attitude has served us well in preserving the illusion of mental balance. If we surrender this attitude, we must face ourselves as "mentally sick."

To what degree do we all have a tendency to take advantage of other people? Do I have to quote examples? Do we create circumstances which serve our self-seeking ends or do we only take advantage of a situation which comes along and permits us to gain an unfair advantage? Do we paint the house merely to cover up its flaws prior to a prospective sale? Do we give false information or do we only withhold unfavorable information? Dirty tricks are not only played in politics. Do we all not at times confuse success with smartness and intelligence and thusly bow to the material aspects of life to the detriment of the emotional values?

The criminal cannot help that he is a criminal. He is only more anti-social than the rest of us. The circumstances of his formative years programmed him into what he turned out to be and, in self-protection, we justifiably try to neutralize his endeavors. This is only proper and as it should be. When, however, we turn away in self-righteous indignation, we almost give the criminal mind just cause to straighten us out. Goethe, in his great dialogue between God and Mephistopheles in his *Faust* has God say, almost in self-justification, that the human mind too readily sinks into self-complacent inertia and the principle of evil prods him out of this unproductive self-complacency again and again, and, therefore, the principle of "Evil," in the highest order of events becomes a constructive force. This is highly poetical and philosophical. The fact remains that, unless we indulge in overbearing self-glorification and unproductive self-idolatry, we must admit that none of us is completely devoid of some anti-social, if not criminal, tendencies. If we apply this principle against other groups with whom we don't identify, we nevertheless offend against the concept of the brotherhood of mankind and indulge in separation of one kind or another.

The criminal or anti-social personality wishes to create and maintain his dominance over other human beings by any means he finds appropriate, regardless of who gets hurt and what cruelty results. The asocial individual will try to gain his ends, but will be less influenced by the need to dominate and destroy. But, disregarding the rights of others, he is driven solely by the desire to fulfill his own wishes.

The sociopath comes from an environment where his basic emotional and physical needs remained largely unfulfilled, and approval was gained when no demands were made. The mother was ill-equipped to furnish the infant with adequate emotional endowment. Somehow, the result is something like: "You have to look out for yourself because nobody else will. Each person is only for himself." This attitude lacks the destructive, forceful connotation of developing dominance over other people. It is a less malignant adjustment which disregards the needs of others if they conflict with self-gratification. To what degree do we all not have some self-seeking sociopathic tendencies? We all feel at times that we have to take care of ourselves, because no one will take care of our needs otherwise. The attitude of *laissez faire* may well apply on the level of the universe, but does not apply on the limited level of the individual. It is a pleasant anesthesia for painful reality but unrealistic, and, therefore, ultimately destructive. Anytime we try to gratify ourselves without giving thought to whether anybody else may be used in the process, we are acting sociopathically. The anti-social individual feels the world is evil, and that he is at his best when he contributes to its dismemberment. He feels powerful to the degree that he can demonstrate his disdain for established rules and society at large unless he can infiltrate them and bend them to his pleasure. The emotional factor of dominion is perhaps more important to the anti-social individual who gains feelings of personal value by being able to subjugate other individuals. The desire to prove our value and strength in competition is as ancient as the human race. It has its origin in the selection of the fittest for the reproductive process and has its biological equivalent in the animal kingdom. The anti-social individual will use any means at his disposal to gain this superiority and will consider fair play an attitude for the sucker who deserves nothing better than to get hurt if he doesn't wise up to the "cruelty" of this world. The victim does not deserve any better because he is so stupid.

The reasonably well-adjusted person also wants to excel and beat the competitor. But he follows the rules of fair play, whether in sport or any other field of human endeavor. Mastery of any field is a socially well-accepted form of proving one's own value. Indeed, it is a highly acceptable form of sublimation.

Criminality is also seen when persons or groups who feel completely frustrated in what they consider their rightful birthright resort to forceful, violent means of weakening or bringing down the hated order. They are considered either heroes or martyrs to a cause on one side, or criminals who wish to succeed in their endeavor by any means at their disposal on the other side. As much as violence is to be abhorred in human relations, only the highest emotional self-acceptance can continue unperturbed in the face of persistent rejection. This total balance of an individual is perhaps more than we can expect from anybody, since it is highly unlikely that we possess this high degree of balance ourselves. Indeed, if we ourselves had this degree of emotional objectivity, many, if not all, social ailments of mankind would have long ago resolved themselves, or never come into existence at all. Since this book is not given to unrealistic wishful dreams, the conclusion can be drawn that—although undesirable—the fight for one's place in the sun is likely to be a violent one. Only as long as violent means are completely impracticable will minority groups profess utterly peaceful means of asserting themselves. The minority may gain the admiration and approval of a selected few, but never total acceptance since ultimately they differ from the surrounding majority and will, therefore, have to pay the price of insecurity at the best and face persecution at the worst whenever they incur the displeasure of the surrounding host. Much of the persecution of the Jews throughout the centuries was based on their apparently deliberate attempt to distinguish themselves from the surrounding majority. The majority viewed this as a stubborn defiance which, although often admired for perseverance, still never permitted total integration. If we in addition consider the differentiation a religious one and if we remember that it is precisely religion which is the crutch of mankind (permitting men to appear normal when in reality psychotic delusion prevails), we can understand that total acceptance could only be approximate on a level where the delusion of religion had little hold on an individual. These individuals, however, were unfortunately very prideful ones, so the interrelationship between them and the Jews was primarily an intellectual and rational one rather than one of warm equality.

The fighter for righteousness needs a cause and so he uses the oppressed and rejected one as a vehicle for his own glorification, truly not a desirable fate although useful at times. The same situation prevails when a minority stubbornly clings to its own language or cultural heritage in a host country. Diversification is considered quaint and interesting, but does not permit identification and therefore integration. There is not one majority host which looks up to a differing powerless minority. Only when the minority becomes close to extinction does the majority magnanimously establish reservations to permit a museum-piece existence for the survivors. The situation develops in the direction of race war when a minority after total effort to be integrated as equal members of a society still meet rejection due to its physical characteristics. If straightening of kinky hair does not appease the host and no drug has been found to bleach out an abundance of pigment of the skin, then equal but different seems a solution if it would be honestly applied. Since, however, this attitude again implies a measure of indulgence on the part of the host, it can only be a working arrangement if a total balance of the power of the two groups prevails. An impasse between the Protestant and Catholic factions resulted in Europe after the Thirty Years' War. A means of coexistence had to be found by necessity since neither group could successfully annihilate the other. On the periphery, intermarriages take place for reasons hinted at in Chapter 9. In Northern Ireland, a stand-off has not been accomplished yet. In similar situations, it is mostly the vigorous, young, and forceful persons who carry on the struggle handed down to them by their approving elders.

The individual member of a minority group cannot find fault with himself. He only turned out to be what he was programmed to be. He feels it is his right as an individual to lead his life in the pursuit of happiness and he cannot perceive that his very existence is, rightly or wrongly, taken as an imposition and intrusion by the host. He feels he has the same rights as the majority although it is highly questionable whether in a reversed situation his attitude would and could prove itself more broad-minded. We truly have to find ourselves on the same raft or sinking ship to close ranks. Differentiations among human beings are the artificially created bones of contention which give men a palatable excuse to vent their frustration on each other. What we have in common—our humanity—is overlooked; what differentiates us is focused upon and seen out of proportion. Who among us is completely free from any prejudicial attitude? And, if we are free from racial, religious, and national prejudice are we not likely to be deficient in humility and rather prideful in our attitude? Human beings cannot be totally balanced; human vanity cannot thus be satisfied.

Now we come to the large if not limitless field of human sexual disturbances. Who among us, once grown up, has not some skeletons of his own to hide in his memory with regard to past or present deviant sexual attitudes and behavior? Are purely biologically normal sex relations throughout one's life possible? Does it not sound like a fairy tale when we postulate that the innocent virgin marries the inexperienced loving young man and they live happily ever after, copulating only when both are so inclined at the same time and giving each other full satisfaction in each approach? Well, mankind is not made this way.

Psychiatry at its best tries to bring home to the patient that there is all the difference between thought and action. Just because I have a passing wish to impose my will on a woman for my pleasure, I am not a rapist yet. The concepts of "how a man thinks, so he is," and "who looks at a woman and desires her has in his mind already committed adultery," are fallacies which impose on mankind the oppressive feeling of sinfulness even in the absence of deviant behavior. Even under prevalent legal conditions, we are not responsible for our thoughts. Those individuals, however, who act out of their desires to the detriment of others we call perverts and deviates.

Again, sex deviation comes in any degree. The measure of the severity of the disturbance is the degree of damage inflicted on the other individual. It seems to me that Peeping Toms represent the mildest form, particularly if the observee never realizes that she has been an object of observation. No force is used and no emotional shock is experienced.

The age of the victim is always of paramount importance in deviant sexual behavior. A child is ever so much more impressionable. A mature woman may be able to shrug off comparatively lightly the exhibitionist who may have a devastating effect on the child. It has to be recognized that the attitude of the child's parents will have a decisive influence on the effect any act of sex abuse may ultimately have on the child.

Unless sexually deviant practices are performed between consenting adults, there is always the anti-social-criminal factor, together with the maladjustment of the sex urges. The offender imposes his will upon the unprepared victim in one way or another and uses the victim as a sex object. This is in clear contradiction to our concept of love which requires the full, conscious consent of the mature sex partner. But are we not all, at times at least, given to fleeting thoughts of domination of others for our pleasure? The sex murderer is an extreme. He wishes for sexual gratification and the destruction of his sex object at the same time. He is driven to seek release from his sexual drive and his hate and fear of the opposite sex who should give him satisfaction are paramount. This concept is a recurrent theme in literature in a somewhat mitigated form. The female who is willing to sacrifice herself for the salvation of her beloved—Senta in the *Flying Dutchman* who brings salvation to him through her sacrifice—or the idea of Beauty and the Beast—are ancient themes.

Perverse as it may be, in death, the victim experiences her highest ecstasy. All this is a perversion of the biological ultimate proof of our worthwhileness. The female animal that risks, and if need be sacrifices, her own life in defense of her cub is the emotional prototype. How much each infant and child wishes to be secure in the knowledge of the unhesitating dedication of his mother to him! To the degree this comforting emotionally secure feeling was never experienced by us, we crave it. In Goethe's *Erlkoenig,* Death says to the shivering child: "If you don't follow me willingly, I will use force." We can paraphrase this for the deviate and sex murderer, who says: "You did not give me what I felt I was entitled to; I will take it by force." He only switches his victim. He means to kill his mother, first sexually using her, but this has been driven out of his awareness, so it is projected upon another member of his mother's sex.

What is the border between an alcoholic and social drinker? All kinds of definitions are given: the need to drink before being able to do any work, the need to drink before noon, etc. I feel it is only a matter of degree where we apply the label of alcoholic to a person. Is it not true that many social visits produce little pleasure unless a drink or two has loosened the tongue and put us in a slight state of euphoria? To what degree does a drink or two on coming home from work, at mealtime, or at bedtime become a time-honored institution? To what degree is alcohol not considered the great relaxer? What are we so tense about? Ordinarily we are not attacked except in our own imagination. We are not really so important that everybody has nothing to do but plot and scheme against us. Or is functioning in itself such a strain on us that we feel unable to carry on from day to day unless we artificially anesthesize ourselves and put ourselves to sleep with chemical help by numbing our nervous system?

From Bacchus to marijuana is only a short step. Don't we set the example and then disapprove when the young generation imitates us but only on their own terms? In our temperate zone, familiarity with alcohol predates by far our relationship to marijuana. But, in general, we do not know much about beetlenuts and mescaline, which Indians have used for the longest time for their own purposes.

Should we criticize the alcoholic who needs help in going through life and who tries to procure this help by himself so that he need not entrust himself to the questionable help available to him? Would any youngster give himself to steady marijuana use if life itself was meaningful enough to him? When the father drinks alcohol and the mother has her medicine cabinet filled with pills and capsules (all promising magic results because physicians prescribed them, responding to a recurrent demand), is the scene not set for the feeling that chemical substances bring forth a state of excitation, fun, relaxation, and personality manifestations otherwise not provided? Is it not true that growing up in the shadow of the hydrogen bomb creates a frenzied obsession to experience life to the fullest before we all are dead? Did similar orgies of lust not take place in the Middle Ages, since, according to some prophets, Armaggedon would soon be upon mankind? How stable must a youngster be to remain unperturbed in such turmoil? To what degree are we not all affected? What rewards does the retired worker reap when he sees his life savings dwindle through inflation? What conclusions can a youngster draw from such examples?

There is a strong difference made between hard drugs and marijuana. Many feel that marijuana is only a stepping stone to more malignant addictions. Still, there has to be the predisposition to be unsatisfied with milder drugs. Great efforts are made to cure the addict. Prevention, long before exposure and before a habit is established, seems the only rational answer. Prevention would have to consist of making life a pleasurable experience to a child instead of the usual nightmare. On the other hand, it is more than questionable whether society can carry the load of making life worthwhile to a youngster who feels rejected, abused, and brutalized from birth on and who develops the attitude that he truly is no good, but indeed bad. Can we, can anything, repair such damage? Are there any answers for human ills except psychosis, sickness, and self-destruction of one kind or another? Who is free from these afflictions? Is it not above all a matter of the degree to which we were made victims or seem to escape somewhat at least from the inexorable forces at work.

Let us say a few words about homosexuals and fanatics. Any physician will assure you that there is no man who does not have some female sex hormones in him, just as every woman has some male hormones. Embryology teaches us that the Müllerian ducts form the original matrix to the genitalia formation of either sex, and no microscopic examination in the first few weeks of fetal existence can determine which sex development will ultimately result. The primary sex characteristics are the gonads. Only testes and ovaries determine the actual sex. The secondary sex characteristics are the organs involved in fertilization and childbearing. Tertiary characteristics facilitate and insure the survival of the infant. Here the female breasts and milk-producing mammary glands are of prime importance. Body build, voice differences, hair distribution differences, different bone (especially pelvic) development between the sexes, and ultimately differences in every cell are only quaternary characteristics. It must, furthermore, be emphasized that each individual, to a certain degree, is a hermaphrodite inasmuch as each sex organ of one sex has a vestigial analogy in the opposite sex. In the prostate gland, there exists a small nob aptly called the utriculus corresponding to the womb. Each female possesses a clitoris, a vestigial remnant of a penis. There are even males with supermammary nipples corresponding to the primitive milk line. Hermaphroditism, therefore, is the norm, although true hermaphroditism, the coexistence of testes and ovaries, occurs in higher mammals and men very rarely.

Who never doubts his masculinity? What woman is always "all woman" and what would that mean? Is it not true that the more doubts we have, the greater efforts we may make to set our doubts at rest? Is the male who has to enlist in the Marines in order to live up to manhood expectations, and thusly jeopardizes his life beyond the call of duty, more masculine than the individual less plagued by this nagging fear of lacking masculinity so that he fulfills his duties but does not feel the need to go beyond them? Are the Casanovas or nymphomaniacs sure of their sex, or do they have to reassert their sex continuously with new objects?

Homosexuality is a matter of self-identification. A man is a man as long as he was born with testes and no gonad transplants are feasible. The amputation of a penis and female sex hormones do not make a female out of a man. Transvestism has been practiced for a long time and these modern operations are, in one sense, only corporally applied transvestism. Now, whether an infant and child can joyfully identify with his innate sex or hates to be what he is, is not based on his own decision but is due to the circumstances which patterned his formative years. Can there be a greater rejection of a father with whom the son does not feel free to identify? Is not the fear of the opposite sex, the mother, implicit if a boy feels he should be more like her and, therefore, more acceptable to her? Is this an implied compliment to the mother or an expression of fear and hate for the fact that he could not be what biologically he was meant to be? The girl who seeks love in a lesbian relationship does not feel free to make love with and give love to a male since the first male in her life apparently had a frightening connotation, hate for the mother because she made the man appear disastrous. To what degree do we all not share remnants of these feelings at least? Is there anybody completely free of homosexuality? Is homosexuality perhaps not a frightening specter of mental abnormality with all its subsequent disastrous consequences? Pederasty and homosexuality have been known since ancient times. Antiquity is replete with examples. From Alexander the Great to Caesar, there is an endless chain of homosexuals.

What are fanatics? People who feel they are right and who are not amenable to any discussion or accountable to opposing views. When their attitude and endeavors are crowned with success, we hail them as inspired geniuses. They are even then difficult to live with, due to their single-mindedness of purpose. Their mates, if they have any, could just as well forego ultimate success in order to suffer less from their obsession. Poets and other artists belong equally to this group at times. If their ultimate aim is constructive and useful to society, allowances will be made for their exclusive and rigid attitude. The situation, however, becomes disastrous when the fanatic has world-improving convictions which are contemptuous of other attitudes. The desire to dominate is ill-disguised behind intolerance. Paranoia hides itself behind the conviction that we know the will of God. God becomes the excuse and justification for almost any attitude we find useful to ourselves. Sometimes mass hysteria follows in the wake of an inspired paranoiac. Our desire to be children again and to follow leaves us open to fascinating rhetoric. Mass hysteria has no bounds. The sun stands still, apparitions appear, objects float freely, the laws of nature are superseded by hallucinatory experiences. And, is any one of us free from such influences? Wars have been declared with singing and flower festivities. Holy wars and crusades are exhilarating experiences except for the very sober individual. Lack of patriotism at times carries the connotation of treason. Who thinks in terms of mankind when the interests of a group are at stake? As long as such attitudes prevail, clashes and confrontations have to follow each other while mankind balances on the brink of self-annihilation. Who is the villain? Who is the saint? Can any distinction be made? The only guideline we have is that whatsoever serves the preservation of the species has to be called useful and acceptable. As human beings, the requirements of the species have to be enlarged from the primitive biological needs to the specific human emotional need of self-awareness and self-respect.

What is the situation with persons who can be described as misfits? They received a programming which does not permit them to act freely upon their impulses. The impulses are anti-social, asocial, paranoid, sexually deviant, or even murderous. They cannot indulge in overtly acting upon their impulses. They have to find clandestine ways to satisfy their urges or live in perpetual frustration. Perpetual frustration is, however, just about unbearable to the nervous system, so an occasional climactic release of the suppressed impulses will take place. (I would like to allude here to ideopathic epilepsy which seems to bring the sudden impulse release upon the individual himself, and, therefore, protects others from his inherent destructiveness.) In suppression of their programmed impulses, the misfits are not happy and in releasing them they are insecure in the fear of being confronted by the established forces of society. In either case, no relaxation and contentment is possible. The more our imprinting and programming fulfillment synchronizes with the aim of the preservation of the species as it applies to human beings, the fewer conflicts will result, the fewer frictions, repressions, sicknesses, and frustrations. On the other hand, it can be said that the misfits are the victims of nature's law of the selection of the fittest. Since we all have a modicum of the "misfitness" in us, we all are, to a certain degree, victims of this law of nature.

chapter 13

THE CONTRIBUTION OF THE MENTALLY SICK TO THE FUNCTIONING OF THE MENTALLY HEALTHY

As a psychiatrist, I am well acquainted with the customary classification and differentiation of human beings into roughly two categories—mentally healthy and mentally sick. I am, of course, very much aware that no sharp demarcation exists between these two extremes. Indeed, it would be much more appropriate to speak of a broad spectrum where, if one chooses to do so, one can catalogue each individual's place according to the adjustment which he was able to make in the setting of the society in which he lives.

We have learned by now that no human being is responsible for the programming he received in his formative years. If we rule out the possibility that chromosomal transmissions genetically preordained us to mental maladjustment with the same inevitability as our physical predispositions are laid down in the DNA molecules, then we have to conclude that our attitude toward life, fellow human beings, and the world at large is due to the environmental exposure which imprint the infant and child from his earliest beginning. We know we are not responsible for the reception which we receive on coming into this world; nevertheless, this reception will form our basic view of the world. We have zeroed in on the mother as the person with overwhelming influence on the pattern formation of the child, either by her presence and attitude or even, paradoxically, by her absence, if this should be the case. If human warmth is an ingredient, which is indispensable to the full, happy emotional development, its absence or inadequate substitution can only leave a child with an emotional deficit commensurate to its lack.

By the very nature of the diversity of human beings, each society has to be quite broad-minded about what passes as acceptable. Some actions must be outrightly rejected and some are permitted to pass as long as the variance from accepted attitude is not too disturbing. Society will show considerable latitude if the variance of an individual from accepted norms is pleasing and brings rewards to society. At times, actors and artists have shown extravagant and eccentric behavior but great allowances have been made according to their accomplishments. Eccentricities are often tolerated within limits to the degree an individual remains self-sustaining or actually commands great wealth or power. If we keep in mind that each individual is patterned and programmed through his mother, whether she was conscious of it or not, exactly as she wanted the child to be patterned according to her own personality imprint, we can, if we are objective enough to perceive it, say that he turns out exactly as the mother subconsciously wanted him to turn out. I can hear all the protestations coming my way from mothers who, erroneously hearing accusation, may feel they have to establish alibis for themselves. I like to be as objective as humanly possible and it is not a question of accusation as was previously clearly established.

Again and again a situation arises in a family when there are several children where most of them, perhaps with the exception of only one, seem to do very well. All seem to adjust very well to life and lead what is generally considered a well-adjusted, successful life. The exception, however, has never adjusted well at all. Perhaps his maladjustment can be traced back to the earliest infancy. We might learn that as an infant he cried continuously and nothing seemed to calm him down; he may have had colic at first and all kinds of diseases may have afflicted him. Later in school, other difficulties may have been present. Toilet training may have come late or not at all. He may have had a difficult time making friends and became a loner early in life. With the advent of puberty, the possibility of deviant behavior grew geometrically. If a breakdown did not take place by that time, the added responsibilities of later life certainly became precipitating factors. The examples and variations which can be enumerated are endless. The fact remains that from the same parents, from the same background, there came a number of apparently healthy individuals and one or more maladjusted ones.

We have to disabuse ourselves of the concept that the parents of several children are the same parents to all of them. The often-used statement of parents that they love them all alike is far from factual. An infinite variety of constellations can arise. A mother may particularly look forward to her first-born child or might have dreaded this first pregnancy with all its implications. She may have sensed the desire of her husband to have a son and be gratified or disappointed as the case may be. She may not have been ready for a pregnancy in the first place or only wanted to please her mother who longed for a grandchild; perhaps her sister had already had several children and she felt second best or left out. In any case, it was highly unlikely that, as in the free animal kingdom, the female in heat copulated with the equally ready male and gestation and delivery followed as a natural sequence of events. Among animals, no forethought of offspring influenced the mating events. Subsequent pregnancies may have taken place under entirely different circumstances. The mother might not have been ready for intercourse (not to speak of pregnancy) after her last delivery and she might have found herself saddled with a new pregnancy when she had barely recovered from her previous one, not to speak of the additional and impossible burden to be satisfactory to one infant while nurturing the next already in the womb. The husband who just had intercourse with her, since he could not contain his sex drive, curses her and the expected child and threatens to leave or actually does so. She may have found out in addition by that time that he was not the Prince Charming whom she visualized in her fantasy but a human and deficient individual, more concerned with his own emotional needs than those of his wife and family. The mother may find herself thrust into a position where she actually has to take over the father's role in addition to her maternal status.

These are situations which don't give themselves to happy solutions. The next child may be a second girl, even though everybody had hoped that this time a boy would come. The same situation, of course, can occur in reverse. Subsequent pregnancies will only complicate the picture. At the same time an event becomes known to us, it loses its threat and we feel less worried than when the unknown had to be met. We can even visualize that a more mature woman may be gratified that she is still in the childbearing and reproductive age and thus welcome a pregnancy, particularly when her earlier born children have outgrown her immediate care.

There are additional circumstances which can considerably complicate the situation. A young widow with children may seek remarriage for a variety of reasons: personal, economic, emotional, or otherwise, and she may have additional pregnancies or, in order to maintain her second marriage, try to influence her own children to an attitude accommodating to her new husband who may or may not have children of his own. In the case of a remarriage of a divorcee with children, the situation seems further complicated. We can postulate a higher degree of maladjustment in a person who married and reproduced with a mate who subsequently was deemed unbearable or at least expendable. Now, according to my thesis, cripple marries cripple and no better emotional adjustment can be expected in a mate who finds himself, unconsciously of course, attracted to a person with emotional flaws. It is quite possible that a man who is basically afraid of women will feel attracted to a woman to whom he considers himself superior and whom he considers will have to depend on him. These thoughts are not coldly calculated premaritally, but they form the matrix on which our desires and attitudes grow. A woman may find herself pregnant without her knowledge or against her wishes, at least on a conscious level.

We see, therefore, that the same parents are not the same to all of their children. Indeed, it is rather the great exception that each child is equally wanted and received by his parents, be it joyfully or the reverse, with the same degree of rejection.

With this different emotional endowment each sibling receives from his parents, a place is assigned to him among the others. At times, the first-born child, male or not, will receive high standing in the pecking order, but, at times, he will become relegated to the role of the patsy, since he is older and should understand better. Any excuse and rationalization can be made to assign any offspring to any undesirable constellation among the other children.

When a rejected child is forced into a role of scapegoat, he serves several purposes. He may subconsciously sense the importance he has to his mother who can vent her hate and impatience on him. We may call such an adjustment by any psychiatric term we choose, but the fact remains that a considerable part of his self-esteem will derive from the fact that he helps his mother by his very existence and to be the fall guy has emotional compensation. We may call such a reaction formation sick but it was unavoidable under the presenting circumstances. Once gratification is obtained from being a fall guy, a pattern is formed which seeks to reenact the same situation over and over again. Not only will our siblings vent their own anger on us for relief of their hostilities (and perhaps indirectly also to gain approval from the mother or parent, which, in turn, equips them to function more successfully with other people), but the rejected child may develop into an individual who feels his purpose in life is to serve as the sacrificial lamb for others.

Mental sickness, like every human disease, comes in degrees. Let us take the example of a chronic schizophrenic patient hospitalized for many years. What can we say about him which he perhaps, indeed probably, is unable to say for himself? There must certainly be a disastrous degree of hate and destructive impulses buried within him because of all the horrible abuse heaped upon him during infancy and childhood to force him to withdraw so totally from contact with other human beings. I once observed two very regressed elderly schizophrenics, completely out of touch with the surrounding world. They stood side by side, pressed against the wall, while one, without any noticeable motion or expression, pressed his fingernails deeply into the flesh of his companion, who neither moved nor gave any noticeable reaction.

What else can we say? Perhaps the mentally sick person feels that he preserved the unity of the family. The parents, using him as the outlet for their hate, were able to coexist with each other and perhaps at the same time did not have the slightest inkling of what, completely unaware, they had inflicted upon their offspring. Under certain pathological circumstances, the parent generation can devour their young. Abraham, to find favor in the eyes of God, was prepared to sacrifice his son. The self-sacrifice of the gods is a recurrent theme in religious thought. The Fisher King as well as the Son of God dies for the benefit of mankind. The theme is recurring.

The schizophrenic about whom we speak may also feel, with considerable justification, that because he served as the scapegoat for his parents and his mother in particular, their ire and scorn became lessened and thus the other children escaped with only a "black eye." Indeed, he also served his siblings, not only as a protecting lightning rod which deflected the disastrous scorn of the parents away from them and thus secured their better acceptance, but the siblings themselves could feel superior to him on the totem pole arrangement of the family and eventually could vent their own frustration on him. He certainly served a very useful purpose in the family constellation, if I am permitted to make such a statement.

Of course, if I were cynical, I could go on and say the schizophrenic might still feel he boosts the morale of many other people by permitting them to feel superior to him and gain a livelihood to boot. We can certainly say that the "mentally ill" make a substantial contribution to the functioning of the so-called "mentally healthy." Somehow, I am reminded of the statement of Abraham Lincoln in the Gettysburg Address, where he questions the right of the survivors to honor those who gave the full measure of their devotion to their duty. If I am perverse enough, maybe some day we should give a day of thanks to the mentally ill who were programmed so that they had to take a place as low man on the totem pole. If I were not so totally devoid of traditional religiosity, I would find myself inclined to say: "Here, but by the grace of God, go I."

chapter 14

THE MECHANICS OF PSYCHOTHERAPY

Once again the question arises: how does psychotherapy work? Patients ask how it can help them to sit and talk while the therapist just sits there and listens. They come for help, but are far from understanding how talk alone is supposed to help them. Indeed, many qualified physicians share this attitude to a high degree. These physicians are willing to go to any length, sometimes in a highly skilled way, to be of help to their patients. But try as they may, the patient may refuse, subconsciously, of course, to feel cured and satisfied under their administrations and may, though reluctantly, find their way into a psychiatrist's office. The symptomatology and degree of disturbance vary, of course, from case to case.

The first thing the psychiatrist has to decide is whether the patient in question can be handled satisfactorily in an office setting or whether short-term hospitalization at least is the treatment of choice. Hospitalization in a private psychiatric setting serves many purposes. In orthodox psychoanalysis, one can ask a patient to come to the office as many as five times weekly, which improves rapport between the psychiatrist and his patient in many instances when weekly interviews would not be adequate. It would be unrealistic not to consider economic feasibility in treatment planning. Short-term hospitalization has at times many desirable effects. The patient overtly accepts psychiatry by the very fact that he consents to hospitalization. (Obviously, I speak here of voluntary hospital admissions.)

Patients who are disturbed enough to lack insight while their actions and behavior become totally unacceptable to society may become subject to involuntary legal commitment to a mental institution. The time is long past when even these commitments would necessarily be considered long-term. As soon as good professional judgment indicates that the patient can again function in an acceptable form outside of an institution, the responsible staff entertains the discharge of such a patient, at least on a trial basis. Out-patient follow-up treatment with or without adjunctive medication is then the treatment of choice. Today, releasing a patient from an institution as soon as good judgment permits, even if later rehospitalization may become indicated, is considered superior to keeping a patient continuously hospitalized. Even the sickest patients will be better served if they spend part of their lives outside hospital walls whenever feasible.

I return to the comparatively mildly disturbed patients who voluntarily admit themselves to short-term psychiatric hospitalization. Many of these patients will form an adequate rapport with the therapist rather promptly, even without adjunctive medication to facilitate their early discharge and subsequent follow-up of expressive and interpretative office psychotherapeutic sessions. No patient should ever be hospitalized if adequate office outpatient psychiatric interviews are adequate. No patient should receive medication if adequate interpersonal psychotherapy can bring about all the desirable results. Medication, if not absolutely indicated, may provide temporary comfort, but precludes the patient's motivation to gain deep-going insight into the etiology of his disturbance and thus bring about a lasting cure in the true sense. Obviously, no patient should ever be considered for electroshock or other similar treatment modalities unless straight psychotherapy or even psychotherapy together with adequate chemotherapy is deemed to be inadequate. The time factor will, of course, also have to be taken into consideration. These are practical considerations which present themselves, and they are open to interpretation by the good judgment of the psychiatrist.

After this short excursion into hospital psychiatry, let us return to the basic principles and mechanics of psychotherapy.

Here again, it must be emphasized that psychotherapy, according to Noyes-Kolb, can be carried out on four basic levels; the demarcation lines are by necessity not sharply drawn but rather fleetingly pass from one level into the next. Elements of the repressive or supportive levels can be found in the expressive and interpretive levels and even in the psychoanalytical level unless the psychoanalyst is so rigid in his own dogma that he cannot unbend, even slightly, to accommodate his patient.

The two nonexploratory levels of psychotherapy are the repressive and supportive. The two dynamic uncovering levels are expressive-interpretive and psychoanalytical. The very terminology describes the greater active intervention by the therapist in the nonexploratory levels because here he will primarily aim to give emotional support to the patient or even tend to repress the symptomatology outright, since he feels this is the most applicable approach. Just as the general physician, when facing a condition in a patient for which at the present time there is no cure available, such as diabetes, rheumatic heart valve disturbances, psoriasis, hemophilia, and many more, tries to support the patient with medication and guidance, so will the psychiatrist be well advised to distinguish clearly between emotional-mental disturbances, which lend themselves to a resolution through deeper insight and disturbances where deeper insight is out of the question because the fragile personality structure of the patient would completely decompensate in facing the underlying emotional etiology of his disturbance. An acute open psychotic break might occur which could culminate in releasing aggressive impulses and destructive urges of such vehemence that the patient himself is swept away or that society could not tolerate them. We have to be very strong emotionally to face up to the murderous and destructive forces deeply embedded in all of us from our formative years on and at the same time have full confidence and security in the feeling of our own inhibiting forces and the good judgment to distinguish between thought and action. It takes a mature individual to distinguish clearly between thought and action and, therefore, not to be frightened by one's own thoughts in the full knowledge that just because we feel one way there is no reason in the world that we have to act upon it if our good judgment tells us that such action is not in our best interest. This maturity we can call objectivity about ourselves and it is the aim of every psychotherapeutic endeavor to approach it as closely as possible if we are not equipped to reach this aim fully. It goes without saying that the therapist must be equipped to permit a patient to reach this goal and this can only happen if the therapist truly knows himself adequately or fully—if this is possible under human conditions. In the uncovering type of psychotherapy, several conditions have to be fulfilled if we hope for positive results rather than mere supportive therapy.

Above all, the most important factor is the motivation of the patient. A patient who has a strong wish to survive and not waste his life away in the face of frustrations which he feels are more than he himself alone can handle and who wishes to gain insight and understanding as to why he is not successful, in the broadest sense of the word, so that he can ultimately lead a more satisfactory life, is the ideal patient for the uncovering type of psychotherapy. The patient is encouraged to express himself freely and the therapist must know when he should only listen and when he should give encouraging signs or even eventually make a few well-chosen interpretations. The timing is also of the greatest importance. As much as the budding therapist has reviewed the literature and listened to his preceptors, ultimately his own personality will come through and will determine the level of insight he is capable of achieving and, therefore, of leading his patient to. It is truly tragic if a patient has the potential to gain deep and relieving insight into his emotional disturbance, but his therapist almost waves him off since deeper insights are not within the therapist's own grasp. It takes a strong and determined patient to perceive the limits of his own therapist and move on to greener pastures under such conditions.

As long as the pursuit of our life was more or less successful or at least deemed so by us, we will lack the initiative and motivation to submit ourselves to a thorough review of our own personality structure, how it was put together and came into existence in the first place, and how it ultimately came to be considered non-operative or at least unsatisfactory by us. Strong will, determination, good intelligence, open-mindedness to new vistas, and an iron will to survive will have to combine to achieve success in such an endeavor. Even partial success will have to be appreciated since: *"ut desint vires tamen est laudanda voluntas"* ("if the strength is insufficient, good intentions must be praised").

Great is the reward of successful psychotherapy. An objective view of the circumstances which conditioned our pattern formation will gradually emerge. We will become objective about our parents and our mother in particular. *"Sine ira et studio,"* that is, without undue emotionalism, we will become objective about ourselves, our parents, and the world at large. Once we have achieved this objectivity we will deal with others on their merits, in other words, appropriately without any undue expenditure of emotion and subsequent concomitant stress reactions, inappropriate defensively paranoid alert reactions, and oversensitizations. Not only will we find emotional security within ourselves, but we will have learned to accept ourselves for what we are. We will have learned that, due to the imprinting, programming forces to which we were subject in our formative years, we could not have turned out differently than we actually turned out and constantly finding fault with ourselves was only justified inasmuch as we did not function to our own satisfaction. With this increased self-acceptance, which we can call peace of mind, and the concomitant increased emotional security, the autonomic nervous system will only be called upon to react appropriately to maintain our emotional and physical equilibrium. The cardiovascular system as well as other organs, directly or indirectly, will be put under less stress and will indeed receive much needed and indicated periods of relaxation so indispensable to safeguard long and satisfactory functioning. Increased insight and subsequent appropriate reactivity will benefit us not only emotionally, mentally, and physically, but we will also benefit on a socioeconomic level. It is self-evident that people will find us more acceptable if we deal with them as fellow human beings on the same ship, the Earth, engaged in the same trip through life as they themselves experience. They will also react favorably to our new-gained objectivity which permits us to deal with them in an appropriate manner as the situation requires and demands. We will not infringe on their rights unjustifiably any more than we see any constructive reason to let others infringe on our rights unless this does serve a constructive purpose or is unavoidable.

When I was a young doctor and underwent my own psychoanalysis (not for training purposes but to find my own emotional acceptance and balance in order not to fail in the goal I had set for myself), I noted in the office of my analyst a picture the significance of which I did not understand at that time. The picture represented a young girl looking into a mirror. Only her back could be seen since she looked full-faced into the mirror. I have long since come to understand the full meaning of the picture. The girl looks into the mirror as if to ask the questions "Who am I?" "What do I look like?" really, squarely, and honestly. We can compare the girl to the patient in the uncovering type of psychotherapy, but I feel it is justified to compare the mirror to the therapist. A good mirror should reflect our picture realistically, neither embellished nor distorted. The more evenly the mirror is polished, the less distorted the reflected image. The mirror reflects the picture objectively, regardless of how much we may posture in front of it to obtain a more pleasing reflection.

The therapist also fulfills other requirements, although these functions come into less play in the dogmatic, orthodox form of psychoanalysis which, after all, was primarily intended to serve the pure anxiety neurosis. All motivation had to originate in the patient and the therapist primarily restricted himself to the role of a listener, who at times went to any degree to maintain this role of passive, permissive listener. Since pure unadultered anxiety neurosis is more a concept than a reality, patients, in spite of the most admirable persistence, finally give up more exhausted than relieved of their symptomatology. Inasmuch as any interference from the therapist is only justified, if and when spontaneous expression of the patient has run its full course and no further, productive expressions can be expected, nevertheless, it is fully justified when such definite deadlock has developed. Such statements from the therapist might amount to no more than encouraging the patient to go on in his search for the facts or some words which convey to the patient that the therapist is well in tune with the patient and understands him. One of the most important aspects of psychotherapy is that the patient develops a feeling that he is not alone and that he can be well understood. The unbearable feeling of lonesomeness goes back to our formative years. When at the earliest age a sense of helpless abandonment pervaded us, on a subconscious emotional level only, this feeling was sensed as a definite threat to our life; the fear of death was underlying it. Once this pattern was set in these earliest stages of our existence, nothing could later erase it. We could surround ourselves with a bevy of people, we could dive into a whirlpool of activity to assuage this gnawing sensation of abandonment, but nothing could quite suffice. We could drown this feeling of lonesomeness at times in the maelstrom of noisy activity, but we only wake up in the depth of the night to the same old dread of death and lonesomeness. Now, in psychotherapy we have a fellow human being, the therapist, who will stay with us through all our ruminations and who will accept us. Although he is only a substitute for the person whose inadequate responses conditioned our lonesomeness, the substitute is better than nothing, particularly if he ultimately leads us to clear understanding of the mechanisms which brought about the pattern formation. At this stage of psychotherapy a deep rapport with the therapist has been established by the patient to the point that the patient may feel his entire life and future depends on the survival and the availability of this specific therapist.

The warmth of the therapist will be an additional factor of the greatest importance. This point should not be misunderstood. By warmth in the psychotherapeutic relationship I only mean the degree of empathy a therapist is capable of mustering with regard to his patient. To the degree the therapist has worked out his own emotional conflicts and does not need the patient to bolster his own unfulfilled emotional needs, he is equipped to serve the needs of the patient and he is able to accept the patient for what he is without showing any signs of inappropriate permissiveness. As I said in another chapter, passive resistance is only employable if we deal with a reasonably well-balanced person since this person will respect our attitude. In the same way, a permissive attitude in psychotherapy can only prevail as long as the expressions of the patient do not become outrightly destructive and abusive.

It is true that a person who does not care at all can tolerate any verbal abuse and expression, simply because he shows no reactivity to them. When we deal with an outright overtly psychotic human being, any therapist will immediately adopt the attitude that whatever abuse the patient may indulge in cannot be taken seriously. When we deal, however, with an individual who wishes to get well but whose pattern is such that he has to be outright aggressive, even if only in a verbal form, a serious impasse is reached. The cold, emotionally uninvolved therapist is unacceptable and unrewarding to this patient in the first place, since he needs to sense the warmth of an empathetic therapist. The empathetic therapist, on the other hand, will eventually respond to the persistent forms of criticism emanating from the patient who cannot be satisfied, no matter what the therapist may do or say. A point of exhaustion will be reached where the therapist, for reasons of self-preservation and serving at the same time the needs of the patient, is wise to suggest that the patient seek another therapist. This is most likely to occur when the patient has a considerable degree of character disturbance-component. The patient has to express and ventilate hostility which goes back again to his own formative years. As long as the release of the hostility reaches only a minor degree, the therapist can tolerate it well. If, after months of psychoanalysis, the patient tells the therapist that he does not look good to him, if he misses an appointment or is late in paying his bill, this too can be tolerated and worked through. In psychoanalytical terms, transference of feelings attached earlier to the significant person in the patient's life to the therapist has taken place, and release of this comparatively mild degree of hostility upon the therapist is well within tolerable limits. Therefore, we can say another function of psychotherapy is the realization and controlled expression of repressed hostility.

If, however, the repressed hostility is of such major degree that its release would become devastating, such release cannot be allowed, certainly not in a psychotherapeutic office setting. There is a broad spectrum of disturbances in which patients sincerely wish to gain better insight into their disturbance, but the degree of the disturbance is such that it becomes only gradually clear that their full expression in the office setting has such destructive connotation that a halt to further expression has to be called.

The following example comes to my mind:

Case History: A 27-year-old white man recently came to see me in my office after referral from a friendly physician. He stated at the outset of the interview that he had felt depressed ever since childhood but that this feeling had recently intensified.

These depressions now seem to affect his work. He suffers from fits of temper; he feels nervous all the time. He finds it difficult to get along with his family, mother, father, brother, and sister. At this point, I asked the patient whether he was married and he said, "Yes," almost as an afterthought. He has a wife and a three-year-old child whom he described as exceedingly bright. He has been married for six years. His wife is slightly older than he, and it is the first marriage for both. He had a college education in music and played the trumpet. He mentioned he had studied a little bit of psychology in college. He added that he was afraid of life. He has trouble in relating to his wife. In addition, he feels he has a good mind which he cannot, however, use. He admitted that he had had some vague suicidal ideas in the past, although nothing definite; he never attempted suicide. He smokes 20 to 49 cigarettes daily. His alcoholic consumption averages about six drinks daily; some weeks he drinks nothing; at other times, he has as many as 40 or 50 drinks a week. He had been drinking less since the birth of his child. His wife consumes about the same amount of alcohol.

He was given some supportive medication and instructed to refrain from alcohol intake if he really wanted to get well and to use the medication as a substitute. Another appointment was made for the next week. Three days later I received an urgent call from his wife. She related that her husband had to leave work and he came home highly agitated, almost in a panic state. He needed immediate help. I suggested hospitalization, which was promptly accepted. The next morning he was greatly improved and had calmed down completely. He said he did not know what had happened the day before. I suggested that I should also see his wife in consultation. The next day his wife came to my office. She gave me much additional information. I learned that his mother had died of a brain tumor when the patient was only two years old. He apparently had had some blackouts and dizzy spells all his life. She also related that once he spent hours at the cemetery to locate the graveside of his mother and did not want to move away from it once he had found it. Once he had supposedly fallen down an elevator shaft. Apparently he had taken Dilantin medication for many years, a fact which he failed to communicate to me. His wife had left him twice during the previous summer, for a few days each time. Two weeks previously he had left his wife for two weeks and she told him he could not come back unless he obtained psychiatric help. After she made this last statement, she wanted to retract it somewhat, implying that her husband reached this decision on his own.

The following day when the patient was seen at the hospital, he looked very well. He assured me that he felt fine and that he wanted to return to work. He could not understand what had happened to him only a few days earlier and he stated definitely that he as well as his wife would come for regular office visits for follow-up psychotherapeutic interviews on a weekly basis. Under these conditions I found it well-justified to discharge the patient from the hospital.

It should be mentioned that an electroencephalogram, brain scan, and skull X-ray were taken. The electroencephalogram had positive findings, confirming mild epileptic seizure activity. The other tests were negative. The encephalographic report read as follows:

"Your patient has nothing in his electroencephalogram to suggest a tumor or other gross lesion in the accessible cortex. The only abnormality consists of small sharp spikes, a mild form of seizure activity which is usually unassociated with structural damage. They are a non-specific, irritative reaction to mild injury; they can be produced by trauma, encephalitis, or vascular disease.

"Seizure discharges of the small sharp spike variety are often asymptomatic but may be associated with infrequent convulsions or 'spells' of some type. Fortunately they are the most benign of the seizure patterns and the seizures which occur in patients with this type of discharge can usually be controlled with Dilantin and phenobarbital, Dilantin and Mysoline, or Dilantin and Mesantoin, and over a period of four or five years they commonly disappear spontaneously."

Three days later the patient arrived punctually at my office. He had not yet returned to work but expected to go back within the next two days. He no longer felt as good as he had before his discharge from the hospital. He stated that he preferred to come to the interview without his wife because it was his problem which he wanted to conquer. I gave him all the support and attention which was called for and tried to be as encouraging as possible. Within a few days the patient returned for his next interview, again alone. He had gone back to work but he started to feel very bad again, and I felt that the interviews with him alone did not bring forth adequate results. I suggested, therefore, that at the next interview his wife should come along because I felt good results could not otherwise be anticipated. Within a few days the patient returned for an interview, accompanied by his wife. It immediately became apparent that both of them were angry. They proceeded into the interview room sullenly without any greeting whatsoever. Upon my question about how he felt, he started to complain that he felt much worse after the last interview. His wife also added that she could not understand why he should grow worse and any explanations I tried to offer did not make sense to them. They found fault with everything I said and the conclusion was unavoidable that they only used me to discharge all their repressed hostility. Indeed, at one point in the interview I pointed out to the patient's wife that a therapist is here to help his patient, but not at the price of becoming a scapegoat and floormat himself. Nothing seemed to make sense and ultimately the wife denied that she had ever said that the condition for his returning to her was that he would seek psychiatric help. I felt that under such conditions I could not continue to be in charge of the case and of further usefulness unless the patient returned to the hospital. The patient refused to consider this alternative since this would cost him his job, whereupon both of them got up and walked out of the office without any further word or farewell.

I realize that this example does not represent a typical case. It is, however, instructive because it raises several pertinent questions. First of all, I like to believe that the patients were greatly helped in spite of the apparent ultimate displeasure. They used me against my intention as the recipient for the release of a good part of their hostility which was a most critical part in the treatment approach which they, so to speak, forced upon me. There was no doubt in my mind that in a way I was used because I leaned backwards in my desire to be of help to them, as far as I could. I had to draw a line when I realized that nothing but an outburst would please them. The destructive urge in both of them was of such magnitude that a halt had to be called. I am sure they will turn now to another therapist who may be very much more successful; however, in reality, only because they previously had been able to discharge a substantive part of their hostility upon me. At no time do I imply that the patient and his wife were conscious of what they were doing. They acted out. He had the motivation for changing his basic pattern, but he acted only upon pressure from his wife who told him he could not come back unless he sought psychiatric help. Both of them apparently had the illusion that just going to the psychiatrist would miraculously and immediately dispel all disturbances and desirable results would be instantaneous. If nothing else, they will show more patience toward the next psychiatrist. Although this case is quite complex, nevertheless, it is a good example to demonstrate some of the difficulties which so often accompany psychotherapy.

In essence, we can say that the adequate psychotherapist for the time being becomes a good parent substitute. After a relationship of trust has been established, which is generally called rapport, the patient gradually proceeds to expose his innermost feelings and thoughts to the therapist. Under no condition does the patient expect and experience rejection of his person by the therapist, although the time will come when the patient and perhaps also the therapist with him will have to re-evaluate an earlier personality pattern which has long outlived its usefulness. Indeed, this reorientation and re-evaluation after adequate review is an essential part of the desirable features of successful psychotherapy.

Only the mildest disturbances qualify for persistent psychoanalysis on their own power and motivation. The more mature the person is, the more willing he will be to make any sacrifices, economic or otherwise, to obtain the best that life can give, self-acceptance and self-respect. One can assemble a group of ambulatory schizophrenic patients still in good contact or their counterparts in institutions and give them daily sessions of group discussion ad infinitum. One can listen to their endless ruminations forever and ever. They will ramble on and on and when they leave they will perhaps have benefited, but only because the effort which went into them was financed and shouldered through public money. The financial responsibility was shifted to society which through taxation provided their sustenance and therapy. Equally, we have to consider the cases of the wealthy from a different angle. The wealthy relatives of a patient find the economic outlay insignificant. Therefore, it matters little to them when psychotherapeutic sessions drag on and on and have basically nothing in common with uncovering psychotherapy but the setting. They are, in reality, only supportive in nature even if this is not clearly understood. If the therapist is aware of this circumstance, he cannot be criticized in continuing a professional relationship which serves a certain modicum of usefulness. Of course, the thought cannot be dismissed that such a situation is similar to that of a highly skilled surgeon who is called on to remove a minor sliver from a superficial wound, an operation which, most likely, any halfway intelligent student nurse could perform equally well. I have great respect for the therapist who feels that his time could be better given to more challenging undertakings.

The point which I wish to make, however, is that there is a broad spectrum of patients, not sick enough to need public support and who certainly do not qualify as wealthy. They can afford sustained, methodical psychotherapy, but there is a modicum of immature aggressiveness in them which makes it plausible to them that this psychotherapeutic help should be given to them free of charge or with only a minimum token amount of outlay on their part.

Mental health clinics have been created all over the country within the last few decades which are meant to accommodate this vast group of persons who seek other psychotherapeutic help and who feel they cannot afford a private psychiatrist or who do not have the strength of motivation to make it possible. I do not wish to go into a discussion of the adequacy of such mental health clinics because, first of all, any generalization is unjustified. On the other hand, there is some truth in the ancient words, "You get what you pay for." The staff personnel may think of themselves as highly adequate but that does not make them necessarily so. Therapists who by definition are not qualified to hospitalize a patient or to administer medication, if this is the treatment of choice, are greatly handicapped in the first place and, secondly, they may be inclined to persist in their own brand of therapeutic approach although objectively it is no longer the approach of choice. I am well aware that these clinics work in close relationship with a psychiatrist, who is called on for advice, guidance, help, and medication, if such is deemed indicated. Nevertheless, it is one thing if the therapist himself is equipped to give medication and another if the therapist serves as a standby who has not formed adequate personal contact with the patient. I am fully aware that compromises have to be made in order to cope with the shortage of therapists. The facts, however, should be stated honestly, and then it can be decided whether something can be done about them or not. Suffice it to say that a certain number of patients will go to a private psychiatrist and be critical if they cannot obtain psychotherapy free of charge, as if it were their innate right to obtain it. These persons can be compared to people who when hungry feel entitled to go to the Waldorf-Astoria restaurant although they cannot pay for it. Their attitude can be understood, but for practical purposes it is a highly demanding, aggressive one with strong paranoid overtones. They feel entitled to the best to make up for the injustice inflicted upon them in earliest childhood when they did not receive the warm reception desirable to us all. They point out by their demand to the psychiatrist and by his refusal to comply with their request how inadequate and selfish he is. Little do they realize that it is not the role of the psychiatrist, nor within his capabilities, to pretend he is the all-healing do-gooder on this earth. He is only an instrument, helpful within the scope of his competence and abilities to the extent of his own degree of empathy.

chapter 15

INTERCOURSE—PRESENT, ABSENT, OR IN BETWEEN

If the preservation of human life on this globe is desirable and the biological and highest basic law of nature is preservation of the species, then only heterosexual intercourse between two mature individuals will do. I am aware that modern gynecology has taken many steps to promote reproduction even in the absence of intercourse. Artificial insemination is only one step in this endeavor. In the absence of patent Fallopian tubes, oophoroscopy has been attempted with the aim of obtaining ova from the Graefian follicle and fertilizing them and reimplanting them subsequently into an available uterus. Ultimately, short of parthenogenesis, which has been successfully attempted in frogs, the ovum must be fertilized by semen and must subsequently develop in an appropriate uterus, if the fetus is to be viable. After all is said and done, the normal physiological-biological process is intercourse.

In the free animal kingdom, the selective and reproductive process follows its own laws characteristic for each individual species. Biologists and naturalists devote much of their energy to the observation and description of the mating habits of animals. The more adaptable a species is to changing climatic and environmental conditions, the greater are its chances of survival. High specialization of the living and nutritive pattern of a species means a greater likelihood of disappearing from the world stage when the conditions alter. The Koala bear, for instance, depends exclusively on the availability of leaves of the eucalyptus tree. The anteater needs termites and ants accessible only to him with his long sticky tongue. The silkworm needs the leaves of the mulberry bush.

In human affairs the selection of the fittest encompasses the satisfaction of our emotional needs. The reproductive process, intercourse, can lead to reproduction and childbirth regardless of the state of mind when intercourse takes place between two biologically mature heterosexual individuals as long as the semen reaches the ovum and both are in fertile condition. The ancient Romans had the saying: *Mater semper certa, pater incertus* ("the mother is always certain; the father uncertain"). The female who voluntarily or involuntarily had sexual relations with several males at one time may find it difficult to identify the impregnator. Modern paternity tests may or may not prove paternity.

It is only to the degree that intercourse is the culmination of the biological sex drive and the fulfillment of our emotional needs and heterosexual companionship that it approaches the highest degree of emotional satisfaction in pure, unadulterated realistic form on this earth. The man who gazes on the countenance of his beloved in the ecstasy of climax will feel the highest degree of affirmation of his masculinity and personal gratification at the same time. The female will find the highest emotional needs of her femininity fulfilled in sensing the enjoyment she is able to provide for her beloved.

Much has been written recently about the desirability of trial marriage and contraceptive methods of all types including vasectomy or tubal ligation. I do not deny that even under most favorable circumstances allowances have to be made with regard to the desirability of offspring or further offspring. Shortcuts in the preparation of food are at times unavoidable but while nutritious edible food will still result, the highest delights of culinary art will not permit such shortcuts. In every human endeavor, shortcuts are at times applied and unavoidable, but true excellence demands no expediency. This also applies to sex, love, and intercourse. It is equally true that only the connoisseur of fine food, of art, or of human achievement will be the true judge of quality, because he alone is equipped to appreciate what is presented to him and he alone would rather forego cheap substitutes if real quality is unavailable. It is only the individual who has experienced the delight of love and fulfilling sexual interrelationships who will not settle for anything short of the optimum. What pleasure can an individual, who experienced or who is qualified to experience the epitome of human fulfillment in the arms of the beloved mate, derive from primitive substitutes which serve only to relieve his tension and which fall short of emotional gratification? If, on the other hand, the emotional gratification and companionship is sought in a homosexual relationship, nobody can consider this biologically unreproductive attitude as conforming to the basic laws of nature. Even homosexuality imitates intercourse in one form or another but the imitation is only partially successful since it denies *a priori* the desirability of the opposite sex. The closest approximation of normal biological sex activity is sex in which the penis enters the vagina and through some contraceptive device semen cannot reach the ovum or if semen or ovum has been previously infertilized.

When tubal ligation is considered, excellent judgment of all prevailing circumstances is indicated. Vasectomy, if considered at all, needs the highest degree of medical judiciousness even perhaps to a higher degree because many times the attitudes held prior to vasectomy and afterwards can vary deeply. Many serious emotional disturbances have been precipitated by ill-advised vasectomies. Physicians at times look mostly at this procedure as a minor operation of no organic consequence but a thorough evaluation of the emotional resources of the partners seems indispensable prior to any contemplated intervention.

The rhythm method has many followers and opponents and nobody can deny that the uncertainty of the practice as well as the interference with spontaneity will leave their marks. To substitute other orifices for the vagina, such as mouth or rectum, uses the sex partner more as an object than an equal partner. The mouth used as a sucking organ in infancy will always have some infantile connotations. Equally, kissing is not practiced in all societies and if used only as sexual stimulant and sexual foreplay, nevertheless, has infantile connotations corresponding to the infantile sucking reflex. Cunnilingus substitutes the female vagina for the breast and therefore is an infantilism in a displaced area.

There is perhaps an easy criterion which can indicate to the involved parties the degree of their emotional maturity and the degree of their emotional fulfillment. The extent of pure joy and pleasure not only sensed in the foreplay and in the act of intercourse itself but above all in the happiness experienced mutually after climax and sexual release is the indicator of the personal emotional degree of human development. When we enjoy the other person and our mate makes us happy, what else can there be?

Shortcuts and substitutions are exactly what the name implies—indicators that we through no fault of our own have not yet developed to the point of appreciating the finest and where we refuse to accept a substitute for the very thing which makes life worthwhile, love. Anybody who seeks above all relief of sexual tensions only uses his mate and should not be surprised to find dissatisfaction or resentment eventually from the mate.

The basic fear of the opposite sex will promote an attitude of self-gratification which connotes not only the fear of the opposite sex but also the anachronistic implication that both sexes dwell within the same individual. At the lowest level of the phylogenetical development this was true. Nevertheless, in masturbatory activity the male imitates the vagina with his hands or other objects just as the female uses her fingers or other objects to imitate the penis. If masturbatory practices are used heterosexually for mutual satisfaction during foreplay they are used only as a substitute for the highest type of exaltation which occurs only in deep mutual and emotional dedication. If such practices are carried to orgasm, masturbation may become the sex activity of choice if a serious organic condition precludes intercourse.

Bestiality avoids human emotional involvement and reveals a strong emotional primitiveness and certainly obviates any possible reproduction.

We have reached the point where we should discuss absence of intercourse altogether. Here the various conditions which determine the abstinence will have to be considered.

It is a well-known fact that under conditions of civilization, economic and educational maturity is reached long after biological maturity. This discrepancy makes these years of adolescence one of the most difficult periods in our lives. The sex drive is present in overwhelming force in these early years but our educational-emotional development lags way behind our drives. We want to belong; we want to be accepted; we yearn for physiological release; but what avenues are open to us? Modern contraception has now greatly decreased the necessity of total abstinence or seeking an outlet by frequenting prostitutes. But just because heterosexual opportunities have increased, the desirable sex partner will not necessarily be available or make herself available. After painful experiences, abstinence under such conditions may still be the approach of choice at least for the time being. There are many other periods in the life of the best-adjusted individual when sexual abstinence is the mature adjustment. Sickness of the marital partner is a point in question. Forced absence in war or peace has equally compelling impact, particularly when the emotional development of the individual has reached a higher degree of maturity which means interpersonal dedication and self-respect.

But sexual abstinence because circumstances demand it is quite different from abstinence because of individual choice. The unattached person of either sex who actually avoids any acquaintanceship as soon as it carries the slightest emotional and sexual connotation makes an adjustment to life, not by his own conscious choice it is true, which is antagonistic to the basic law of the preservation of the species. If he or she reaches out for help to gain readjustment, the etiological forces which patterned this attitude may easily become discernible. In the absence of such motivation, his or her life may at times have great merit from a social viewpoint, but friendships cannot totally substitute for the epitome of happiness embodied in an emotionally highly satisfactory heterosexual union.

The total dedication of religious celibacy to idealism instead of reality has by its own definition the connotation of unreality which is delusional.

The Vestal Virgins were dedicated to their goddess and nuns are called the Brides of Christ.

Indeed, sexual abstinence is often considered more virtuous than physiological intercourse. This attitude is reminiscent of the belief that this life represents only the vale of tears which we have to pass through in order to reach eternal bliss. Is it not apparent to the blindest that delusional hope is used to compensate for the deficiency of the realistic presence? Is it not self-evident that such an attitude, although understandable, is nevertheless unrealistic and therefore psychotic?

The sex act in itself, depending on how it is performed or whether it is performed at all, can be considered the quintessence and summary of our own emotional adjustment to life.

When Freud first evolved his libidinal concept, he found much rejection. Only gradually did it become clear that genital and libidinal sex could not be used interchangeably. Genital practices without the adequate heterosexual emotional concomitants of mature involvement are unworthy of the human potentialities and therefore have to be experienced as debasing and unsatisfactory. Mature love ennobles the biological urges and drives.

chapter 16

FLEXIBILITY, RIGIDITY, AND PERSEVERANCE

The imprinting which we receive in our infancy and childhood is the matrix for our personality pattern with which we have to live our lives for better or worse. The more our mere presence gave joy and pleasure to our parents, the more it pleased our mother to see us develop in an adequate fashion, the more we are likely to turn out self-accepting and fit to take our proper place on this earth. Under these conditions we will not be patterned to serve the emotional needs of our mother; whereas under less favorable conditions, she would have, unaware, used us to substitute for the emotional needs existing from her own childhood, and ultimately not fulfilled by her mate. We will sense the emotional need which our mother has attached to our existence. We will feel torn between our innate biological striving toward independence and our emotionally conditioned symbiotic relationship with our mother. We cannot let our mother down even at the price of self-destruction.

Enlightened psychiatry places less emphasis on the specific features of an emotional and mental disturbance and goes to great lengths to classify secondary symptomatology, describing a variety of disease entities which basically have one common etiological denominator. The more disturbed our emotional background was, the less our own emotional mature needs were part of the pattern formation. We were not wanted; we provided no joy for our parents; we were experienced mostly as burdens, and we either had to knock ourselves out in the vain hope of finding acceptance and a gleam of joy in the eyes of our mother, or we took the pattern placed before us—everybody for himself. Nothing that happened to us subsequently could supersede this early programming. We will follow this imprinted pattern with the greatest inflexibility, regardless of how unsatisfactory the responses may be. Indeed, it can truly be said about individuals who fall into this category that they are unable to learn from mistakes.

Flexibility implies that we received a pattern formation which permitted us to adapt ourselves to the exigencies of a changing environment. This adaptability equipped us to bend with the needs of a changing world as the willow tree is able to bend with the storm and thus survives. This adaptability and flexibility is only another expression of the selection of the fittest.

Rigidity, on the other hand, results when the early imprint upon us is of such nature that we were to serve the emotional need of our mother. To the degree this was the case, we were patterned to unyieldingly serve this purpose. Although this pattern formation was in constant conflict with our own biological needs and, therefore, resulted in persistent conflict, once established it left little room for subsequent adaptability.

Changing environmental requirements did not find us conditioned to bend with the wind, so to speak, and when the pressures became too strong, we were more likely to succumb and break than to ride out the storm. An unyielding rigid attitude is on the surface many times very impressive and perceived as a sign of great strength whereas, if inappropriately applied, it is basically a self-destructive force.

The question finally boils down to resisting pressures with all one's might when indicated and appropriate in the constructive sense, but yielding appropriate adaptability when such resistance is only self-serving and an expression of one's own stubborn rigidity. The difference is a question of judgment and adequate judgment will serve realistic constructive ends whereas deficient judgment is steeped in serving one's own emotional needs.

It is truly tragic when we see human beings who follow, unknown to themselves, a personality pattern for the formation of which they were not responsible in the first place, for which in human vanity they blame themselves, and yet which sooner or later leads them to unhappiness and self-destruction.

The natural law of the selection of the fittest truly applies to mankind, just as it applies to all other forms of life. Only on an emotional, subconscious level can these individuals feel gratification because they serve their mother either as an outlet for her displeasure which gave her some relief or as an emotional crutch which again gave her some comfort.

This rigid inflexible attitude is mitigated to the degree our birth and existence gave comfort, pleasure, and even joy to our mother. Let us speak of the optimal condition and then we can always determine how far our own pattern formation falls short of this optimum.

Under optimal conditions, our mother will feel exhilarated to have the good fortune of being pregnant by her beloved mate and being instrumental in keeping life going on this earth (thus contributing to the preservation of the species) and, in so doing, recreating the image of the beloved mate and herself which is the only realistic form of immortality on this earth, limited as the concept of immortality may be in this respect.

The child will sense the joy his mere presence creates in his mother. He will sense that he is treated as an individual, dependent and helpless though he may be at first. He will develop self-acceptance and self-esteem. He will sense only to a lesser degree that he has to serve the purpose of his parents but will not feel guilty because his parents were dedicated to him since they enjoyed him by so doing. He will in his own good time be as ready as his parents were to be an adequate parent to his own children and at the same time feel full of gratitude to his parents for all their joyful dedication. In this respect he cannot help but love his parents. Love does not come about upon command and demand but freely, spontaneously given as the most natural sequence of events.

Such a fortunate individual will not feel tied down by his emotional attachment to his parents. He will be equipped to deal with each presenting situation objectively according to its intrinsic merits or demerits. He knows that what is good for him will please his parents whose emotional gratification is secured by his success and happiness. He can be flexible enough to adjust himself to the exigencies of a changing situation and this adjustability will secure a better chance of survival and success. He does not have to prove anything—neither his strength nor his existence in the face of hopelessness. We have to be strong enough to surrender in the face of hopeless defeat, when further resistance is tantamount to suicide. Distinguishing between a hopeless situation and one where persistence can be useful is at times difficult and crucial.

Animals of the same species usually do not fight to the point of annihilation but, if they feel defeated, they honestly acknowledge this fact either by leaving the field of contest or by expressing outright an attitude of total surrender by rolling on their backs and exposing their jugular vein to the victor. The animal is generous—the victor has prevailed—he does not seek the destruction of his erstwhile opponent. Only in human affairs do we want to deal once and for all with a situation and show at times little compassion for the vanquished. Our fear of being confronted again by the same challenge makes us ruthless at times. However, it is exactly this ruthlessness which will recreate ill will and resentment and this in turn will subsequently jeopardize our own chances of survival. Utter ruthlessness is a sign of inner weakness and fear and is only a camouflage to hide our emotional weakness. The ruthless masters present a pitiful picture when they find themselves in difficulties. The emotionally strong person will accept the inevitability of an unfavorable fate and face up to it squarely.

If we decide to serve another person dear to us, there may be no limit to the extent to which our judgment tells us we should go. On the other hand, if we try to prove a point in itself insignificant only to demonstrate our strength and unbending inflexibility (which we mistakenly consider good signs of character), then we cannot be surprised when we find that we ultimately have little to show for all our efforts but our own emotional self-gratification.

We can simplify these statements to the point that any attitude is justified and mature when it serves a realistic purpose and we are fully aware of its factual and realistic implications.

If, on the other hand, our attitude is primarily inspired by emotional considerations, we are not realistic. If we try to date a girl because she is pleasing and appealing to us, any persistence is justified as long as the answer is not a clear "no." If, on the contrary, we only try to prove a point, whatever this point may be, the emotional motivation of our persistence will have an unsatisfactory outcome even if on the surface we seem to succeed.

Stubborn persistence and inspired perseverance are two qualities completely opposite to each other. Whereas the former only serves to preserve the emotional self-gratification of unyielding strength without any worthwhile realistic purpose, the latter disregards completely the emotional implications. Realistic perserverance is goal-directed. It will not deviate from the indicated path under any conditions as long as the value of the desired end is greater than the difficulties.

The qualifications of a person can be measured by his dedication to a desired goal. At times it appears that long years of study to obtain certain degrees and titles serve just as much to eliminate less dedicated applicants from obtaining the desired status as the imparting of objective knowledge.

In a horse race, running on the flat and clearing hurdles, persistence and stamina are tested as much as the temporary burst of energy. In a wonderful monologue-aria in Wagner's *Die Meistersinger,* Hans Sachs, the old master, explains to the young radiant knight, Walther Stolzing, "Who is a real master? In youth we can all sing and write poems; it is spring itself which bursts forth; however, as we get older in spite of all the vicissitudes which life brings us, who then still sings a song, He is the real master!"

The concept of maturity and conversely immaturity should be understood in the same context. Maturity connotes nothing but that we have learned to function independently of our parents, emotionally as well as physically, to the greatest satisfaction of all concerned. We were endowed in our formative years with the acceptance and warmth which equipped us to develop into self-accepting, functioning human beings able to take the center stage and to enjoy it to a high degree as well as to rejoice in the responsibility which we are now equipped to shoulder. We are entitled to get tired at times. Nothing is perfect and night follows day. But after the night there is another day and we carry on until finally our life's work is done and we can look back on a worthwhile, well-spent life.

Immaturity, on the other hand, is a sequel to a formative period in childhood where our emotional independence was never considered. Immature parents raise immature children and the emotional requirements of the parents impose their own needs upon the helpless dependent child who in a way is victimized. A pattern is therefore imprinted upon the child which will become his personality structure. The child's own emotional needs remain unfulfilled and he will go through life as far as his path leads him with this void. He will sense responsibilities as burdens and impositions and will run into difficulties anytime performance in the face of the slightest stress is expected. These individuals act as though the world owes them a living. They will complain that nobody cares; they will show physical or emotional stress reactions if they attempt to face up to a stressful situation in a constructive fashion. If the home situation in the formative years was forbidding, the immaturity will take a pattern where self-gratification, regardless of who gets hurt, be comes the imprint. Indeed, the unbearable feeling of immaturity may grow to such disastrous proportions that only the inflicting of pain upon others gives the feeling of strength and power. If we are so disposed, we take a gun and try to impose our will upon other people. With a gun we obtain the feeling of power and manliness, the absence of which was completely unbearable to us. We call a hardened criminal an individual who does not readjust his thinking processes in the face of all punishing experiences. Lack of virility is viewed by such individuals as equivalent to mental disease, which in fact is a quite realistic evaluation. Therefore, some of these absolute rigid individuals are not equipped to bend in the slightest way but prefer to shoot it out to their ultimate annihilation rather than surrender and give themselves to a review of their basic pattern formation. Indeed, in dying they will try to victimize as many persons at the same time as possible. Recently, a convicted murderer who attempted a break-out by holding hostages, argued that the authorities gambled with their lives by not immediately giving in to his requests. It does not occur to such an individual to question the justification of his own attitude which used hostages for his own end, in the first place.

chapter 17

PUBERTY: AN ATTEMPT TO BECOME INDEPENDENT

Let us first consider ideal conditions but never lose sight of the fact that these conditions are only hypothetically assumptive and can at best only be approximated, but never fulfilled in the imperfect world of human affairs.

Let us assume that the two parents thoroughly, deeply, and completely approved of each other and in love conceived a child. This child will be cherished by both parents. The parents will be well aware of the needs of the infant and deal with him properly. Although this infant is totally helpless and dependent on the administrations of his parents, they in turn will treat him as a precious individual and the fact that the infant and child totally depends on them will in no way influence them in their consideration of him as a human being, an individual in his own right. The child will grow up with no difficulty in feeling himself to be a person. He will readily go to his parents for advice and guidance whenever the situation calls for it. What he feels capable of doing, he will do, and he will not feel the need to take inappropriate risks to prove his value. He will stay with his parents as long as his development requires it and will become self-sufficient as soon as he is ready to do so.

We see that in the animal kingdom such a condition prevails but the human feature of feeling "I am somebody" is, of course, missing.

Ideal parents never try to speed up the maturation process of the child nor try to retard it, consciously or unconsciously. Only those who feel privileged to bring up a new generation will at no time experience this as a burden. The growing child will never feel the inclination to be rebellious and defiant toward his parents, sensing perfectly well that his personality needs are fully considered by his parents to the point that they wish him to mature and become independent of them in due course. They will not be in need of his emotional attachment to them, since their own emotional requirements have been adequately fulfilled by each other. The love and appreciation of the child will be spontaneous and unavoidable for work well done by his parents. No commandments will have to be issued to force him into an attitude which is inappropriate for the circumstances which surrounded his upbringing. The child will not develop guilt feelings and doubts in his own appropriate reactivity when he notices the discrepancy between the expected love for his parents and his own feelings of being unfairly treated by them.

Of course, we know that all parents do the best they can, horribly inadequate though it may be. They cannot be faulted for their attitudes toward the infant. However, the parents are the infant's gods and he cannot be expected, certainly not in the early all-important years of formative development, to make allowances for the shortcomings of his parents. Sadly enough, parents have to plead later on for indulgence from their children to whom they owed a full measure of dedication. The discrepancy between the reality of circumstances and the condition which is desirable is obvious.

We know, and it cannot be repeated often enough, that the parents are only the result of their own upbringing and the emotional endowment which they received in their own early years. But, deplorably deficient and devastating as their own emotional endowment was, to the same degree they are unable to be emotionally adequate for their offspring but are rather more likely to be disastrously damaging. A reversal of the basic law of nature will take place. Instead of the parent generation totally serving the justified needs of the new generation (and generation will follow generation and in maturity each will unhesitatingly fulfill its requirement to its own offspring and thus repay its parents indirectly), the new generation will start on its way on this earth in an emotionally crippled condition. The child will be called on by his parents to serve their emotional needs. He will be kept in a dependency situation long after such dependency is no longer called for. He will be discouraged from showing manifestations of his own individuality and any attempt at self-assertion will be vehemently, if not violently, opposed. The parents will be unable to perceive the emotional need for self-manifestation and will feel greatly hurt, if not outraged, by such a desire to lead an independent, self-respecting existence. Parents will impose rules of behavior upon their children long after a general understanding of human coexistence should have been obtained. They will use any method available to them to bring about results comforting to them. The iron fist in the velvet glove will at times use sickness and ill health, real or imaginary, to exert pressure on the children to make them malleable to the parents' own wishes and needs.

I know a school teacher in her forties who never married and who lives with her mother who tells her that there are plenty of women who marry only when they are fifty years old. Each time her daughter shows any signs of freeing herself from this bondage, the mother becomes totally exhausted. It is as if the child has to atone for the sin of being born and the mother feels justified in making the child pay for the inconvenience if not revulsion she experienced at time of intercourse, gestation, delivery, and ever after. Now, being grown up, the child becomes useful to her and since the child was never perceived as an individual in her own right, no qualms accompany this attitude of the mother. The child serves her and the child is destroyed at the same time. This is the brutal fact.

We can see again and again that precisely those children who were least desired in a family constellation and who were, so to speak, considered the black sheep, will in later years, or in the old age of the parent, go to any lengths in their striving on behalf of the parents despite discomfort to themselves in the subconscious and vain hope that the mother ultimately may utter the deeply longed for words, "I love you; I am glad I had you; I am glad you are my child."

The resulting reaction formation of the child will depend on the relationship between the parents. If the mother is of a dependent personality pattern who remains with the husband in spite of her serious disapproval of him, the child will perceive the father as the fearsome enemy whom he must defeat for his own salvation and to rescue his mother from overpowering oppression. The child will equally resent the weakness of the mother whose dependency needs stop her from standing up to her mate openly, frankly, and courageously. Many times, in similar cases, real or surmised physical difficulties arise and it is here that modern medicine serves best as a face-saving alibi. For emotional dyspareunia, some physical excuse has to be found, whether it is a tilted womb, some questionable adhesions, or some minor fanciful deviation from what is considered the norm. In similar cases, at times a woman may put up little fight to preserve her womb. Hysterectomy at times becomes a very desirable solution, although nobody would part with an eye as readily and under such weak indications without consulting another physician. The surgery and the concomitant attention will be experienced as salubrious certainly as long as it justifiably seems to account for the need of special consideration. If the emotional need of such an individual is not adequately fulfilled by such surgical procedures, a situation can arise in which the surgeon wishes he had never started any procedure at all. Such a person with unfulfilled emotional needs together with a strong tendency towards aggressiveness may put herself in the framework of thinking that all her "real" troubles only started with the surgical procedure. She then has an apparently logical excuse justifying her persistent feeling of resentment which, however, has been projected on an immaterial side issue. Just as the psychiatrist is at times at his best when he is used as the outlet for the projected resentment of his patient, so the surgical procedure is incriminated, usually falsely, in subsequent difficulties. At times, the dependency need of the woman will go so far that she stays with her husband although she faces an unbearable situation, intolerable to the point that realistic contact with life is seriously impaired. Mental hospitalization then becomes indicated and electroshock treatment or other physical-chemical methods of treatment may also be indicated, depending on the speed "recovery" is expected.

How must a child feel at seeing his mother hospitalized in a mental institution and perhaps having to undergo electroshock treatments? All depressions are self-limited in duration, unless suicide intervenes, and one is prepared to wait even years for their resolution.

The situation can, of course, be completely reversed. A man can be completely dependent on his wife who is perhaps the only person who permitted him to have sexual intercourse with her and thus gives him the illusion of manliness. We can only speculate how such a woman feels any time such a man approaches her with sexual desire. She may feel that he is oblivious to her feelings and only tries to satisfy himself. She is likely to treat him with great disregard and when he eventually dies of a heart attack, she may think that he has finally proved that he was a good man after all, or, conversely, that he was inconsiderate in leaving her inadequately provided for.

The variations between the parents are endless. Alcohol, adultery, or total submersion in church or professional activities are only a few of the expedients resorted to at times to permit the continuance of a situation which in itself has become intolerable.

This is the background against which the children grow up and are even expected to thrive. If two parents merely put up with each other for the sake of the children, they at least make an effort toward decency although the child will sense the strain on his parents and blame himself for it. Few are the parents who seek professional psychiatric help consistently and determinedly enough to become objective about themselves and, therefore, about their companion in order to reach a point of self-acceptance compatible with adequacy toward their children. Strictly speaking, all these parents are at crossroads. Will they continue in the pattern their own parents imprinted into them and thus preserve the sense of loyalty to their parents even though at the same time they remain, emotionally at least, immature children and serve the past generation? Or will they now emancipate themselves from their early programming for the sake of the future generation, their own children? Here the empathetic potentialities of the psychiatrist will be of the utmost importance. He has to sense when he should listen and when he should speak and if he speaks every word and expression has to convey his sense of deep understanding. Studies and learning, however, can never substitute for the kinship of experience.

We can make an almost dogmatic statement to the effect that the more seriously disturbed human beings are the less they will be available or make themselves available to the uncovering types of psychiatric approaches. Medication and other forms of treatment modalities will be acceptable but deep-going insight cannot be hoped for.

Children grow up in environments which vary from deplorable to disastrous. If parents wish to fool themselves about their adequacy, they may. Providing for the material needs of the family ought to be a joy and privilege, not an exhausting burden on the bread-winner. The maintenance of a home should equally be a joy to the woman. Any time life is less than a joy, it is inadequate. I am not so unrealistic as not to realize limitations, but without even a touch of joy, life is a dull experience.

To the degree the child feels his existence interferes with the well-being of his mother in particular and his parents in general, he must feel compelled to leave the family situation. Many children run away long before they are equipped to be self-supporting and to know adequately the pitfalls of life. Disturbed and unhappy as they are, they attach themselves to any individual or group which gives them the semblance of independence. Their bodies can become the means of support and it is not surprising that at times they fill the emergency rooms of hospitals after having taken excessive doses of all the various drugs which are so easily accessible to the young in our day. Drug consumption is an escape from unhappiness and unbearable reality but it is more than that. "I want fun in this life and I don't care what price is demanded or who pays the price." It is hedonistic pleasure-seeking without any scruples whatsoever. How self-centered and self-seeking must the parents have been to produce such end results!

Children and juveniles have always been eager to be on their own. There is nothing wrong in a child wanting to be grown up. Little girls try on the shoes of their mothers and cherish dolls and playing "house" is their favorite pastime in early childhood. Boys have their own games which they consider manly. In the past, they adventurously went to sea, joined the Army, or left for new shores. Alcohol was used extensively as so many drinking songs attest to. Wayfaring journeymen were a common sight in many countries, expressing the restlessness of youth similar to students who attended various universities as a welcome pretext for restlessness. It is conceded that leaving home became a necessity at times due to limitations of living conditions. Even as apprentices in a trade, they had to live in different households.

Girls at times get married so early that they are certainly not prepared for all the responsibilities of such an undertaking. The overriding motivation is to get away from home and the young husband could be considered used as much as he uses his immature wife. When pregnancy takes place, a disaster is not far behind.

It is true that increased civilization necessitates long-term educational dedication and prolonged dependency on parental support, which, in a way, is unacceptable to large cross sections of adolescents. The rebellion of youth will at times take the form of outright law-challenging and law-defying behaviors. Indeed, if they belong to groups which they consider underprivileged, they will think themselves important when they indulge in destructive activities. Their attitude, although not acceptable, is understandable in view of their persistent frustration. After all, men want to feel equal, particularly if realistically or self-consciously they feel relegated to inferior status on the totem pole arrangement of the social order. It is easy to preach with a full stomach and it is equally easy to establish laws which tend to preserve one's own prerogatives. And the do-gooder, the Francis of Assisi, is disturbed in the first place. This rebellion is equally and perhaps surprisingly found among the children of the well-to-do. Many times such rebellious behavior is kept under wraps since the parents are equipped to cover up either by restitution or by availing themselves of legal and psychiatric advice and help. The question can be raised: in the rebellion of the well-to-do, is there not a modicum of social justice discernible?

If in puberty there is the first chance for independence, this independence from parents is merely switched to dependency on other persons or institutions. If welfare or other agencies have to fill the void, the independence was only an imaginary one and consisted of nothing but getting away from home while dragging the cord behind them. In the animal kingdom, the cubs are left to their own devices as soon as their mother deems them ready for independent existence. In human affairs, this natural law of succession is greatly disturbed because of human emotional inadequacies.

Youthful rebellion, in a rather harmless way, can express itself in styles of clothing, hair styles, and special artistic expressions such as musical forms and rhythms and all sorts of innovative artistic manifestations. An essential part in all these attitudes is the shock effect on the parent generation. We must do our own thing, like it or not, and as long as it does not become self-destructive and basically unacceptable, this outlet of rebellious self-expression is within tolerable limits.

chapter 18

THE GENTLE ESCAPE—THE ARTS

In the southern part of France and in the Spanish Pyrenees, in the green valleys of the Vegere and Dordoyne at Altamira in Spain, there are magnificent limestone cave paintings going back to about 30,000 years B.C., the late Paleolithic times. These paintings arc primarily found on walls and ceilings of caves, the entrances to which are barely noticeable to the unsearching eye and narrow to the point that one has to enter them in a crouching or crawling position. Inside the caves deep darkness soon surrounds the visitor. At times, the passage narrows down again, then suddenly, in tremendous natural halls, these magnificent wall paintings become visible by artificial light. Animal outlines of bears, bison, rhinoceroses, and horses, and paintings of hunting scenes predominate. The earliest representations are outlines cut in stone and burnished. There are pictures of animals with arrows piercing them. Traps drawn next to these animals can also be identified. More than sixty such caves have been found in France, Spain, and Italy. Darkness and humidity helped to preserve the magnificent pictures. Natural pigments were used to fill in the outlines of the figures. The caves contain no trace of having served as abodes for human occupancy. Scientists have, therefore, come to the conclusion that these sacred caverns were places of religious worship and rites and the animal paintings were a predominant part of these exercises. Bleeding wounds are very realistically depicted in red ochre. Actual spear holes perforated other animal outlines. This represented an outright killing of these animals. Primitive man had the delusion that through sympathetic magic, as anthropology calls it, he had the power of success in the hunt. Sir James George Frazier in *The Golden Bough* identifies sympathetic magic as a belief based on the assumption that like produces like—the law of similarity. It is implied by the magician or shaman that any effect desired can be produced by imitating it. Incantations were probably used by shamans in much earlier periods of human development going back roughly 80,000 years to the Mousterian culture. The shamans ministered to the physical ills of men. They tried to placate or exorcise the evil spirits with incantations and magical spells. Stone Age men tied up the corpses of their dead at times to assure that their wandering spirits would not reanimate the body and thus endanger the survivors. They placed weapons, food, jewelry, and red ochre (which symbolized life in their religious paintings) into the graves of the dead, hoping to sustain and placate the spirit in its new existence.

Hundreds of large open-air sanctuaries which were enclosed by large slabs and pillars of rock have been found in Scandinavia, Ireland, France, Britain, Spain, Portugal, Italy, and Malta. These big stones are called "megaliths." The most famous of these sites is Stonehenge in England. These sites came into existence when, at the end of the Paleolithic Age, the glaciers receded and men emerged from their caves. The basic form of the megalithic architecture is upright stones topped by a slab. There is a resemblance to a tomb but their gigantic dimensions suggest other usage, probably worship or implied studies. Some definite arrangements of the megaliths at Stonehenge coincide with the winter solstice—the moment when the sun god dies and subsequently is reborn, according to belief. As man emerged from his dark caves because of climatic changes, he lifted his eyes toward the sun.

This chapter is not meant as an outline of the fascinating anthropological development of man since his earliest beginnings, nor do I mean to follow art through all its history and the various forms of its manifestations. In this chapter I only wish to hint at the well-known fact that art in its earliest beginnings was intimately related to, if not a substantial part of, magical thinking and beliefs. This relationship is probably not only confined to a specific area nor to a specific period of time but is universal, including all primitive peoples of any time and geographical location whether they have been dead for 30,000 years or whether they still survive in remote areas.

Out of magical beliefs religions evolved. The early food gatherers, who developed into hunters over thousands and thousands of years, eventually acquired the skill and understanding to plant seeds and to domesticate animals. Earlier, they had developed the bow and arrow, which allowed them to stalk and kill swift prey while remaining unseen. They had learned to build fish traps and to dry the surplus for future use. All these developments followed after the glaciers began to recede mysteriously about 20,000 years ago. Trees took root in the warming earth; lakes and rivers were formed from the melting ice. Life outside of caves in the open was easier and more abundant.

All these developments were still unrecorded since man had not yet learned the art of writing. It is believed that agriculture and domestication of animals occurred first in the Old World in the sunny areas between modern Asia Minor, northern Iraq, Iran, and southern Asia. Probably these developments can be dated as having taken place between 6,000 and 7,000 years B.C. Agriculture developed independently in the ricelands of the Far East. It also came to the Americas. The Biblical Garden of Eden was said to have been located in the area of highest fertility between the Euphrates and Tigris rivers. In Neolithic times the climate there was warm and dry as today, but verdure more abundant. The land had not yet been ravaged by later generations of man. It was studded with trees and meadows of wild wheat and barley. The basic crops were present in a wild state, and so were the basic animals —sheep, goats, cattle, pigs. The rainfall was adequate for grain. Villages developed.

Slowly, three great civilizations arose in the fertile valleys of the Old World. The Nile overflowed its banks each summer year after year and deposited rich black silt which permitted two or even three harvests in the mild climate. Along the banks of the Euphrates and Tigris, the cities of Sumer developed —the "land of Shinar," in the words of the Old Testament. It was later known as Mesopotamia.

The Indus in the area which today forms part of Pakistan and India is the third site of an emerging civilization. This early Indus civilization left few traces except for physical remains of their towns and cities and other excavations. It flourished for about 1,000 years and probably succumbed to invasions by Asians generally called "Aryans." Unlike the Sumerian and Egyptian civilizations, the Indus civilization had little impact on Western civilization but did influence the later Hindu people of India.

The time came when the long prehistory of man from its earliest dawn drew to its close. The Egyptians had learned to adorn the tombs of noblemen with hieroglyphic texts, praising their lives on this earth and expressing hopes for their continuation in the next. They had invented ink and papyrus reeds were found in abundance along the Nile.

The Sumerians used bricks made of clay as their main building material. At an early stage, they used sharpened reeds and made pictographs of human heads, fish, trees, birds, and spears on rough tablets. Gradually, these symbols no longer represented actual things but turned into abstract signs. Over another thousand years, the old pictographs were changed into wedge-shaped impressions made on soft clay by a cut reed. This was cuneiform or wedge-shaped writing.

There also was writing in the early Indus civilization but little of it has come down to us and it has not yet been deciphered.

From its earliest beginning, when primitive tools and implements were adorned with scratched-in pictures and cave walls were adorned with highly artistic pictures, art was put into the service of magic. Perhaps art in itself was the magic or sympathetic magic, as Frazier calls it.

The development of music and dance as a form of human activity is hidden in the mysterious ages of primitive man. He certainly heard the songs of birds. Many animals stamp their feet in rhythm or flap their wings in dance-like motions. Gorillas beat their chests. Most animals, unless forced to fight by hunger or in defense, prefer snarling and growling to outright fighting and possible mutilation. Man had ample opportunity to observe the animals and, using sympathetic magic, to imitate them. Rhythmic beating of implements had the realistic purpose of bringing game into the open for the kill, but it also served to arouse war-like spirits, to stir up war-like and killer instincts in man. The monotonous repetition of a sound has a tendency to bring about a trance-like sensation in the exposed individual which was well known to the early shamans who put themselves into a spiritual frenzy which had its infectious effect on the participants in rites and ceremonies. Mass hysteria initiated by fanatical leaders has always required martial music and drums. The rhythmic march-step of soldiers from the Roman legions to our day is infectious. The rhythm of a mother's heartbeat is the cradle song of life.

Writing a complete history of the arts, the creative arts and the performing arts, in each civilization, can only be attempted, never completed. In this chapter I only wish to point out that creative as well as performing arts have their origin in the fathomless eons of man's emergence from the animal kingdom and seemed magical in themselves.

However, there seemed to come a time when the artist became self-serving and his creations and renditions became enjoyable for their own sake. Man, who was no longer satisfied to be a creature of this earth like all his fellow forms of nature, wanted in his vanity to find a purpose and meaning to his life. But, as this meaning was elusive and when best maintained, it served only to glorify God, life became meaningless and empty to all those who were realistic enough not to completely submerge themselves in psychotic-unrealistic concepts. Art became a solace, a refuge, an escape. It became *Ars pro arte,* or, as Schiller's poem, so beautifully set to music by Franz Schubert, states, the thanks which the artist owes to his art for helping him over the vicissitudes of life. I cannot indulge here in hairsplitting discussions about what is true art or who is a true artist. Suffice it to say that true art has a universal appeal and is timeless. There are few individuals who are not deeply touched before Laocoön or when gazing at the Parthenon, staring up at the ceilings of the Sistine Chapel, or standing in awe before ancient Incan and Mayan art. The Greek tragedies, Homer's epics, Dante's *Divine Comedy,* Shakespeare's plays—all have a timelessness which has its origin in appealing to the most human features in all of us.

Art, as well as artists, comes in all degrees of skill and dedication. "Enthusiasm" is derived from the Greek word meaning to carry God within ourselves. Perhaps "possessed," "totally dedicated," and "fanatical" can all be used interchangeably. Yes, these artists may be disturbed when viewed from an objective, analytical perspective, but so too was Freud himself who tried to overcome his own deep-seated sense of emotional insecurity in a most dedicated effort to become objective about himself and, thus, about others. These great artists create and perform and by so doing serve themselves and the beholder. They assuage the monotony of life, not necessarily with power struggles where other people are hurt and destroyed to achieve the goal. Nor are they so withdrawn from the progress of life that they wish to have no part of it. They are part of life, and, at the same time, lead their own lives which do not hurt anybody, but serve to help us over our own hours of indifference or depression.

The songs of Orpheus gained him admission into Hades, and the Greek priests were not ill-advised when soothing songs were heard in their temples where emotionally and mentally distressed people sought refuge. I feel that artistic forms of self-expression cannot be emphasized enough in the treatment of emotionally and mentally disturbed individuals and the performing arts can play a larger role in mental institutions. Anything which contributes to making this life appear more pleasant in a realistic way contributes to an improved adjustment of an individual and his outlook on life.

There are additional features. Anybody who has observed a disturbed person digging his fingers into a glob of damp clay, which he had been invited to form into shapes of his own choosing, notices the strong aggressive element contained in his approach. Indeed, it has been said that at times the artist furiously attacks his canvas, or the sculptor the material with which he works. Great masters, at times, unsatisfied with their own performances, have destroyed their own handiwork. Is it not better to slash a painting or tear up a poem than to commit suicide? Many times the efforts of psychiatrically oriented people are directed to the young and in particular to persons with whom they can readily identify as well as to people with whom verbal communication is possible; in other words, to people who are in good contact and with whom they wish to reason. In the first place, reasoning is only possible if the other person is emotionally open-minded enough to widen his viewpoint.

When I was a young psychiatric resident in a state hospital, I initiated a weekly program of community singing. Elderly chronic patients were assembled in sizeable numbers in the recreation hall, which was usually reserved for activities of the younger and less chronically afflicted patients. The lyrics of very popular old songs were projected on the large screen on the podium. The help of a very dedicated organist was obtained and with zest and gusto—however lacking in vocal qualifications as I was—I tried to stir up this old and forgotten, backward population to life and song. It was inspiring to see how, for a short time at least, some life seemed to return to these ancient ruins who did not know of any better adjustment to the vicissitudes of their existence than to become totally defeated. And even those who did not sing—and there were many—seemed to beat the tune with their feet and fingers. They all returned willingly week after week to this experience of music and enthusiasm. The superintendent, in the true tradition of administrative caution, said he would keep an eye on me, apparently fearing repercussions which might result from this undertaking. Ultimately, the nurses and aides who were needed to supervise the smooth transfer of the patients could not be spared from other duties and so the program came to an end.

Children, newly introduced to the ways of this life, have a great affinity for make-believe, play-acting, painting, playing with such plastic substances as clay, sand, and later carving, chiseling, etc. It gives them not only imaginary companions which they lack in reality, but also a mode of expressing their feelings in an unrestrained, genuine fashion which they have learned is mostly unacceptable in real life. They can vent their feelings in the true tradition of sympathetic magic. They certainly like to beat noisily on any object that is available and pots and pans are their special delight. The phylogenetic development of mankind is relived in every child in his early period.

Art is the salve of life. It does not cure its ills but it makes them bearable. It can even create a feeling of well-being and ecstasy, reminiscent of true orgasm. It is a substitute but one which does not hurt anybody and which can be shared by many. The joy of life "for life's sake" is a rare commodity. We have to be tuned into ourselves and must come to accept ourselves quite well to approximate even this state of emotional equilibrium. Art is one of the most acceptable forms of a crutch that helps us through this life. Titian, the great Italian painter, had to wait for the plague before he finally died at the age of 99. Picasso, Pablo Casals, Toscanini, and many other great artists have reached very ripe old ages. Of course, there were many who consumed themselves in early years, like Mozart, Schubert, and Lord Byron. Some artists, in spite of their art, finally fall into mental oblivion. Robert Schumann and Vincent Van Gogh come immediately to mind. It is equally true that artists are not necessarily the easiest people to live with and their personal adjustments to life show great inadequacies. We are little concerned whether Michelangelo had homosexual tendencies, whether Goethe had innumerable love affairs or, at least, fell in love all the time, and for ten years courted a married woman, or whether nobody could live with Beethoven who left us the *Choral Symphony,* or whether Richard Wagner married Cosima, the wife of his best friend, etc. Great prices apparently have to be paid for singular performances.

Top achievements in any field require exclusivity at the expense of other qualifications. This holds true not only for the arts but for other human endeavors too. An example is sports, which in a way are akin to art. Indeed, it becomes debatable whether accomplished figure-skating is to be considered a sport or an art. Gymnastics also belong in this in-between land. The appealing beauty of the performance of an Olga Korbut combines body control, skill, and grace to the highest extent.

When we speak of style in any sport, it is the minimum expenditure of brute force combined with highest results which seems appealing. We call such a performance a thing of beauty. Diving is another such sport. Grace here also is the ultimate prerequisite.

Anybody who has ever witnessed the performance of the Spanish Riding Academy of Vienna, the famous Lippizan stallions, cannot deny that the artistic endeavor can manifest itself even in the performance and training of animals. Appropriately, classical music accompanies their performances. Their quadrilles and minuets are in the best tradition of the dance.

In the arts, we can relive our most tender feelings and give unqualified expression to all the fury a human being is capable of. Murder, as long as it is expressed in music, drama, painting, or sculpture, is eminently acceptable. The poet will turn into the most sensitive verses his longing for a maiden who just went off and eloped with someone else. If it were not for the verse, we would call him insane, thoroughly in love with himself. That he projects his feelings on paper or canvas or stone is the saving grace. He may be celebrated and famous; he alone knows what he is lacking.

In the performing arts, women abound. In ballet, one male dancer is outnumbered by many females although perhaps in modern dance some change may occur. On the stage, women have held their own for a long time although originally young boys had to take female parts in opera and drama. Composing, painting, sculpting, and architecture until very modern times—with few exceptions—were male domains. It almost seems that from the time of stone age man—when the female fertility goddess was first replaced by the overpowering male gods, from Zeus to Wotan to Yahweh and all the other war gods—to the present time when the blessing of God is invoked before any war-like encounter that the male of the species has arrogated to himself a place of dominance extending apparently even to a high degree into the art world.

Or could it be that women after all are somewhat more realistic than men? If the mother, as previously outlined, for all visible purposes is the more dominant and significant figure in the early life of an infant, then the girl can look forward in direct line to succeed her mother, whereas a boy has first to find pleasure in her eyes to feel he is somebody. Please don't misunderstand me—I don't intend to say that it is not equally important to the girl to awaken pleasure in her mother to become self-assured. But she is of the same sex as the mother and, therefore, may find it easier to identify with her. Many times women seek help from wherever it may come. They feel less compunction about fraternizing with enemy soldiers than their brothers. They seek out help in churches, in doctors' offices, and in psychiatric sessions more readily than men. Help is what they want; their pride is not the same as a man's who confuses pride with self-love. Anybody who is in need of help and seeks it is more realistic than the one who in self-love has to believe he can do it alone. If the aforesaid is true, and I am not convinced that it should not be open to discussion, this may provide a reason why women did not have to escape into the creative arts as much as men. Nor, to their glory, did they play as active a role in magic and religion, although their role in witchcraft was undisputed. They were only rarely the leaders; they were the inspired followers perversely secure in the leadership of men.

Just as there is a considerable difference in the emotional personality structure between an individual who becomes a shaman, a priest, a medicine man, or crusader and his followers who believe and take certain comfort in their administrations, so there is a degree of difference between the fanatically dedicated artist and the surrounding world which enjoys his creations. As I previously pointed out and as it is generally agreed upon, we human beings differ from one another not in the quality of our various personality traits but in the quantity and degree of their distribution and development within us. "Know thyself" and as you know thyself you will find every feature represented within you which you previously found in your fellow human beings. This is the reason we get along better with other people to the degree we understand ourselves. We become less critical of them and they in turn instantaneously respond with lessened defensiveness.

What are the conditions which create a great artist? The example of Mozart is often cited. At the age of four years he was already the darling of the European courts. His father was an accomplished musician. Interestingly enough, his sister "Nannerl" was also extremely gifted in music. It is safe, therefore, to assume that his mother very much approved of his father's endeavor to give both children an excellent musical education at the earliest age possible. There are many examples where father and son are equally famous in the arts. Two Hans Holbeins, the Elder and the Younger, a father and son, are examples in question. Richard Strauss was the son of a leading hornist who in turn had played under Wagner's direction. Strauss received the most thorough musical education.

Many young balletophiles are brought to their early lessons by their eager and ambitious mothers who wish to capture fame and fortune in a way which had escaped them. Early exposure to artistic excellence, striving for imitation and surpassing it to win greatest appreciation of the significant person, seems to have come together paired with the single-mindedness of fanaticism. These seem to be the qualifications which create the great artist, not special neuron distribution in vaguely circumscribed brain centers. Beethoven became the foremost composer whether he could hear his own tunes or not. I go so far as to postulate that a great painter would become and remain a painter even if he should find himself without the use of his hands. Renoir might be considered as such an example in his old age.

chapter 19

THE PSYCHOSIS OF POWER

Inadequacy and insecurity are the fate and characteristic of mankind. To maintain his self-vanity in the face of the merciless destructive forces of nature, he created his own unrealistic system of magic, magical cults and rituals, sacrifices, and supplications. These early, rather primitive attempts to maintain a sense of importance and adequacy (which from time to time enjoyed a renaissance even in higher cultures) were followed by theistic concepts by which omnipotence was invested into a single Deity. However, man tried to make himself acceptable to this very deity whom he projected in his fantasy beyond the reach of mortals. The mechanism was more subtle but essentially unchanged. The prime characteristic of the monotheistic God is his omnipotence. The First Commandment states that this God will not tolerate any other gods, and, therefore, He above all must be adored.

"The more powerful I am, the less can I get hurt." Achilles was only vulnerable at his heel where his mother Thetis had to hold him when she dipped him into the river Styx.

Siegfried, the Nordic hero, bathed in the blood of the dragon which he slew. This made his entire body invulnerable with the exception of his shoulder which was accidently covered by a leaf.

We see that the concept of invulnerability is an old wishful dream of mankind. Mythology wisely made allowances for human imperfection. Perhaps we are justified in saying: "The more insecure we feel, the more secure we wish to feel." This feeling of security can be obtained, realistically or not, in many different ways.

To the degree we did not get a joyful reception in our infancy and childhood, commensurate sensations of insecurity will result within us—a point which was developed in the chapter on basic anxiety. Anxiety in itself is almost intolerable to man and one mechanism or another will take place to convert it into a more bearable form. Psychoneurotic conversion into body symptomatology is well recognized. Any form of sociomental maladjustment, most organic diseases through the pathway of the vegetative autonomic nervous systems, and any unrealistic attitudes have one and the same origin and one and the same purpose—alleviation of the unbearable sensation of anxiety. Little does it matter whether this transformation of anxiety serves a realistically useful purpose. The usefulness from the viewpoint of the afflicted individual is the relief from unbearable suffering. Just as we yearn for death in the face of unbearable agony, so any adjustment is superior to permanent anxiety even if the relief is paid for by the acceptance of unreality or impairment of other functions.

In this chapter I wish to concentrate on the relief which the striving for power, influence, and supremacy brings, as well as compensatory feelings of value and importance. Power can come in many forms. It can be political, military, financial, economic, physical, or spiritual, based on education or training, obtained by arduous persistent striving, or bestowed in the cradle as a God-given right. Beauty and good looks, as well as physical strength and prowess, are largely endowments which come with birth but they require consistent total dedication to be kept in effective shape. Therefore, it is justified to consider the effort which has to be invested into maintenance of physical beauty and physical strength and skills and prowess and equal to other efforts for power and influence. The striving for power has another deep root. The obtaining and preservation of territory by the Alpha male in various animal settings is typified especially by the baboons, whereas the chimpanzees have a rather loose, friendlier social order. This territorial dominance serves, of course, as a matrix for the mating purpose and thus, ties in with sexual gratification.

Before I go into more detail about the ways men aspire to power, I wish to elaborate on the way emotional insecurity makes itself felt above all. This emotional insecurity must be clearly distinguished from a realistic insecurity. To live at the foot of a known volcano, to live in an area where natural disasters like earthquakes, tidal waves, hurricanes, floods, etc., are likely to occur will result in a very realistic and justified feeling of insecurity which has to be faced up to and the best adjustment feasible will have to be made dependent on the overall situation. The same will hold true for miners in deep mines, for steel workers on high skyscrapers, and for those in similar professions carrying a relatively high-risk factor. A certain justified insecurity will also prevail if a person has to live surrounded by unfriendly or even hostile neighbors or groups. Innumerable examples can be made of such conditions.

Emotional insecurity is something totally different. It is based on an original rejection by the significant person, mostly the mother, and subsequent incorporation of doubt in our own self which can reach intolerable degrees. Not everybody is inclined to consider self-destruction the desirable solution. The doubt and rejection of ourselves is likely to create doubt about our manhood if we are men, and about our femininity if we are women. The more doubt I have about my manhood, the more I have to prove my masculinity. A Casanova is driven daily to new exploits in order to prove again and again his manhood. The nymphomaniac is equally unsure of her femininity which only an ongoing sequence of conquests can assauge. Of course, the destructive impulse toward the opposite sex is implicit in either case. Masculinity is confused with power; femininity with the ability to get men to do one's bidding. The less I consider myself a man, the more I have to aspire to power to compensate for this dreadful feeling. Emotionally and sexually well-adjusted males lack the overriding obsession to wield more and more influence. Not until after his death did it become a matter of general knowledge that Adolph Hitler had a mistress whom he married at the hour of his death. I do not know whether there exists any creditable account of his actual sex performance. Mussolini, who apparently had a somewhat more conventional sexual adjustment, was certainly the more humane and less fanatical dictator. A desire to impress one's wife with one's importance is certainly the key to understanding fanatical persistence in the relentless striving for power. If I am unable to bring about climatic orgasm in my wife, if I am unable to impress her adequately with my manhood so that intercourse with me is desirable to her, I have to find a method of impressing her with my power.

Primitive men liked to abduct women by force. The Sabine women are a good example inasmuch as they ultimately seemed to enjoy the experience. To win the favors of women, kings have been known to lay their kingdoms at their feet. Jacob had to serve twice seven years to win his beloved Rachel. A ten-year war, according to Homer, was fought over Helen, a war which ended in the destruction of Troy. King Edward VIII abdicated his throne for the woman he loved. History is replete with similar examples where men go to any length to obtain confirmation of their value from the woman of their choice. Crimes and murders have been committed to obtain the woman deemed singularly fit to confirm the value and masculinity of a man. Innumerable murders of passion and jealousy come to mind where only total vengeance and destruction can reestablish the shattered illusion of self-esteem of the jilted vanity which became unbearable.

What was the emotional attitude of a woman, on the other hand, who found a man with such a weak concept of his manhood desirable in the first place? Obviously, a solid, emotionally well-balanced mate was unacceptable to such a woman. She had to feel superior to him. She was so unsure of her own femininity that she would have felt outclassed and in an unbearable position had her mate not depended on her, say, for the affirmation of his manhood. She was too afraid of men to get herself into a predicament where she would have had to give herself totally into the hands of a man. This attitude, of course, was conditioned by her own upbringing and programming. She could only marry a man who was not threatening to her, to whom she felt superior and whom perhaps she could move and manipulate at will. The price which had to be paid was sexual dissatisfaction. Intercourse became a duty at best, and eventually it became loathsome and repulsive. Only as this mate obtained apparent great power and importance, did he gradually gain stature and masculinity in her eyes. Is it any wonder, therefore, that men at times will go to any lengths to obtain this most cherished feeling of manhood and vicarious self-esteem from the female of their choice whom they endowed with the power to decide their evaluation? We know what motivated Alexander the Great. The earlier conquests of his father became a spur and a thorn in his flesh which could only be assuaged by surpassing his accomplishment. The boy always wants to outdo the father to obtain, in fantasy at least, the favors of the mother who is the implicit oedipal love object.

We can only speculate about the love life of latter-day politicians and other ambitious personalities when we consider their relentless and obsessively goal-directed striving which recognizes only one issue—success in reaching one's aim and maintaining the power once obtained.

The single-mindedness of the true artist I have already discussed in a previous chapter.

The religious leader, the religious fanatic, deserves some consideration here. There is one thing which all religious leaders, regardless of creed or denomination, have in common—the striving for influence and therefore power. What they lack in conviction about their own manhood or womanhood, they make up in aspiring to feel paternal or maternal towards all, or at least toward their flock. They are the shepherds which, of course, makes the rest of us the sheep which have to be led or which wish to be led. The meek religious who goes out and humbly seeks acceptance by God through self-sacrificing action and self-effacing attitudes is only the foot soldier with whom the generals of his church play chessboard politics. In another sense, their apparent meekness is only a handy disguise to forcefully obtain what they deem useful to the church with which they identify themselves and which ultimately is only their vehicle for obtaining self-serving gratification. They are totally brainwashed into unobjectivity toward their parents; parents cannot do wrong, certainly not the mother. They are psychotically incapable of independent objective evaluation of the circumstances which patterned them. Religious leaders are the high priests of the insanity which walks upright and claims to have the ultimate truth. Ruthlessly, they feel justified in destroying everything and anything which stands in their way or threatens their adjustment. The only inhibition they may have is the realistic appraisal that their attitude may be openly censured and harm their standing. They are fanatically dedicated to the issue which permits them to avoid seeing themselves as they really are—the truly insane without any insight into their own insanity. All human beings, by necessity, have a modicum of unreality and, therefore, psychosis. These high priests have the full measure of it and pass as highly acceptable members of society. They were always next to the throne, from birth to grave. They had to have the last word. A marriage without their blessing was a sacrilege. Ill-begotten money became sanctified if duly turned over to the church and directly or indirectly they tried to steer the ship of state. The man who spoke in the name of the Lord, who knew His thinking and attitude, was from time immemorial a madman or a charlatan. In either case, he was seriously disturbed.

And yet, there is in every insanity a modicum of useful constructiveness. The murderer for passion teaches, in a way, the unacceptability of faithlessness and adultery. The ruthless politician will try to serve his country if for no other reason than to maintain his public acceptability. Even Hitler was highly acceptable to the majority of his own people as long as he served their own purposes. I am sure even today some, more or less secretly, consider his days the days of glory and exaltation in Germany. The contributions of the religious cannot be minimized. For centuries, all education and higher learning was in their hands. Their welfare agencies for their own are at times unequalled. Many hospitals and schools are only in existence because they were founded and run by their followers. It is difficult ultimately to determine to what degree insanity and unreality is creative art or unavoidable in human affairs. Once the die was cast and we descended from the trees, became erect, and thus developed our vainglory, unreality became unavoidable. Man is a psychotic animal but he is, at the same time, the only animal with self-awareness and a system of self-esteem. Like so many other poets, Henrik Ibsen pointed this out succinctly in his *Peer Gynt.* We cannot retrace our steps into the animal kingdom whence we came. We have to follow the fate of mankind wherever it may lead us, even if ultimately the earthly existence and emergence of man is nothing but a glorious failure. To make the best of it as long as the day lasts is probably the best which can be said. A show which we like to see may only last a couple of hours. We know it will be over soon but, as long as it lasts, we are careful to select a good performance with comfortable seats in good surroundings. Life in itself can be viewed similarly. Anyone who feels it is not worthwhile because it does not last on and on forever misses the boat entirely. It is not his fault admittedly, but he misses the reality of the situation. He was not endowed to be realistic, objective, sane. Psychosis and unreality was his adjustment reaction to permit him existence as long as it lasted.

chapter 20

THE NEGATIVE DELUSION— DENIAL

We can divide delusional assumptions into positive and negative aspects. When the delusion is positive, our basic vanity drives us to create concepts which serve to maintain our sense of grandiosity and self-importance. From time immemorial, man has created concepts of magic which he endowed with the ability to influence and bring about desirable results. This mechanism, although unrealistic and therefore psychotic, helped to preserve the sense of mightiness in men which, as I pointed out previously, originated in the new-found mastery over other creatures, the animals.

Magic can be either positive or negative. The positive magic required the observance of certain acts or rituals or the employment of charms to be effective; negative magic required the omission of certain acts or words which became taboo so they would not cast their disastrous spell. These taboos are implicitly believed by primitive man to regulate the course of nature independently of human will. Taboo is a negative application of practical magic. Negative taboos are just as unrealistic as positive magic or sorcery. Religion subsequently moved into the realm of magic and employed positive orders as well as negative prohibitions to achieve the desired end. Actions pleasing the god are intended to promote favorable consideration; omission of certain specific actions is intended to avoid offending the deity. Each religion has its own rules and avoidances. As time progresses, all religions try to increase their influence by enlarging their scope of activity beyond their intercession with the deity to direct influence on human interrelationships. In the name of the deity with whom their priests alone can properly communicate, they convey to ordinary mortals the will and intent of the deity, even when they speak mystically or in riddles as the priestesses of the Delphic Oracle did on so many occasions. Indeed, duplicity could at times be charged as when the Delphic Oracle prophesied to the unsuspecting King Croesus of Lydia that he would destroy a great empire if he went into battle. The prophecy came true in an unexpected way. He lost his own empire. Under such conditions, the oracle can hardly be wrong.

I am well aware that in established textbooks on psychiatry, denial is considered to be a defense mechanism by which individuals on an unconscious level try to protect their personality from facing up to unacceptable impulses or unbearable features of reality. Defense mechanisms in the psychiatric sense are mental mechanisms which serve to allay intolerable anxiety. Usually, denial is considered a psychoneurotic defense mechanism designed to preserve the intactness of the personality and prevent outright psychotic decompensation. Some of the other common defense mechanisms are repression, rationalization, reaction formation, projection, fixation, introjection, sublimation, regression, dissociation, conversion, etc. Usually, sublimation is considered the most desirable defense mechanism because it converts a threat to one's own personality into constructive application. Aggressive impulses can thus be converted into competitive sports or military exploits, both of which are highly acceptable to society. The entire evaluation of these defense mechanisms deserves a thorough review and re-evaluation. The defense mechanisms are unrealistic devices employed on a subconscious level which promote only the illusion of an intact personality. Any unrealistic device can just as well be considered psychotic. We must not shirk from the unavoidable logical conclusion that inasmuch as most (if not all) human beings employ one defensive mechanism or another, to a certain degree at least, nobody is entirely free of a modicum of psychotic, unrealistic adjustment. This conclusion is neither surprising nor far-fetched, if we consider the thesis and basic concept put forth in this book. No human being, by the very fact of his development phylogenetically and individually, can be totally realistic and any unreality is tantamount to delusion and psychosis.

I will not indulge here in a discussion of the various modalities of defensive mechanisms. These aspects are well covered in all conventional textbooks on psychiatry and the uninitiated reader will find all desired definitions and specific explanations there.

I shall restrict myself to the discussion of denial which implies by its very definition that an individual cannot admit and face up to the fact of his own emotions and the objective facts of some features of reality which he meets. If we close our eyes we don't see an object before us, but it would be unrealistic to surmise that closing the eyes makes the object actually disappear. It is true that when we close our eyes the object subjectively disappears for the beholder and he may have freed himself from viewing the disagreeable features of this object. Similarly, the refusal to observe unacceptable features within ourselves will only relieve us from viewing ourselves objectively and realistically and gives us a sense of higher acceptability at the price of self-delusion. The highest precept of self-awareness and self-knowledge is thus negated and fleeting comfort is obtained while deep insight is forfeited.

Just as a delusional assumption is psychotic, it can be said that delusional denial is a psychotic mechanism. As the magician conjures up objects and then makes them disappear, a delusion can have a positive manifestation or a negative one. The similarity to positive magic and negative magic of the primitive man is obvious.

The question immediately arises as to whether there is a difference between denial and lying. Much will depend on the connotation given to the meaning of a word. We can consider a malingerer who feigns sickness to obtain his ends a sociopath but not psychotic in a legal sense; however, we have to admit a healthy, emotionally well-balanced individual disdains to employ such trickery under ordinary conditions since he deems such an attitude incompatible with the greater good of his self-esteem. Still, we have to differentiate a psychosomatic reaction of immobilization in the fact of great peril from a consciously pretended condition of paralysis to avoid facing up to the same danger.

The relationship between denial and lying seems to run parallel to this situation. In denial, a subconscious, unrealistic, and emotional mechanism takes over which makes a fact or factual situation actually disappear from the perspective of the beholder. It is a delusion in reverse which, in fantasy at least, makes a fact disappear and the individual's concept of himself remains unchallenged. When lying, the individual is well aware that he consciously and deliberately misrepresents a certain fact or occurrence. He will do so because he feels that he thus serves his ends best by obtaining unfair advantages or avoiding the painful repercussions of speaking the truth. "I cannot tell a lie" almost always prevails only if the rendition of the true circumstances of our acts or thoughts is not followed by dire consequences. The child who is punished as a consequence of his truthfulness cannot be expected, unless he is already seriously disturbed, to invite more punishment for additional truthfulness. Lying and truthfulness are adjustment reactions to our early life experiences. Nevertheless, in lying, we postulate an awareness of his act by the offender which again, in legal terminology, would qualify him as being non-psychotic. There is a narrow margin between denial and lying, mostly in the realm of quantity and degree of the underlying disturbance rather than in quality. As any disturbance in human life is subject to the degree of affliction, so too is the delusion of denial of the existence of a disturbing aspect. Psychosis comes in degrees of severity just as do measles and theft.

Is lying at times a sign of healthy adjustment? Obviously, yes, if disclosure of true facts would bring about disastrous results to oneself or to other people—results out of proportion to the disputed fact in question. If a fact, whatever it may be, is used by an authoritative force as an outlet for his own emotional tensions and frustrations, then I am well adjusted if I withhold such information from such authority since it would only serve as a trigger mechanism—loosening upon me an avalanche of recriminations or physical abuse, completely out of proportion to the infraction. Where the line should be drawn becomes immediately a matter of personal judgment, based upon one's own experiences in the formative years of life. If we have been sensitized to unusual and cruel punishment for minor misdeeds in these early years, we will develop a tendency to be defensive by conditioned reflex and react later on in life instantaneously in a paranoid defensive way at the slightest hint of threat or inconvenience to us which a less sensitized individual would be perfectly able to overlook and ignore, thus confirming his sense of security. This insecurity becomes our own undoing since it conditions our overreaction to irritants, long after the period of sensitization has passed. Fredric Schiller, in his *Braut von Messina* put it beautifully in stating: "This is the curse of the evil deed that it reproduces evil effects on its own in succession."

From generation to generation, shortcomings are passed on. Each generation of parents does the best they know how, depending on their own imprinting, horribly inadequate as this imprinting proves to be. We have innumerable approaches to the alleviation of resulting symptomatology—from medication to religious and philosophical beliefs—but cure in its true sense can only come from clear exposure and delineation of the disturbing forces. It is only when we are true to ourselves that it follows that we can be true to other people, to paraphrase Shakespeare.

We cannot deny the fact that priding oneself on truthfulness at any price can become destructive and even disastrous. A sea captain whose ship has run into an iceberg and takes on water and which is in serious danger of sinking is well advised to minimize, if not outright deny, the damage if he can thus avoid a disastrous panic among the passengers which might greatly diminish their chance of survival. If we are truthful with other human beings even in the face of our own exposure or the exposure of other people, we had better thoroughly evaluate the objectivity of the correspondent and his potential reactivity to avoid disastrous consequences. To speak "the truth" under any conditions is nothing but self-glorification and vanity. It is not necessarily constructive because its motivation is not a realistic consideration of cause and effect but self-pride and self-love.

chapter 21

THE DESIRE TO KILL

Dr. L. S. B. Leakey, the British anthropologist who worked in the Olduvai Gorge in Northern Tanzania, has identified the fossils of a tool-using individual whom he calls *Homo habilis,* dating from the earliest dawn of mankind. During the Pleistocene Age (from about 2,000,000 years B.C. to 30,000 B.C.), there were great climatic changes on this globe, including several ice ages. Tropical Africa was more temperate than it is today. This promoted hunting in this area and in others.

Experts on dental structure are best equipped to draw intelligent inferences about the type of food which early man had to depend on for his sustenance. Herbivorous and carniverous animals have different dental constructions. Man has been called the killer ape. His dental structure is such that he can depend on a vegetable as well as a meat diet. He depended on food gathering long before he became an accomplished hunter. And, even much later when every piece of evidence points to his excellent hunting skills, he certainly used edible roots, fruits, and leaves as additional food supplies.

Hunting certainly set the scene for killing. Indeed, we can postulate that the skilled and experienced hunter was highly rated and could aspire to an influential position in his group. Similar respect is accorded to powerful leaders in animal herds by their fellow animals.

Cannibalism is practically unknown in the animal kingdom. Fights among rival members of the same species are a daily occurence but, if snarling and threatening gestures do not suffice to establish the superiority of one individual over his rival, a short fight will ensue which usually ends in the surrender or flight of the defeated animal and this is the end of the altercation. With few exceptions, no animal will come to the conclusion that he should totally annihilate the opponent so that he may not have to fight another day. The "final solution" is a human specialty. Crushed skull fossils have been found in abundance by anthropologists and we comparatively can only wonder how so many similar remains can be accounted for.

Suffice it to say that the great civilizations developed in the Neolithic period out of small hunting groups. Villages given to agriculture and domestication of animals developed and these villages closed ranks to form state and cultural entities. Cohesion of its members was essential, if for no other reason than to preserve the new-found integrity. It is to this period of time that we can trace back the emergence of the great moral codes of Hammurabi and all other better or lesser known laws of the various cultures and empires which followed each other. Religion, of course, became deeply concerned with the acceptable rules governing the acts and the interrelationships of men.

The concept of "Thou shalt not kill" is one of the highest and most profound tenets imprinted into man from his early beginning. Nobody can doubt that without its powerful impact chaos would reign, not the law of the jungle because the jungle has its own law, which is the survival of the fittest and the ecological balance of its inhabitants, but much worse, killing for emotional reasons. The animal, unaffected by the specific human vanity of grandeur, acts appropriately, even in its killing instinct. The specific human vanity knows no bounds when it fights for its establishment and preservation. "Surrender or I shall kill you" is the ancient cry and frequently even surrender does not suffice.

Is this murderous inclination an instinctual endowment, as Carl Jung postulated, and phylogenetically determined or is it above all a reaction pattern experienced by the infant on the most subconscious vegetative nervous system level in the earliest period of his formative state? Probably both aspects are true and one does not exclude the other.

Let us restrict ourselves from here on to the specific human factor represented in each infant and child. We have stated in the chapter on Basic Anxiety that even under optimal conditions no infant is ever totally accepted by his parents and especially the mother, his significant person at that time. To the degree the child was not accepted, he was experienced as a burden and imposition. We, on a subconscious level at least, would like to do without a burden and this wish is sensed intuitively by the infant and child and perceived by him as a death threat. These seem to be strong words, but the reader must keep in mind that we are speaking here of a condition which varies in intensity from faint to severe. If I own a horse and lose my temper and beat it in anger only once, it will never forget my potentialities and all assuaging and apologetic words subsequently cannot erase the experience. The child who has experienced the ill-temper of his parents only once will be imprinted for life with the fear which was engendered in him. He may forget the incident completely or the event may even have taken place before memory could develop, but the irreparable imprint was made, and only a long period of placid existence can, to a certain degree at least, cover the wound, once inflicted. The husband who has struck his wife even once will never be able to totally erase this memory from her mind.

At first on the vegetative nervous system level and later on a subconscious or even conscious level, the child will appropriately react to and cope with any threat to his existence by the wish to defend himself, even if this should imply the wish to eliminate this threat once and for all; that is, kill the originator of the threat. Since this threat mostly, if not totally, originates from the mother directly or indirectly, the child harbors death wishes against his mother. Death wishes against our father do not seem to upset us as deeply. We wonder many times why our mother married him in the first place, totally forgetting he had something to do with our existence.

At the same time, the mother is the source of life for the infant and child, if not life itself. We can see right here the unsolvable dilemma which a clash of emotions within us so totally opposite must produce. We come to the conclusion that either we are no good at all and should not exist in the first place or we must be insane to harbor such sensations within us, which are considered the most despicable on the human emotional scale. Murder of a father sounds bad enough, but murder of one's own mother is an unthinkable act. The thought of it alone makes us shiver and to postulate here that to a certain degree the thought is unavoidable due to the human circumstances which accompany birth will challenge many imaginations.

Suffice it to say that it is present whether we like it or not and whether we can face up to it or not. Indeed, the more clearly we are able to face up to its existence, the stronger we are and the less likely to divert or project it upon innocent and incidental fellow travelers.

Whether the killing instinct so overtly expressed in hunting is a carryover from early ancestral instincts or is a diversion of one's own individual killing instincts on harmless and helpless animals is open to debate. Marksmanship may be excellent in killing an animal at a great distance with a high-powered rifle but this marksmanship can be displayed in a less deadly way. The feelings of power and virility of these latter-day huntsmen seems unjustified by the circumstances.

All our teachings and indoctrinations are, in reality, moral straitjackets into which we are put in the formative years to repress and contain the killing instinct against other human beings. Unless we are emotionally very strong and capable of knowing ourselves realistically, we are not able to face up to our own selves squarely and, therefore, this destructive impulse—killing—is repressed. Repression does not eliminate the desire but only pushes it out of sight, keeps it out of our awareness, and displaces it in other directions and onto other targets. Under the disguise of service to one's country or to the maintenance of law and order sublimation can take place which converts aggressive hostile domineering impulses into socially highly acceptable ones, even highly esteemed ones, since now they have been made subservient to society. From Brutus to Principe, who, by assassination of the archduke Ferdinand, touched off the First World War, to the murderer of Walter Rathenau to Lee Harvey Oswald to Sirhan Sirhan, each social or political or religious murderer feels he serves the highest interests of his own group or that he actually represents this group's conscience. He feels his own ideology is far superior to the one he opposes or which he may perceive as so oppressive that only murder can remedy the condition.

As long as one society is pitched against the other, with whatever connotations this takes place, bloody conflicts are likely to occur. A more cynical observer may wonder whether differing attitudes have to appear in mankind. If they were not present, perhaps they would have to be created to give the killing impulses of man a face-saving justification. If individuals find themselves on a life raft or under similar conditions, they wonder what their previous differences were all about.

Human beings basically have the biological wish to survive. They are stuck with their own hostile impulses. It is not very wise to vent these on more powerful individuals and risk serious repercussions unless we toy with our own destruction. Is it not, therefore, the most logical undertaking to ventilate one's aggressive and even destructive impulses on the weak, dependent, and defenseless? The animals could sing a long song of human inhumanity. It is not necessarily a delight from an animal's viewpoint to share this globe with *Homo sapiens.* Children too are defenseless. Unless the neighbors hear their pitiful cries and unhappiness and call the police in extreme cases, they can be the targets of the venom and hateful destructiveness of their elders who, however, as we know by now, were only the recipients of similar treatment a few years earlier. "This is the way my father and mother raised me. I became a 'decent' citizen. What was good for me, is good for you." Forgotten are all the tears and nightmares of childhood. Observe the way children are raised in their formative years. Even the most patient mother becomes impatient and short-tempered at times. It is all very understandable but deplorable, nevertheless.

I once read in a composition, written by a 10-year-old boy, that parents only have children to take out on them what was done to them when they themselves were young.

How deep the killing instinct is embedded in mankind we can see in the development of magic and religion.

The often quoted *Golden Bough,* by Frazier, is replete with examples of kings and god kings being killed at the first sign of waning power or even before to prevent their souls from becoming unavailable to their tribe but rather properly and promptly transferred to their successors. The gods themselves had to die and revive yearly in an obvious parallel to the seasonal changes. In the Eastern Mediterranean area, the cradle of civilization, the rites varied slightly from place to place but basically remained the same. Osiris, Tammuz, Adonis, Attis, etc., represented yearly decay and, therefore, death and subsequent revival. The ancient Mexicans offered the hearts of human victims to the sun as the source of all vital forces. They called the sun god Ipalnemohnani "he by whom men live," but in order to be able to give life he needed to receive life. The bleeding hearts of their victims were offered to this god, symbolizing life to renew his own energies. Animals, of course, were used abundantly as sacrifices and scapegoats throughout both history and prehistory. Bloody and delusional is the story of mankind.

Killing and the watching of killings were not only magical and religious preoccupations but were outright exciting and exhilarating experiences. "*Panem et circenses,*" cried the Roman mob, as they hastened to the Colosseum to see a few gladiators kill each other or to see other victims being eaten up by the lions. What accounts for this blood-thirsty pleasure in violent death? Is it an exhilarating feeling of power to watch the destruction of another human being? What brutal primitive killing instincts are awakened in us when bloody executions are performed? The Spanish-speaking peoples made the bull fight an event of fine art and high skill and daring.

Our boxing arenas are filled with screaming crowds although they have to be satisfied with a good knockout. For centuries offended honor could only be saved by bloody, deadly duels. Human sacrifices and cannibalism were not only practiced in ancient days but into modern times by more primitive tribes. Frenzied worshippers of Bacchus tore animals and men into pieces and devoured them raw. Since Bacchus or Dionysus was represented by a goat they believed they were eating the body and blood of the god. Eating parts of the victim was not intended so much as nourishment but was believed to transfer his strength.

Modern language in a supposedly much more civilized time uses the term "killing" for more peaceful pursuits. We speak of a "killing" in the stock market or in a successful speculation. The expression, "I could kill you," is mostly an expression of one's own feelings and is not necessarily meant nor understood as a real threat.

We know that many soldiers find it difficult to kill in combat, even when ordered to do so and may subsequently suffer serious emotional difficulties and find it impossible to reconcile their action with their own upbringings. Conscientious objections to killing have been mostly associated with certain religious convictions but to a high degree, unless clearly contradicted as a self-defensive measure, can be considered justified for reasons of conviction alone. The confrontation of opinions will ultimately take place between those who feel that the national interest or patriotism should have preference over an attitude of universality which considers all human beings fellow travelers on this earth.

Individuals have been executed throughout history not only for treasonable behavior which implies favoring the fortunes of opposing forces but at times for refusing to participate in what is considered the common effort. The military code has to be applied firmly in time of emergency to keep divergent opinions under control. Martial law is the first thing to be called into existence in the face of a natural disaster or emergency. It has been said that only the law stands between man and the jungle. It is unrealistic to dream that human beings can coexist without law to govern and direct their behavior and actions. Anarchism, which means the absence of any government, is an unrealistic fantasy when it applies to human beings as is "Utopia," the ideal state, or the concept that all human beings love each other. The reality is that all human institutions are imperfect and realistically we have to deal with human beings as they are and not as our wishful fantasies would imagine them to be. Hypothetically, we can assume that if there were perfectly mature human beings they would all act perfectly, they would be considerate of each other, and nobody would have to tell anybody else what to do or what not to do.

This book has concerned itself with pointing out the inevitable delusion of mankind and stressed that allowances have to be made for its existence. It took mankind several million years to develop into societies governed by religious laws. It was a great step forward when the law divorced itself from religion and became independent of supranatural connotations.

chapter 22

LIFE, SEX, AND LOVE

Life on this planet is a fact. Anybody who indulges in thoughts of his own about the developments of mankind should first take a thorough course in human embryology. He will soon learn that at the fetal age of a few weeks the bronchial arches and pharyngeal pouches correspond to the gills of fishes and some amphibians. At times they even rupture, thereby completing the gill-slit. The coccyx is called the "tail bone" with good reason. In herbivores the cecum colon is highly developed. It corresponds to the vermiform process (also called the appendix) in the higher apes and human beings and it is comparatively larger at birth than after a few years of life. Several pairs of mammary glands normally occur in mammals (pigs, dogs, etc.). They form along the so-called milk line. Accessory mammae are found only as anomalies in human beings. They occasionally form along the embryonic milk lines. Supernumerary mammary glands, also called hypermastiae, are quite infrequent but accessary nipples (hypertheliae) are fairly common in both sexes. Traces of them supposedly occur in as many as one percent of the population.

As long as we speak of a "theory" of evolution, we miss the point. It is no more a theory than the fact that stoneage men used to populate this earth or that, under certain circumstances, wood will petrify. If we have so little faith in our own observations that we prefer to lean toward wild, unfounded assumptions because they seem to satisfy our emotional needs and our bottomless insecurity rather than objective findings, then we cannot hope to develop the self-confidence which springs from faith in our knowledge. We do not know all, we never will know all, but what we know, limited as it may be, should not be considered a theory—otherwise we will lose ourselves in self-doubting nihilism on the one hand or in emotionally conditioned attitudes of rigidity on the other. These attitudes are void of rationality and are founded only on the bottomless insecurity of human beings who, because of their basic vanity, find it intolerable to see themselves as infinitesmally insignificant particles in an unimaginable universe.

I postulate that it is precisely the degree of emotional insecurity which determines the degree of rigid belief, no matter what the belief may be. Belief is the salve of the gnawing pain of insecurity. Belief is an emotional crutch needed by man to give the appearance of walking on his own feet. As human beings, we all need a crutch of some sort. The degree of our dependence on the crutch determines the degree of our emotional insecurity. The more insecure we basically are, the more heavily we have to lean on the crutch. The reasonably well-adjusted person will only occasionally feel the need to fall back on some support. His sense of reality appreciation will prevent him from embracing a drunken sense of self-glorification.

Once life had developed on this planet, it continued to develop. Under differing environmental conditions, a wide range of manifestations of life developed. They all had one thing in common. Since protein in itself ages and finally falls apart, preservation of life and later of the species demanded a reproduction process. In primitive unicellular organisms, reproduction occurs through cell division—that is, each organism divides in half and forms two "daughter" cells. At an early stage in fetal development, a differentiation into two separate but similar forms in a species takes place. These two forms are complementary to each other. When they come together, the preservation of the species is secured through copulation. Only extraordinary changes in external conditions are sufficient to frustrate this sequence of events and terminate a form of life which we can call a species.

Human beings are mammals, first and foremost. The female carries the seed in her womb, gives birth to living offspring, and nurses them on her breast in the earliest and most tender period of their lives. Many ingenious substitutions have been employed from wetnurse to bottle-feeding to attempts at placental transplants to using incubators to compensate for fetal environment. Substitutions are useful but at the best inadequate, whether we think of dental or body prostheses, optical appliances, hearing aids, etc. Goethe, in his *Faust,* described the experimentally created homunculus precariously existing for a limited time. Man, in his vain self-glory, tries always to best nature; he attempts first to learn her secrets and then to become independent of her laws. But sooner or later she catches up with his endeavors and relegates him to his place. Modern ecological understanding is a point in question. All mammals left to their own devices procreate only by sexual copulation. I am well aware of the fact that in animal husbandry artificial insemination is widely practiced. I would like to raise a very subtle question which perhaps has not been discussed so far. The cow that is artificially inseminated with the semen of a prize bull procreates, to be sure. Obviously, the end-product is desirable or the practice would have been abandoned by now. However, I cannot help but feel that the excitation and glandular interplay in normal copulation must have some purpose in addition to the strictly mechanical function of creating vaginal lubrication. Insignificant as this missing element may be, is it not conceivable that over long periods of time, it may have an accumulative effect? I realize this point is far-fetched, but I find it difficult to assume that artificiality will not have some repercussions in one way or another, even if the resulting calves are bigger and meatier, and, therefore, more marketable.

In human affairs, this point becomes much more tangible. In the animal kingdom we can lightly dispose of any emotional factor; in human affairs, this factor is essential. Because this emotional factor must be taken into account in human artificial insemination, it is desirable to mix the semen of the donor with the ejaculate of the husband, infertile as it may be, in order to preserve the illusion that the resulting offspring after all could have been derived from a lonely lost sperm not totally dead in his ejaculate.

We have learned that in higher animals there are courtship games or rituals performed which apparently serve the purpose of proper selection for the mating process. There may be outright fights for the privilege of mating which certainly serves the law of selection of the fittest. To my knowledge, in their natural habitat, untouched by any human interference, neither rape nor homosexuality exist among animals. All kinds of perversions can be observed only when this natural existence is disturbed. Mating does not take place unless the female is ready and willing to participate wholeheartedly. No cub is forced to serve as an object for sexual release or pleasure by a more mature though frustrated individual. These deviations would only contradict the natural law of the selection of the fittest and preservation of the species. The animal has no need to indulge in sex play prematurely. The cub need not prove its sexual identity, whether it be masculine or feminine. Incidentally, at this point, it can also be pointed out that higher animals, as predatory as they may be, never indulge in cannibalism. This is a human speciality developed not so much for food as for delusional reasons. The heart and other organs were consumed to acquire by ingestion the strength, courage, or other qualities of the sacrificed victim. Harmless colloquialisms go back to this sinister past—"I love you so much, I could eat you up" is a very endearing expression. "Bloodthirsty" might have a similar origin.

Let us speak here for a while about human perversion before we consider the high point of human potentiality—love. The infant is born with the sucking reflex. The gladly offered productive nipple of the mother is the natural source of food. Even if all human beings were bottle-fed, this still would not be normal—average, yes; normal, no. Therefore, it is equally inadequate to call masturbation normal just because practically all boys have indulged in it at one time or another. It is not, however, a catastrophe and, therefore, a parent ought not to hit the ceiling when he finds out that his son has masturbated. Because the sex drive is assumed to be stronger in male youngsters at an earlier age and because the female has to be aroused before responding sexually, masturbation is probably more frequent in boys than in girls. There is, however, quite a difference between a young boy who masturbates from frustration and a married man who prefers to masturbate rather than approach his ready and potentially willing mate. As long as masturbation is perceived as a poor substitute for normal intercourse, the attitude of the individual does not become greatly deviant. He may lack self-control, but he does not feel that self-gratification not only is a desirable substitution for a heterosexual relationship but actually preferable to it. The law of preservation of the species, which is the biological drive of mankind, is also totally defied when masturbation becomes the practiced sexual activity of choice.

This goes hand in hand with withdrawal from human interrelationships, and certainly any visitor to the back wards of mental institutions can bear witness to this fact. If bestiality is practiced, an animated object, however without self-awareness, is used instead of an inanimate one. In homosexuality, whatever else can be said about it, the fact remains that the preservation of the species is ruled out *a priori.* I fully realize that when two sexageneraians have intercourse with each other, no offspring will result, but a deviation or perversion is exactly what the name implies. *Via* in Latin means "way." Deviation is straying from the way. *Vertere* in Latin means to turn; *pervertere,* to misturn, to make a wrong turn. There is a yardstick to measure the degree of a perversion as every ailment is characterized by the degree of severity of the affliction. Besides age, frequency of practice, and whether the perversion is only practiced under mitigating circumstances or as a method of choice, we can say that masturbatory self-gratification does, above all, only remove the individual from proper participation in his expected socially contributory relations.

Fetishism should be mentioned here. When a part or an object, which previously had some sort of relationship to the love object, becomes the love object itself, this is a fetish. The sentimental dedication of a lock of hair, for instance, serves as a reminder to the lover of his absent beloved and is a romantic gesture. When it becomes the love object itself, disturbance has started. When force is used to obtain it, we could almost speak of minimal rape. The Latin expression *pars pro toto* ("a part for the whole") best describes fetishism.

Then we can classify whether the mate is selected from the same equal species or from the animal kingdom. Even when the same species is involved, it has to be established whether the partner is an undeveloped human being, a child, immature or adolescent, an invalid, or an imbecile without adequate orientation to life, which is greatly reminiscent of a helpless animal which becomes the victim of the perversion. The question arises as to whether the mate is selected heterosexually or is of the same sex. Lastly, the type of perversion has to be considered even if the mate is heterosexual, mature, and willing. In many perversions, the mouth, lips, and tongue are involved, a throwback to unsatisfied early oral gratification. From early pacifiers to thumbs, pencil ends, cigarettes, winebottles, to excessive food indulgence, it is a continuous sequence which is only called a perversion when cunnilingus or fellatio is practiced. We can say that a deviation is most mild when it is practiced between two mature consenting heterosexual individuals involving the genitalia. The deviation becomes more severe if the body orifice or involved organ is inappropriate or if heterosexuality is replaced by homosexuality; free consent of two mature individuals replaced by immaturity, incompetency, or force. Bestiality does not hurt other human beings, and, therefore, loses the criminal aspect which characterizes the forceful subjugation of another person to our gratification. These elements, of course, can overlap, and all these factors will be a measure of the severity of the disturbance. In defense of adult homosexuality, it can be said that the human emotional factor may be preserved. It is then only a total rejection of the opposite sex, although even then normal intercourse is imitated. Suffice it to say that deviation only takes place when the *via*—the "way"—seems uninviting or forbidding. The individual becomes the victim of environmental conditions which imprinted and programmed him. He sees himself as a derelict; he feels like an outcast; he feels incapable of communicating his condition to anybody. He is sure of rejection and aversion. Perhaps he brazenly flaunts his condition, challenging society. He is torn by the drive for self-preservation and the self-destructive urge behind his basically asocial or anti-social attitude. Hate is all-pervasive in these individuals. Was not "nature" unfair to them? Why should they be singled out for such injustice? It is difficult to be a victim and to believe in justice at the same time. Human vanity does not permit this. If anybody looks for justice, he must enlarge his scope to a truly universal level. We all share the fate of the universe. Short of this, the laws of nature are unyielding.

When we speak of mature heterosexual love between two human beings, we must remember that the very requirements of the term "maturity" implies heterosexuality. We can postulate that it is difficult to perceive full self-acceptance in either partner if the biological requirement of intercourse in the only form that leads to reproduction does not ultimately take place. Superimposed is the specific human factor of emotionally acceptable gratification or, even better, the highest fulfillment of one's own potential. The human being is at his best when he can identify himself with other human beings. We have learned that this propensity depends greatly upon whether he, although totally dependent, was treated as an individual in his formative years—that is, introduced to the ways of the world since his unavoidable inexperience demanded it, but who was considered an individual, a human being, not without reactivity. If we were fortunate enough that our mother actually enjoyed us for no ulterior motive except that our mere existence gave her pleasure, then we certainly belong to the select few (if any) who are the favorites of the gods. So, let us not look for perfection, let us be satisfied with the closest approximation of this happy state; the emotional connotation of love is total approval of the other person. The message is something like this: "I totally approve of the way you are—your way to be is a most desirable one. I consider myself fortunate beyond description to be considered as worthwhile by you—it will prove to me that I am worthwhile. I shall go to any extent to preserve you and what you stand for, risking even my very life in this pursuit, if necessity dictates. To be united with you is the epitome of fulfillment this life has to offer." Reproduction from this union is the sequence which occurs by the natural biological forces at play. Emotionally, intercourse serves no other purpose but the culmination of mutual delight and enjoyment. "He enjoys me—I feel fulfilled; I am a woman." Or perhaps, "She enjoys me—I am a man, no doubt about it. In her arms I receive confirmation of my manhood and humanity." Let me emphasize once more that an approximation to this happy state is already highly desirable. Even if such approximation has taken place only occasionally, we can feel at the end of our days that we have known life. The person who has, sometimes at least, given us this delight can never become insignificant to us again.

How does this situation change when reproduction takes place? The female companion becomes the mother and now her infant totally depends on her. Here comes the true test of marital and human love and maturity. To what degree is the man satisfied that his mate has chosen him to be the father of her children? Is it not in itself the highest compliment a woman can pay to a man by implicitly stating, "You are my man. I choose you to become the father of my children. I find it worthwhile that you should live on in your children. I provide you with the opportunity of the only realistic approximation to immortality." As mother, she is indispensable to her children. She can no longer serve the needs of her husband first, and, to the degree the man is sure of his personality, no further proof is necessary. Indeed, the man would want to see the total dedication of his wife—now a mother—to his children. Inevitably, it will follow that the mother conveys then to the children the high regard by which she is bound to her husband. Through the eyes of the mother, they will see him. Ultimately, it is not decisive whether the father is actually present *in corpore* or only represented to the children through the views of the mother. The old sea captain, away on voyages for years, even the soldier killed in battle, can provide children with a reasonably adequate means of identification or substitution as long as the mother conveys her high regard for him. His absence may be felt, but no disastrous consequences will follow.

It is always daring when a man takes it upon himself to describe the emotional feelings of a woman. Men and women are human beings. In this respect we want the same objectives. We want to feel that we are somebody. We may differ in our approach as to how we obtain this feeling; the avenues may differ, but not the goal. I daresay, to be desired by the man whom the woman esteems as desirable, makes her feel that she is somebody, that she is a woman. For this man she will do anything to preserve this feeling of being wanted and approved of. When she has his children, she wants her son to be like him and the daughter to be like her, which means that she will eventually marry a man like her mate was. This is the song of love—from man to woman, from woman to man. This is the rhapsody of the ages. I am not a poet but a psychiatrist, and, therefore, I cannot indulge in concluding on this high note.

Let us look at the opposite side—impotence. After all is said and done and all books and studies on this subject are finished, the message is clear: "You are not a desirable person in my eyes. I cannot make love to you because I do not consider you lovable." Impotence comes in several forms and degrees. The male may not have an arousal reaction, the penis remains completely unerect or partial, inadequate erection may take place. An orgastic ejaculation may take place prematurely—that is, extra-vaginally, or after short contact with the vagina. Male impotence is very obvious. Any degree of inadequate response to appropriate sexual stimulus falls into this category. We see, therefore, that impotence, like any other disturbance, comes in various degrees. It can be partial or total; temporary or continuous; relative or absolute with regard to one individual or the opposite sex altogether. The degree to which spermatogenesis is influenced by emotional factors deserves much further study. If spermatogenesis and ovogenesis can definitely be shown to be under emotional influences, as I would suppose them to be, this would go a long way toward explaining infertility. In this case, infertility could be considered equivalent to impotence. Consciously and in performance, the partners seem like love birds; physiologically and subconsciously, self-castration has taken place. The appearance is safeguarded but nature is not fooled. These are strong and startling concepts which one can only reach if one clearly perceives the all-penetrating power of emotions through the autonomic glandular nervous system.

We can see the extent to which the desire to win approval from the mate is involved in the case of a patient who was under my care. It started when a 12-year-old boy was brought to my attention when he showed tendencies toward transvestism, fetishism, and sexual aggressiveness by grabbing for the breasts of a passing woman. The parents entered therapy also. Now it became overt that the mother in 13 years of marriage never had experienced orgasm and the father, in order to force orgasm in his wife, remained in the vagina up to two hours, hoping, so to speak, that she would ultimately relent. In the course of therapy, it became obvious that the woman had devastating urges against the male sex, and the vagina truly became a battleground. Female impotence can vary from absence of final orgasm to total revulsion at the mere thought of male contact.

I wish to use an example to illustrate how the female, consciously or subconsciously, perceives male impotence. The beloved man who perhaps in wartime suffered cruel injury to his genitalia, with a resulting physical inability to have intercourse, will be viewed totally differently by the woman than the mate who lies in bed next to her, turns to his side, and begins to snore, or the male who prefers alcohol, fishing, or his business to her. The degrees of these activities, of course, have to be kept in mind.

When we get the message from our mate through overt impotence that we are not lovable, several avenues are open to us. We can react with hate toward our humiliator and take revenge of one type or another to restore our sense of self-value, or we can ask ourselves what lies within us which makes us unacceptable. This approach will touch on the deepest layers of our personality, of course, and it is questionable whether or not we can again find favor in the eyes of the mate. But life has to go on and ultimately we cannot make ourselves totally dependent on the evaluation which another human being is disposed to bestow upon us.

Here, perhaps, a word is justified about the distinction between love and falling in love. Love, in my vocabulary, encompasses the highest form of approval of another person. To fall in love, in my concept, means to be almost in an unrealistic trance where we wish to appear so lovable that we will ultimately gain our desired objective. To fall in love has, to me, self-serving connotations. Love in itself, to me, signifies primarily the concern for another human being. Our reward is the fulfillment of our own potential.

I turn to a more sordid example which ties in with impotence. The rapist who ejaculates prematurely before the penis enters the vagina may feel humiliated. He set out to have his way by force but some unconscious mechanism of social responsibility prevented his ruthlessness. The impotence was thus an expression of higher social and emotional qualities within him than he would have given himself credit for. Equally, the man who experiences impotence while frequenting a house of prostitution or when trying to seduce a female for whom he feels no emotional dedication will be ill-advised if this is viewed as an expression of true impotence or lack of masculinity. I would go so far as to postulate that the man of highest emotional fulfillment will be impotent in the face of any other love object but his beloved. An aversion to other temptations can be postulated. I do assume that the same reaction will be present in a woman under equal emotional conditions. She will go to any length to preserve herself for her beloved.

chapter 23

SELF-ACCEPTANCE AND MENTAL BALANCE

Our yardstick is quite clear by now. The closer an infant comes to the ideal circumstance of total and joyful acceptance by his mother, the more the infant or child senses he is a source of joy to his mother, the more he will accept himself and will feel, "I am somebody—my mere existence gave joy to my mother." Do I need to reemphasize that the joy of the mother will depend upon how much joy her existence brings to her mate? We have established that in the courtship days, mates test each other out for their emotional needs. The less disturbed we are, the less we are attracted to disturbed potential mates. At the highest level of emotional maturity, we seek out our mate to increase our enjoyment of life, not to satisfy hidden emotional needs.

The search for identity is almost an obsession with young people. Who am I? What is the purpose of life? What is my purpose in life? Simple factual answers don't seem to satisfy. Is this all there is to life? is asked when the facts of life are pointed out. Basic human vanity is not satisfied with a factual answer. Human beings find it difficult to view themselves only as forms of creation. Their sense of psychotic grandeur forces them to see themselves as god entities; and they find it painful, if not intolerable, each time they are forced to be realistic. Even if all the hydrogen bombs in existence should literally blow up our earth, what will this matter to our galaxy or other distant galaxies?

God is a concept used by primitive men to come to some relationship with the cosmos. Modern cosmology leaves the last answers open but goes as far as human scientific thinking can lead us at this time. Peace of mind and self-acceptance imply the same thing. Our self-concept and self-evaluation is not completely misled. We can numb it or ignore its gnawing comment which we sometimes like to call conscience and which, as the word implies (*scio* = "I know," in Latin), is our own self-critic. Of course, we realize that it is composed of what Freud liked to call the "superego," the code of behavior and action programmed into us. So perhaps self-acceptance is present when we live up to this code within us. Historians, commenting on the Carthagenian Hamilcar who made his sons, Hannibal and Hasdrubal, take a solemn oath that they would take vengeance on Rome, like to remark that never was an oath more faithfully fulfilled. In this case we have to assume that Hannibal and Hasdrubal were satisfied with themselves. Rebellion against the teachings of our parents has then two aspects. In one way we feel compelled to dissociate ourselves from their attitudes in order to satisfy our illusion of independence. On the other hand, by doing so we offend the demands of the superego which calls for conformity to the imprinted concepts.

We are again caught in a dilemma from which, for practical purposes, there is no escape. Many times, when we are older and establishing a feeling of individuality, which long ago lost its urgency, we regret that we did not follow the concepts to which we were exposed in our formative years. Little do we realize that in reality we had no choice in the matter. Our basic human vanity requires the delusion that we had a choice in the matter. In psychoanalytical therapy, an effort is made to review our formative years objectively in the hope of recognizing that we could not have turned out differently than we did, due to the prevailing circumstances at the critical time. With this new-found objectivity about ourselves and about our own prevailing pattern formation, a sense of self-acceptance develops. The gain of this endeavor consists in our freeing ourselves from earlier guilt feelings which resulted from the discord between our indoctrination and subsequent attitudes. If the psychoanalysis or deep-going psychotherapy was truly successful, we can recognize a changed life-style in the recipient since he can then freely choose for himself attitudes and actions which he deems useful, despite earlier pattern formation. Psychoanalysis is selective and is built on the concept that it is only fully applicable to pure anxiety neuroses in which the patient brings forth all the motivation for the necessary insight and the role of the therapist is restricted to an understanding listener. This concept of pure anxiety neurosis is perhaps a misconception because other elements of disturbances, such as obsession, phobic reactions, conversion reactions, and depressive and paranoid features, are interwoven. These features to be resolved do not yield to the objective listening of the therapist. The best psychoanalysis or psychoanalytical approach is, therefore, more likely to end in the final exhaustion of the patient who comes to the conclusion that he has to live with his symptomatology. A certain active interference by and participation of the therapist will, therefore, be the optimal approach for the patient. However, it should be well understood that, although this interference and interpretation will be indispensable at times if curative results are expected, these active interferences and interpretations should be held to the very minimum needed for further insights by the patient. Here the tact, compassion, and self-knowledge of the therapist will be of the utmost importance, and no teaching can supersede the degree of the therapist's self-knowledge. Unfortunately, in psychiatric practice there does not exist an objective yardstick to measure the personal quality of a therapist. Scholastic knowledge and education will only result in following theoretical concepts presented previously by others, but the personal ability to identify with the patient will be missing.

Now, a most interesting phenomenon takes place. The better the therapist, the clearer his concept and self-knowledge—the better his ability to identify with his patient, the more likely he is at an early stage to perceive the causes of the disturbances in the patient. Although he refrains from lightly exposing his insights to the patient, hoping that the patient through persistent therapy will gain these insights himself, sooner or later he divulges his insights and understandings of the disturbing influences to the patient, since otherwise the results would fall very short of the potential optimum. Logically, one would expect the patient to be grateful for these insights. This appreciation may follow much later, perhaps long after therapy has been concluded, but, for the moment, the patient is much more likely to act as kings did in ancient days—when a messenger brought them unfavorable news, they chopped off the head of the messenger. Depending on the degree of his disturbance, the patient may only express himself unfavorably to the therapist. The therapist should be equipped to handle this but, on occasion, the patient may act out much more vindictively. He may go back to the referring physician complaining about the treatment he received. The destructive intent is noticeable. If a physician repeatedly gets complaints from erstwhile referrals, he will come to the conclusion that the psychiatrist is deficient in his approach. Considerable damage to the psychiatrist's practice and livelihood can thus result, almost at times in reverse proportion to his skill and abilities as a therapist. Inadequate therapists may at times have much more popular appeal because the referring physician does not have his own emotional inadequacy painfully, although indirectly, brought home to him. Of course, it may happen (almost miraculously and quite unpredictably) that patients who at first seemed very unhappy become valuable sources of referrals in later days, with greater objectivity.

The vindictiveness of the patient or his angry outbursts at learning about and perceiving himself with clearer objectivity can take many forms. Interrupting therapy, going to another therapist to finish and bringing the treatment to a successful end there, apparently out of the original therapist's hands, overlooks the fact that the release of the patient's hostility upon the first therapist was actually the essential part of the therapy. Nonpayment of bills is another form of hidden vindictiveness. The better the therapist, the more likely he is to end up as the scapegoat since his desire to help forces him to expose himself to possible painful experience to a certain degree. He must determine for himself where he feels he has to draw the line for the simple reason of self-preservation. The scapegoat principle is an ancient one. Innocent animals have been sacrificed by man for such purposes. Since time immemorial, kings had to die for their people in ancient traditions and the self-sacrifice of the gods is an ancient principle.

Obviously, all these projective techniques are unrealistic and, therefore, delusional. The goat and the therapist don't deserve the wrath of the afflicted. They are used as convenient outlets. The therapist, if he is really good, does not enjoy serving as an outlet for the repressed hostility of his patients, but, as long as the release of the repression is not devastating, he will bear up under it and regain his strength after some painful reactivity. The anger and hostility were, of course, originally meant for and directed at those persons directly involved in our unhappy imprinting—our parents. But this realization was never permitted to dawn upon us. We think rather—"Our parents—these wonderful creatures who sacrificed and worked for us—how evil we must be to doubt their perfection!" Is it not a sin against Almighty God not to honor your father and mother? Why does the commandment not say that we will do so freely without compulsion if they deserve our love and honor? Is it our fault that they indulged in intercourse and were unprepared to live up to its consequences? Yet, we are expected to give them love and honor, regardless of how emotionally and even physically mutilated we become in this process! Is it not possible that the very essence of the Fourth Commandment is nothing but putting the new generation into an emotional straitjacket so that later on (when the parental generation has lost its teeth and power, so to speak, and the child generation has grown up) the children do not take bloody vengeance on the causes of their affliction?

We cannot become objective about parents, particularly about our mother. We can, however, perish in our own frustration, develop sicknesses of all sorts, or project our repressed hate for the suffered injustice and deprivations of emotional warmth upon innocent victims. The more emotionally deficient the mother was, the more rigidly we will be patterned not to become objective about her and to her deficits which caused our own disturbances. The reader knows by now that her devastating influence upon us was not willful or even conscious in any way. She did the best she could but it was horribly inadequate. We feel somewhat more free to be objective about our father. Even in legal practice, the ultimate in depravity is not patricide, but matricide. As previously mentioned, I created the analogy to the Freudian concept of the Oedipus complex in the Orestes complex. According to Greek mythology, Orestes avenges his slain father, Agamemnon, by killing Clytemnestra, Agamemnon's wife and Orestes' mother, at the urging of his sister, Electra.

What degree of objectivity is necessary to recognize and deal successfully with all these horrifying emotions in oneself? Is it any great wonder that there is a time in successful psychotherapy when the patient has to go through the emotional horror of viewing himself as a monster? Is there not a time in successful psychotherapy when the patient has the definite sensation that he is going to die, and is it not a fact that only after he has braved this and his motivation has become strong enough, in spite of these frightening contingencies, that self-acceptance and a more joyful outlook on life takes place? Motivation is the most important factor in psychotherapy. The greater the motivation, the less significant the quality of the therapist. A therapist must be very deficient to deter a determined, well-motivated patient. The patient gains insight even if the therapist is only inclined to sit and listen attentively. On the other hand, the quality of the therapist will be taxed as therapy progresses and the question of resolution of the disturbance or resignation to it arises. Although psychoanalysis has as its noble aim deep insights and ultimately self-knowledge, unfortunately, all too frequently it ends up only as supportive therapy, falling far short of its inherent potential.

"Know thyself" are the ancient words of wisdom. Apparently, since the dawn of mankind, human beings have recognized that total objectivity about oneself is almost impossible. What we know of ourselves, what we feel and think, can be compared to the tip of an iceberg visible above the water, while nine-tenths remains submerged.

Is a definition of mental balance possible? I shall attempt to give one. When we have made peace with ourselves, when we know ourselves pretty well, when our attitudes and actions are synchronized to the point that we feel, whatever the prevailing circumstances in each case, we have done the best rationally acceptable; when we have learned to forgive ourselves for our imperfections and shortcomings, then we can speak of mental balance. This attitude rules out the obsessive neurotic striving for unreachable perfection and subsequent guilt feelings for one's inability to achieve this ephemeral concept of perfection. We have to be ready to make concessions to human frailty and imperfection. Otherwise, we become self-destructive through exhausting frustration. If we do not try our level best, we fall short of the specific human factor of justified self-esteem.

chapter 24

DEATH, FINALITY, IMMORTALITY AND PSYCHOSIS

This final chapter will state only what the attentive reader of this book by now expects me to say. Modern science draws only a narrow margin between organic and inorganic, between living and non-living substances. It is certainly not my assignment to go into all the various theories of life on this earth, nor will I attempt to repeat the scientifically accepted theories of the development of life forms from their most primitive beginnings in the sea to the mammals, anthropoids, and *Homo sapiens.* We can, of course, only speak of life on this earth. We can only speculate whether similar or dissimilar conditions on other celestial bodies have brought forth life in forms like or totally unlike those we know. We speak of birth and death and we certainly do not agree at what precise moment we should start counting or pronounce when death has taken place.

Does life start at the moment of delivery and first spontaneous breath or at the time of germ cell copulation? But the germ cells individually were alive prior to copulation, etc. This question is even less answerable when we go to the primitive forms of life which reproduce and keep their species alive by nonsexual division and splitting off from a parent cell. The tobacco virus, for example, probably changes from inorganic to organic.

Strictly speaking, we can talk then only of a continuum of life from the earliest beginning to a distant (hopefully) future. In this sense, birth and death are artificial demarcation marks in the chain of life composed by links certainly going back at least to the very start and serving the law of preservation of the species. In this sense, I am almost tempted to say that death does not occur unless a branch of the chain ends by lack of reproductivity.

It could be imagined that for a human individual, for instance, who had led a really fulfilled and satisfactory life to the very last breath, death is not feared but accepted as the termination of one's own highly satisfactory life experience. This attitude is rather universally accepted. If, after a long, well-lived life, death finally comes to an individual who was well respected and loved, the survivors feel rightly little sorrow or regret and almost envy him for the rich and rewarding life experience he was fortunate enough to have passed through. He had known life, he had experienced all that life had to offer, and nothing remained unknown. The time had come and that is all there was to it. One does not look for either a compensatory reward or for a frightening punishment for actions and thought patterns for which, as we have learned, we were not responsible in the first place. Death as the end of life refers only to the individual links in the chain of life. We can feel compensated in that our works will carry on after us even in the absence of direct descendants. All this, of course, only seems to appease the unsatisfied vanity of the individual. It was unbearable to man since his dawn that he should disappear from this earth unsung, traceless, and with total finality.

When we look into the past, as early as we can trace history and prehistorical times, and wherever we turn geographically, we find mankind given to the fantasy of some form or other of existence after death. The basic human vanity simply cannot be reconciled to the realistic fact that personal life has come to its end and the physical substance of the body melts back into the great chemical reserves. The ancient Egyptians erected the most grandiose pyramids as dwelling places for their pharoahs in afterlife. The ancient Greeks, whose mythology is so well known, had a place where the souls or shadows of the deceased assembled, although the shadow of Achilles expressed little pleasure at being called even a king in Hades. The Teutonic heroes assembled in Valhalla where great joys awaited them. Each tribe visualized afterlife in its own peculiar way, from Happy Hunting Grounds to Eternal Bliss or Damnation. Indeed, some attitudes outrightly perceive earthly existence only as a proving ground or a vale of tears one has to endure to qualify for the bliss to come.

We can postulate that the less rewarding the present existence is to an individual, the more he may look forward to the compensatory mechanism of later reward, just as an unsatisfactory main course of a meal makes us hope for a compensating dessert. All these imaginary compensatory mechanisms have no justification other than making unbearable reality acceptable by falsifying it into psychotic delusion.

The concept of an afterlife which mankind reserves for itself is, interestingly enough, not quite acceptable yet to young children who still feel great kinship to their beloved pets. A child might find Heaven an undesirable place to be if his beloved Fido or kitty cannot ultimately be admitted there too. Animal funerals and pet cemeteries are, in a way, revolutionary attitudes to the exclusive vanity of human beings. We see that ancient Egyptians made exceptions for cats.

The threat of punishment in the afterlife is, of course, meant to act as a deterrent to undesirable action just as much as the reward to be gained in the afterlife (in the form of a promissory note) is to act as an incentive for desirable actions here and now. It is a built-in conditioned reflex responsive to imaginary reward or pain. The argument that nobody has yet come back after death and, therefore, the possibility of our afterlife cannot be totally dismissed, lacks all justification of logic. A wild assumption has no more resemblance to reality than unrealistic fantastic speculations are founded on facts. On the other hand, it is not adequately perceived that mature responsible reactivity is its own reward inasmuch as it makes human existence a worthwhile, perhaps even joyful, experience.

POSTSCRIPT

I was born in Vienna, Austria, in 1907. I was the second-born son of a middle-class merchant and his wife—the daughter of a highly respected Viennese physician of good standing and quality. I developed my inferiority feelings as second-born son and for a good part of my life, I endeavored to overcome these difficulties. I started my medical education belatedly; then, as I was about to take my final examinations at the University of Vienna, I was overtaken by the well-known political events of 1938. I arrived in the United States and finished my medical education in Chicago. After the War, I practiced medicine for about ten years. In the meantime, I had married and two wonderful children were born to this marriage. My wife left me after the birth of the second child, returned to her parents with the children, and obtained a divorce over all my protestations. I loved these children dearly and never agreed to the divorce. I had told myself that I would rather die than fail to remain a father in their eyes. I persisted in this determination for two and a half decades and still follow this course, having no inclination to deviate from it. This persistence forced me to mobilize within myself all emotional resources in order to persevere. My thinking, therefore, became more and more psychiatrically oriented. After I had my own prolonged psychotherapeutic exposure, I decided to become a psychiatrist. I took the necessary additional training requirements and became a diplomate of the American Board of Psychiatry. For a short time I was Chief of Psychiatry of the Veterans Administration Hospital in San Francisco; later I became Superintendent of the Peoria State Hospital and Assistant Professor of Psychiatry at the Chicago Medical School; and for the last ten years I have been engaged in the private practice of psychiatry in Chicago, Illinois.

My earlier book, *Basic Anxiety, A New Psychophysiological Concept,* was published by the Philosophical Library, New York, N.Y., in 1962.

SELECTED BIBLIOGRAPHY

1. Alexander, Franz; Ross, Helen, eds.: *Dynamic Psychiatry.* The University of Chicago Press, Chicago, Illinois, 1953.

2. American Medical Association: *Nostrums and Quackery.* Reprinted from JAMA.

3. Ardrey, Robert: *African Genesis.* Atheneum, New York, 1963.

4. Ardrey, Robert: *African Genesis.* Dell Publishing Co., New York, 1963.

5. Arey, Leslie Brainerd: *Developmental Anatomy.* W. B. Saunders Co., Philadelphia, 1946.

6. Aristotle: *Politics.* 384 BC – 323 BC.

7. Asimov, Isaac: *The Wellsprings of Life.* The New American Library, Inc., New York, 1960.

8. Barnett, Lincoln: *The Universe and Dr. Einstein.* The New American Library, New York, 1962.

9. Bauer, W. W.: *Potions, Remedies and Old Wives Tales.* Doubleday & Co., Garden City, New York, 1969.

10. Bulfinch, Thomas: *The Age of Fable or Beauties of Mythology.* The New American Library of World Literature, Inc., New York, 1962.

11. Burdick, Jacques: *Theater.* Newsweek Books, New York (Europa Verlag), 1974.

12. Burkhardt, Dietrich; Schleidt, Wolfgan; Altner, Helmut: *Signals in the Animal World.* George Allen and Unwin, Ltd., London, 1967.

13. Casson, Lionel: *Ancient Egypt.* Time, Inc., New York, 1965.
14. Clark, Ronald W.: *Einstein: The Life and Times.* The World Publishing Co., 1971.
15. Coleman, James A.: *Modern Theories of the Universe.* The New American Library, New York, 1963.
16. De Beauvior, Simone: *The Second Sex.* Knopf, New York, 1953.
17. Durant, Will: *The Story of Philosophy.* Garden City Publishing Co., Inc., 1943.
18. Eckstein, Gustav: *The Body has a Head.* Harper & Row, New York, 1969.
19. Eiseley, Lorin: *The Invisible Pyramid.* Charles Scribner's Sons, New York, 1970.
20. *Encyclopaedia Britannica:* Encyclopaedia Britannica, Inc., William Benton, Publisher (The University of Chicago), 1968.
21. Engel, Carl: *Music of the Most Ancient Nations* (select bibliographies reprint series), 1909.
22. Engel, George L.: *Psychological Development in Health and Disease.* W. B. Saunders Co., Philadelphia, 1962.
23. Farago, Peter; Lagnado, John: *Life in Action.* Random House, New York, 1973.
24. Fenichel, Otto: *Psychoanalytic Theory of Neurosis.* W. W. Norton, New York, 1945.
25. Foucault, Michel: *Madness & Civilization; a History of Insanity in the Age of Reason.* The New American Library, New York, 1967.
26. Frazier, Sir James George: *The Golden Bough.* The Macmillan Co., New York, 1971.
27. Freedman, Alfred M.; Kaplan, Harold I., eds.: *Comprehensive Textbook of Psychiatry.* The Williams and Wilkins Co., Baltimore, Maryland, 1967.
28. Freud, Sigmund: *Collected Papers, Vol. I.* The Hogarth Press, London, 1956.
29. Freud, Sigmund: *Mourning and Melancholia.* Standard Edition of Complete Psychological Works of Sigmund Freud, Vol. 14, p. 243. Hogarth Press, London, 1957.
30. Freud, Sigmund: *Totum and Taboo.* (Strachy, James, trans.) W. W. Norton, New York, 1952.
31. Gamow, George. *One, Two, Three, Infinity.* The Viking Press, New York, 1962.
32. Gardner, Martin: *Relativity for the Million.* The Macmillan Co., New York, 1962.
33. Garre, Walter J.: *Basic Anxiety.* Philosophical Library, Inc., New York, 1962.
34. Goethe, Johann W.: *Faust, drama; Erlkoenig, poems.*
35. Harrison, Jane E.: *Ancient Art and Ritual.* Greenwood, Conn., 1951.

36. Holbrook, Howard M.: *The Golden Age of Quackery.* The Macmillan Co., New York, 1959.
37. Horney, K.: *Neurosis and Human Growth.* W. W. Norton, New York, 1950.
38. Jung, C. G.: *Collected Works.* Pantheon Books, New York, 1953.
39. Kanner, Leo: *Child Psychiatry.* C C Thomas, Springfield, Illinois, 1972.
40. Kaplan, Harold I.; Sadock, Benjamin J.: *Comprehensive Group Psychotherapy.* The Williams and Wilkins Co., Baltimore, Maryland, 1971.
41. Kiernon, Thomas: *Shrinks, etc.* The Dial Press, New York, 1974.
42. Kraepelin, Emil: *Dementia Praecox and Paraphrenia* (reproduction of the 1919 edition). Krieger, 1971.
43. Kraepelin, Emil: *General Paresis (nervous and mental diseases monograph series #14).* Moore, J. W., trans. Johnson Reproductions, 1913.
44. Kraepelin, Emil: *Lectures on Clinical Psychiatry (history of medicine series, Vol. 33).* Hafner, 1968.
45. Kuznetsov, B.: *Einstein.* Phaedra, New York, 1970.
46. La Barre, Weston: *The Human Animal.* The University of Chicago Press, Chicago, 1954.
47. Le Cron, Leslie M., ed.: *Experimental Hypnosis.* Macmillan Co., New York, 1954.
48. Le Shan, Lawrence: *The Medium, the Mystic, and the Physicist.* Viking Press, New York, 1974.
49. Life: *The Epic of Man.* Time, Inc., New York, 1961.
50. Magnus, Hugo: *Superstition in Medicine.* Funk & Wagnall Co., New York, 1905.
51. Maltz, Maxwell: *Psycho-cybernetics.* Prentice-Hall, Inc., New York, (Pocket Books, Inc.) 1960.
52. Menzel, Donald H.: *Astronomy.* Random House, New York, 1970.
53. Munitz, Milton K.: *Space, Time and Creation.* The Free Press, 1957; Collier Books, New York, 1961.
54. Newman, James R., ed.: *What is Science?* Simon and Schuster, New York, 1955.
55. Noyes, Arthur P.; Lilb, Lawrence C.: *Modern Clinical Psychiatry.* W. B. Saunders Co., Philadelphia, 1958.
56. Oppenheimer, J. Robert: *The Open Mind.* Simon and Schuster, New York, 1963.
57. Ostrander, Sheila; Schroedler, Lynn: *Psychic Discoveries Behind the Iron Curtain.* New York, Bantam Books, 1971.
58. Rado, Sandor: *Adaptational Psychodynamics, Motivation and Control.* Jameson, Jane; Klein, Henriette, eds. J. Aronson, 1969.
59. Rado, Sandor; Daniels, G. E.: *Changing Concepts of Psychoanalytic Medicine.* Grune & Stratton, New York, 1956.

60. Rheingold, Joseph C.: *The Fear of being a Woman.* Grune & Stratton, Inc., New York, 1964.
61. Rheingold, Joseph C.: *The Mother, Anxiety and Death.* Little, Brown & Co., Boston, 1967.
62. Robbins, Stanley L.: *Textbook of Pathology with Clinical Applications.* W. B. Saunders Co., Philadelphia, 1957.
63. Roheim, Geza: *Magic and Schizophrenia.* Indiana University Press, Indianapolis, 1962.
64. Rouze, Michel: *Robert Oppenheimer, the Man and his Theories.* Fawcett Publications, Inc., Connecticut, 1965.
65. Rowe, Clarence J.: *An Outline of Psychiatry.* Wm. C. Brown Co., 1972.
66. Russell, Bertrand: *A History of Western Philosophy.* Simon & Schuster, New York, 1945.
67. Russell, Bertrand: *The ABC of Relativity.* The New American Library of World Literature, New York, 1962.
68. Ryze, Milan: *Parpsychology.* Hawthorn Books, Inc., New York, 1970.
69. Sachs, Cut: *Rise of Music in the Ancient World.* W. W. Norton, New York, 1943.
70. Schiller, Friedrich: *Die Braut von Messina Drama.*
71. Sendrey, Alfred: *Music in the Social and Religious Life of Antiquity.* Fairleigh Dickinson, New Jersey, 1971.
72. Simon, Brian, ed.: *Psychology in the Soviet Union.* Stanford University, Stanford, California, 1957.
73. Stillman, John Maxson: *Paracelsus.* Chicago, 1920.
74. Talbot Rice, David: *Concise History of Painting.* Praeger, New York, 1968.
75. Thomas, Lewis: *The Lives of a Cell.* The Viking Press, New York, 1974.
76. Tillich, Paul: *The Courage to be.* Yale University Press, New Haven, Connecticut, 1965.
77. Wiener, Norbert: *Cybernetics; or Control and Communication in the Animal and the Machine.* M.I.T. Press, Boston, 1976.
78. Wiener, Norbert: *God & Golem, Inc.* The M.I.T. Press, Boston, 1969.
79. Wiener, Norbert: *The Human Use of Human Beings.* Avon, New York, 1967.
80. Wittkower, Eric David; Gleghor, Robert Allen, eds.: *Recent Developments in Psychosomatic Medicine.* Lippincott Co., 1954.
81. Zetzel, Elizabeth R.: *Capacity for Emotional Growth.* International Universities Press, 1971.
82. Zetzel, Elizabeth R.; Meissner, W. W.: *Basic Concepts of Psychoanalytic Psychiatry.* Basic Books, New York, 1973.

INDEX